Deep Learning
for Natural Language Process

Deep Learning for Natural Language Processing

STEPHAN RAAIJMAKERS

MANNING
SHELTER ISLAND

For online information and ordering of this and other Manning books, please visit
www.manning.com. The publisher offers discounts on this book when ordered in quantity.
For more information, please contact

    Special Sales Department
    Manning Publications Co.
    20 Baldwin Road
    PO Box 761
    Shelter Island, NY 11964
    Email: orders@manning.com

 Manning Publications Co.
    20 Baldwin Road
    PO Box 761
    Shelter Island, NY 11964

Development editor:	Dustin Archibald
Technical development editors:	Michiel Trimpe and Al Krinker
Review editor:	Ivan Martinović
Production editor:	Keri Hales
Copy editor:	Tiffany Taylor
Proofreader:	Katie Tennant
Technical proofreader:	Mayur Patil
Typesetter and cover designer:	Marija Tudor

ISBN 9781617295447
Printed and bound by CPI Group (UK) Ltd, Croydon, CR0 4YY

brief contents

contents

PART 3   ADVANCED TOPICS 161

7   *Attention   163*

8   *Multitask learning   190*

9   *Transformers   219*

preface

Computers have been trying hard to make sense of language in recent decades. Supported by disciplines like linguistics, computer science, statistics, and machine learning, the field of *computational linguistics* or *natural language processing* (NLP) has come into full bloom, supported by numerous scientific journals, conferences, and active industry participation. Big tech companies like Google, Facebook, IBM, and Microsoft appear to have prioritized their efforts in natural language analysis and understanding, and progressively offer datasets and helpful open source software for the natural language processing community. Currently, deep learning is increasingly dominating the NLP field.

To someone who is eager to join this exciting field, the high pace at which new developments take place in the deep learning–oriented NLP community may seem daunting. There seems to be a large gap between descriptive, statistical, and more traditional machine learning approaches to NLP on the one hand, and the highly technical, procedural approach of deep learning neural networks on the other hand. This book aims for bridging this gap a bit, through a gentle introduction to deep learning for NLP. It targets students, linguists, computer scientists, practitioners, and all other people interested in artificial intelligence. Let's refer to these groups of people as *NLP engineers*. When I was a student, lacking a systematic computational linguistics program in those days, I pretty much pieced together a personal—and necessarily incomplete—NLP curriculum. It was a tough job. My motivation for writing this book has been to make this journey a bit easier for aspiring NLP engineers, and to give you a head start by introducing you to the fundamentals of deep learning–based NLP.

I sincerely believe that to become an NLP engineer with the ambition to produce innovative solutions, you need to possess advanced software development and machine learning skills. You need to fiddle with algorithms and come up with new variants yourself. Much like the 17th-century Dutch scientist Antonie van Leeuwenhoek, who designed and produced his own microscopes for experimentation, the modern-day NLP engineer creates their own digital instruments for studying and analyzing language. Whenever an NLP engineer succeeds in building a model of natural language that "adheres to the facts," that is, is *observationally adequate*, not only industrial (that is, practical) but also scientific progress has been made. I invite you to adopt this mindset, to continuously keep taking a good look at how humans process language, and to contribute to the wonderful field of NLP, where, in spite of algorithmic progress, so many topics are still open!

acknowledgments

I wish to thank my employer, TNO (the Netherlands Organisation for Applied Scientific Research) for supporting the realization of this book. My thanks go to students from the faculties of Humanities and Science from Leiden University and assorted readers of the book for your feedback on the various MEAP versions, including correcting typos and other errors. I would also like to thank the Manning staff—in particular, development editor Dustin Archibald, production editor Keri Hales, and proofreader Katie Tennant, for their enduring support, encouragement and, above all, patience.

At my request, Manning transfers all author fees to UNICEF. Through your purchase of this book, you contribute to a better future for children in need, and that need is even more acute in 2022. "UNICEF is committed to ensuring special protection for the most disadvantaged children—victims of war, disasters, extreme poverty, all forms of violence and exploitation, and those with disabilities" (www.unicef.org/about-us/mission-statement). Many thanks for your help.

To all the reviewers: Alejandro Alcalde Barros, Amlan Chatterjee, Chetan Mehra, Deborah Mesquita, Eremey Vladimirovich Valetov, Erik Sapper, Giuliano Araujo Bertoti, Grzegorz Mika, Harald Kuhn, Jagan Mohan, Jorge Ezequiel Bo, Kelum Senanayake, Ken W. Alger, Kim Falk Jørgensen, Manish Jain, Mike F. Cuddy, Mortaza Doulaty, Ninoslav Čerkez, Philippe Van Bergen, Prabhuti Prakash, Ritwik Dubey, Rohit Agarwal, Shashank Polasa Venkata, Sowmya Vajjala, Thomas Peklak, Vamsi Sistla, and Vlad Navitski, thank you—your suggestions helped make this a better book.

about this book

This book will give you a thorough introduction to deep learning applied to a variety of language analysis tasks, supported by actual hands-on code. Explicitly linking the evergreens of computational linguistics (such as part-of-speech tagging, textual similarity, topic labeling, and Question Answering) to deep learning will help you become a proficient deep learning, natural language processing (NLP) expert. Beyond this, the book covers state-of-the-art approaches to challenging new problems.

Who should read this book

The intended audience for this book is anyone working in NLP: computational linguists, software engineers, and students. The field of machine learning–based NLP is vast and comprises a daunting number of formalisms and approaches. With deep learning entering the stage, many are eager to get their feet wet but may shy away from the highly technical nature of deep learning and the fast pace of this field—new approaches, software, and papers emerge on a daily basis. This book will bring you up to speed.

This book is not for those who wish to become proficient in deep learning in a general manner, readers in need of an introduction to NLP, or anyone desiring to master Keras, the deep learning Python library we use. Manning offers two books that fill these gaps and can be read as companions to this book: *Natural Language Processing in Action* (Hobson Lane, Cole Howard, and Hannes Hapke, 2019; www.manning .com/books/natural-language-processing-in-action) and *Deep Learning with Python* (François Chollet, 2021: www.manning.com/books/deep-learning-with-python -second-edition). If you want a quick and thorough introduction to Keras, visit https://keras.io/getting_started/intro_to_keras_for_engineers.

How this book is organized: A road map

Part 1, consisting of chapters 1, 2, and 3, introduces the history of deep learning, the basic architectures of deep learning for NLP and their implementation in Keras, and how to represent text for deep learning using embeddings and popular embedding strategies.

Part 2, consisting of chapters 4, 5, and 6, focuses on assessing textual similarity with deep learning, processing long sequences with memory-equipped models for Question Answering, and then applying such memory models to other NLP.

Part 3, consisting of chapters 7, 8, 9, and 10, starts by introducing neural attention, then moves on to the concept of multitask learning, using Transformers, and finally getting hands-on with BERT and inspecting the embeddings it produces.

About the code

The code we develop in this book is somewhat generic. Keras is a dynamic library, and while I was writing the book, some things changed, including the now-exclusive dependency of Keras on TensorFlow as a backend (a Keras backend is low-level code for performing efficient neural network computations). The changes are limited, but occasionally you may need to adapt the syntax of your code if you're using the latest Keras version (version 2.0 and above).

In the book, we draw pragmatic inspiration from public domain, open source code and reuse code snippets that are handy. Specific sources include the following:

- The Keras source code base, which contains many examples addressing NLP
- The code accompanying the companion book *Deep Learning with Python*
- Popular and excellent open source websites like https://adventuresinmachine-learning.com and https://machinelearningmastery.com
- Blogs like http://karpathy.github.io
- Coder communities like Stack Overflow

The emphasis of the book is more on outlining algorithms and code and less on achieving academic state-of-the-art results. However, starting from the basic solutions and approaches outlined throughout the book, and backed up by the many practical code examples, you will be empowered to reach better results.

This book contains many examples of source code both in numbered listings and in line with normal text. In both cases, source code is formatted in a `fixed-width font like this` to separate it from ordinary text.

In many cases, the original source code has been reformatted; we've added line breaks and reworked indentation to accommodate the available page space in the book. In some cases, even this was not enough, and listings include line-continuation markers (➥). Code annotations accompany many of the listings, highlighting important concepts.

You can get executable snippets of code from the liveBook (online) version of this book at https://livebook.manning.com/book/deep-learning-for-natural-language-processing. The complete code for the examples in the book is available for download from the Manning website at https://www.manning.com/books/deep-learning-for -natural-language-processing, and from GitHub at https://github.com/stephanraaij makers/deeplearningfornlp.

liveBook discussion forum

Purchase of *Deep Learning for Natural Language Processing* includes free access to live-Book, Manning's online reading platform. Using liveBook's exclusive discussion features, you can attach comments to the book globally or to specific sections or paragraphs. It's a snap to make notes for yourself, ask and answer technical questions, and receive help from the author and other users. To access the forum, go to https://livebook.manning.com/book/deep-learning-for-natural-language-process-ing/discussion. You can also learn more about Manning's forums and the rules of conduct at https://livebook.manning.com/discussion.

Manning's commitment to our readers is to provide a venue where a meaningful dialogue between individual readers and between readers and the author can take place. It is not a commitment to any specific amount of participation on the part of the author, whose contribution to the forum remains voluntary (and unpaid). We suggest you try asking him some challenging questions lest his interest stray! The forum and the archives of previous discussions will be accessible from the publisher's website as long as the book is in print.

about the author

STEPHAN RAAIJMAKERS received his education as a computational linguist at Leiden University, the Netherlands. He obtained his PhD on machine learning–based NLP from Tilburg University. He has been working since 2000 at the Netherlands Organisation for Applied Scientific Research (TNO), an independent organization founded by law in 1932, aimed at enabling business and government to apply scientific knowledge, contributing to industrial innovation and societal welfare. Within TNO, he has worked on many machine learning–intensive projects dealing with language. Stephan is also a professor of communicative AI at Leiden University (LUCL, Leiden University Centre for Linguistics). His chair focuses on deep learning–based approaches to human-machine dialogue.

about the cover illustration

The figure on the cover of *Deep Learning for Natural Language Processing*, titled "Paisan de dalecarlie," or "Peasant, Dalecarlia," is from an image held by the New York Public Library in the Miriam and Ira D. Wallach Division of Art, Prints and Photographs: Picture Collection. Each illustration is finely drawn and colored by hand.

In those days, it was easy to identify where people lived and what their trade or station in life was just by their dress. Manning celebrates the inventiveness and initiative of the computer business with book covers based on the rich diversity of regional culture centuries ago, brought back to life by pictures from collections such as this one.

Part 1

Introduction

Part 1 introduces the history of deep learning, relating it to other forms of machine learning–based natural language processing (NLP; chapter 1). Chapter 2 discusses the basic architectures of deep learning for NLP and their implementation in Keras. Chapter 3 discusses how to represent text for deep learning using embeddings and focuses on Word2Vec and Doc2Vec, two popular embedding strategies.

Deep learning for NLP

This chapter covers

- Taking a short road trip through machine learning applied to NLP
- Learning about the historical roots of deep learning
- Introducing vector-based representations of language

Language comes naturally to humans but has historically been hard for computers to grasp. This book addresses the application of recent, cutting-edge deep learning techniques to automated language analysis. In the last decade, deep learning has emerged as the vehicle of the latest wave in artificial intelligence (AI). Results have consistently redefined the state of the art for a plethora of data analysis tasks in a variety of domains. For an increasing number of deep learning algorithms, better-than-human (human-parity or superhuman) performance has been reported: for instance, speech recognition in noisy conditions and medical diagnosis based on images. Current deep learning–based natural language processing (NLP) out-performs all pre-existing approaches by a large margin. What exactly makes deep learning so suitable for these intricate analysis tasks, in particular language processing? This chapter presents some of the background necessary to answer this question and guides you through a selection of important topics in machine learning for NLP.

We first examine a few main approaches to machine learning: the neural perceptron, support vector machines, and memory-based learning. After that, we look at historical developments leading to deep learning and address vector representations: encoding data (notably, textual) with numerical representations suitable for processing by neural networks.

Let's start by discussing a few well-known machine learning–based NLP algorithms in some detail, illustrated with a handful of practical examples to whet your appetite. After that, we present the case for deep learning–based NLP.

1.1   *A selection of machine learning methods for NLP*

Let's start with a quick (and necessarily incomplete) tour of machine learning–based NLP (see figure 1.1). Current natural language processing heavily relies on machine learning. Machine learning has its roots in statistics, building among others on the seminal work by Thomas Bayes and Pierre-Simon Laplace in the 18th and 19th centuries and the least-squares methods for curve approximation by Legendre in 1812. The field of neural computing started with the work of McCulloch and Pitts in 1943, who put forward a formal theory (and logical calculus) of neural networks. It would take until 1950 before learning machines were proposed by Alan Turing.

All machine learning algorithms that perform classification (labeling) share a single goal: to arrive at *linear separability* of data that is labeled with *classes*: labels that indicate a (usually exclusive) category to which a data point belongs. Data points presented to a machine learning algorithm typically consist of vector representations of descriptive traits. These representations constitute a so-called *input space*. The subsequent processing, manipulation, and abstraction of the input space during the

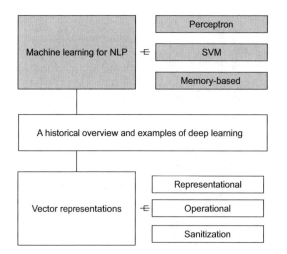

Figure 1.1   **Machine learning for NLP. A first look at neural machine learning, plus background on support vector machines and memory-based learning.**

learning stage of a self-learning algorithm yields a *feature space*. Some of this processing can be done external to the algorithm: raw data can be converted to features as part of a preprocessing stage, which technically creates an input space consisting of features. The *output space* consists of class labels that separate the various data points in a dataset based on the class boundaries. The essence of deep learning, as we will see, is to learn abstract representations in the feature space. Figure 1.2 illustrates how deep learning mediates between inputs and outputs: through abstract representations derived from the input data.

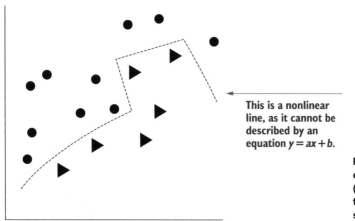

Figure 1.2 **From input space to output space (labels). Deep learning constructs intermediate, abstract representations of input data, mapping an *input space* to a *feature space*. Through this mapping, it learns to relate input to output: to map the input space to an output space (encoding class labels or other interpretations of the input data).**

Training a machine learning component involves learning boundaries between classes, which may depend on complex functions. The burden of learning class separability can be alleviated by smart feature preprocessing. Learning the class boundaries occurs by performing implicit or explicit transformations on linearly inseparable input spaces. Figure 1.3 shows a non-linear class boundary: a line separating objects in two classes that cannot be modeled by a linear function $f(x) = ax + b$. The function corresponding to this line is a non-linear classifier. A real-world example would be a bowl of multicolored

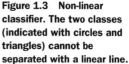

This is a nonlinear line, as it cannot be described by an equation $y = ax + b$.

Figure 1.3 **Non-linear classifier. The two classes (indicated with circles and triangles) cannot be separated with a linear line.**

marbles mixed in such a way that they cannot be separated from each other by means of a straight plate (like a flat scoop).

A linear function that separates classes with a straight line is a *linear classifier* and would produce a picture like figure 1.4.

We now briefly address three types of machine learning approaches that have had major uptake in NLP:

- The single-layer perceptron and its generalization to the multilayer perceptron
- Support vector machines
- Memory-based learning

While there is a lot more to the story, these three types embody, respectively, the *neural*

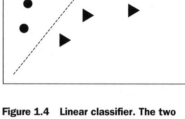

Figure 1.4   Linear classifier. The two classes (indicated with circles and triangles) can be separated with a straight line.

or *cognitive*, *eager*, and *lazy* types of machine learning. All of these approaches relate naturally to the deep learning approach to natural language analysis, which is the main topic of this book.

1.1.1   *The perceptron*

In 1957, the first implementation of a biologically inspired machine learning component was realized: Rosenblatt's perceptron. This device, implemented on physical hardware, allowed the processing of visual stimuli represented by a square 400 (20 by 20) array of photosensitive cells. The weights of this network were set by electromotors driving potentiometers. The learning part of this perceptron was based on a simple one-layer neural network, which effectively became the archetype of neural networks (see figure 1.5).

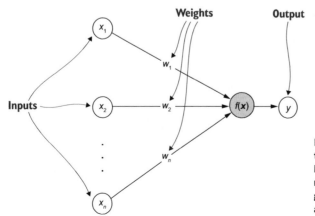

Figure 1.5   Rosenblatt's perceptron: the fruit fly of neural machine learning. It represents a single neuron receiving several inputs and generating (by applying a threshold) a single output value.

Suppose you have a vector of features that describe aspects of a certain object of interest, like the words in a document, and you want to create a function from these features to a binary label (for instance, you want to decide if the document conveys a positive or negative sentiment). The single-layer perceptron is capable of doing this. It produces a binary output y (0 or 1) from a weighted combination of input values $x_1 \ldots x_n$, based on a threshold θ and a bias b:

$$f(\mathbf{x}) = \begin{cases} 1 \text{ if } \mathbf{w} \cdot \mathbf{x} + b > \theta \\ 0 \text{ } else \end{cases}$$

The weights $w_1, \ldots w_n$ are learned from training data consisting of input vectors labeled with output labels. The thresholded unit is called a *neuron*. It receives the summed and weighted input v. So, assume we have the set of weights and associated inputs shown in table 1.1.

Then their summed and weighted output would be

$$3 \times 10 + 5 \times 20 + 7 \times 30 = 340$$

$$v = \sum_{i=1}^{n} w_i x_i$$

Table 1.1   Weighted input

Weight 1	3
Weight 2	5
Weight 3	7
Input 1	10
Input 2	20
Input 3	30

This simplistic network is able to learn a specific set of functions that address the class of *linearly separable problems*: problems that are separable in *input* space with a linear function. Usually, these are the easier problems in classification. It is quite common for data to be *heavily entangled*. Consider undoing a knot in two separate ropes. Some knots are easy and can be undone in one step. Other knots need many more steps. This is the business of machine learning algorithms: undoing the intertwining of data objects living in different classes. For NLP, the single-layer perceptron nowadays plays a marginal role, but it underlies several derived algorithms that strive for simplicity, such as online learning (Bottou 1998).

A practical example of a perceptron classifier is the following. We set out to build a document classifier that categorizes raw texts as being broadly about either atheism or medical topics. The popular *20 newsgroups* dataset (http://qwone.com/~jason/20Newsgroups), one of the most widely used datasets for building and evaluating document classifiers, consists of newsgroup (Usenet) texts distributed over 20 hand-assigned topics. Here is what we do:

1 Make a subselection for two newsgroups of interest: *alt.atheism* and *sci.med.*
2 Train a simple perceptron on a *vector representation* of the documents in these two classes. A vector is nothing more than a container (an ordered list of a finite dimension) for numerical values.

The vector representation is based on a statistical representation of words called TF.IDF, which we discuss in section 1.3.2. For now, just assume TF.IDF is a magic trick that turns documents into vectors that can be fed to a machine learning algorithm.

Don't worry if you don't completely understand the following listing right now. It's here to give you an idea of what the code looks like for a basic perceptron.

Listing 1.1   A simple perceptron-based document classifier

```
from sklearn.linear_model import Perceptron          ← Import a basic perceptron
                                                        classifier from sklearn.
from sklearn.datasets import fetch_20newsgroups       ← Import a routine for fetching the 20
                                                        newsgroups dataset from sklearn.
categories = ['alt.atheism', 'sci.med']     ←  Limit the categories
                                               of the dataset.
train = fetch_20newsgroups(å
subset='train',categories=categories, shuffle=True)
                                                       Our perceptron is defined. It will
perceptron = Perceptron(max_iter=100)              ←  be trained for 100 iterations.

from sklearn.feature_extraction.text import CountVectorizer   ←  The familiar
cv = CountVectorizer()                                           CountVectorizer is fit
X_train_counts = cv.fit_transform(train.data)                   on our training data.

from sklearn.feature_extraction.text import TfidfTransformer  ←  Load, fit, and deploy
tfidf_tf = TfidfTransformer()                                   a TF.IDF transformer
X_train_tfidf = tfidf_tf.fit_transform(X_train_counts)          from sklearn. It
                                            The perceptron       computes TF.IDF
perceptron.fit(X_train_tfidf,train.target)  ← is trained on the  representations of
                                            TF.IDF vectors.      our count vectors.
test_docs = ['Religion is widespread, even in modern times', 'His kidneyå
failed','The pope is a controversial leader', 'White blood cells fightå
off infections','The reverend had a heart attack in church']

X_test_counts = cv.transform(test_docs)         ←  The test data is vectorized
X_test_tfidf = tfidf_tf.transform(X_test_counts)   first to count vectors and
                                                   then to TF.IDF vectors.
pred = perceptron.predict(X_test_tfidf)

for doc, category in zip(test_docs, pred):                       ←  The results
    print('%r => %s' % (doc, train.target_names[category]))         are printed.
```

Obtain documents for our category selection.

Our test data

The perceptron is applied to the test documents.

This produces the following results:

```
Religion is widespread, even in modern times => alt.atheism

His kidney failed => sci.med

The pope is a controversial leader => alt.atheism
```

```
White blood cells fight off infections => sci.med

The reverend had a heart attack in church => sci.med
```

Apparently, these few short texts can be linearly separated by a simple, weight-based algorithm. This example is a huge simplification: the topics chosen are quite distinct. In real life, linear algorithms fall short in separating topics that overlap and share similar vocabulary.

The multilayer perceptron (MLP) generalizes the single-layer model of the original perceptron to a model with at least three layers: an input layer, one or more hidden representational layers, and an output layer (figure 1.6).

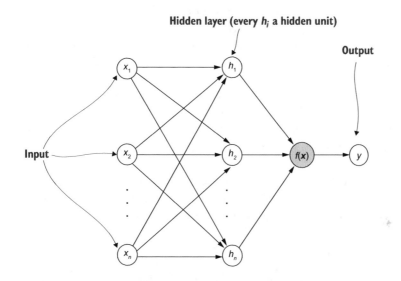

Figure 1.6 A multilayer perceptron (MLP) with an input layer, one hidden layer ($h_1...h_n$), and an output layer. Multidimensional input is processed by neurons $x_1...x_n$. These neurons are like singular perceptrons, the difference being that instead of thresholding their activation and producing a label, they send their activations to neurons in the hidden layer. Finally, the threshold function $f(x)$ gathers all the input and predicts an output y. Every connection between input and neurons, and between neurons, is weighted, and weights are learned during training the perceptron.

1.1.2 Support vector machines

As mentioned, machine learning algorithms that perform classification (the labeling of objects with classes) attempt to arrive at linear boundaries between data points. Recall figure 1.4 for such a linear boundary. Imagine seeing two objects (like an orange and an apple) on a plate, one of which partially obscures the other. If you close one eye, you lose 3D stereovision, and you cannot separate the two objects in 2D. If you open both eyes, you can separate the two objects. Support vector machines

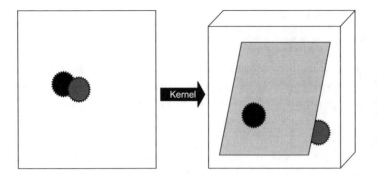

Figure 1.7 From 2D to 3D with a kernel. The kernel leads to linear separability in 3D of the two data points, which are linearly inseparable in 2D. The hyperplane in 3D can be described with a linear function.

(SVMs) routinely perform this migration to a higher dimension, separating objects in this space. Their secret weapon: *kernels* (figure 1.7).

An SVM is a binary classifier that implicitly maps data in feature space to higher dimensions in which data becomes separable by a linear plane called a *hyperplane*. This mapping is implicit and is carried out by a *kernel function*. This is a function that transforms the original input space to an alternative representation that implicitly has a higher dimensionality, with the aim of disentangling the data and making it linearly separable. But this transformation is implicit in the sense that it takes the form of a similarity function applied to two feature vectors, just computing their distance. This is called the *kernel trick*.

You should already be familiar with the dot product of two vectors. If not, please see https://en.wikipedia.org/wiki/Dot_product for a refresher. To recap, the standard dot product of two vectors a and b is the sum of the cross-product of the two vectors:

```
def dot_product(a,b):
  return sum( [a[i]*b[i] for i in range(len(a))])
```

So, a dot product is just a multiplicative operation on two vectors that produces a single number. Kernels are generalizations of this dot product between vectors: they compute the dot product between *altered* versions of these vectors. The nature of the alteration is specified by a kernel function. Generally speaking, a kernel function takes two vectors, mixes in a constant (a kernel parameter), and adds some kernel-specific ingredients to produce a specific form of a dot product of the two vectors.

Let's return to our orange and apple. The objects are described by pairs of coordinates (x,y) since the table they're lying on is a flat XY-plane. Like other types of kernels, the *polynomial kernel* maps lower-dimensional spaces to higher-dimensional ones. You may recall from high school math that a polynomial function produces a value using addition, subtraction, multiplication, or positive exponentiation only, like $y = 4x^2 + 10$. Polynomial kernels work on two input values (vectors of numeric values) and (usually) a constant. They compute a result using a polynomial.

For instance, a simple *quadratic* kernel K that uses a constant c and addresses the two two-dimensional XY-vectors describing our orange and apple

$$x = (x_1, x_2)$$

and

$$y = (y_1, y_2)$$

looks like this:

$$K(x,y) = (c + x^T y)^2 = (c + x_1 y_1 + x_2 y_2)^2 =$$
$$c^2 + x_1^2 y_1^2 + x_2^2 y_2^2 + 2c x_1 y_1 + 2c x_2 y_2 + 2 x_1 y_1 x_2 y_2$$

Notice the superscripted T: that is *vector transposition* (swapping columns and rows), necessary for vector multiplication. What does the kernel do? It computes a product between two vectors. This product is a number expressing a relation between the two input vectors. But the tedious expansion of this kernel shows that we actually operate in a six- (not even a three-!) dimensional space. Count the factors separated by the plus sign in the result; we have six such factors. In this case, the kernel function K implicitly computes its dot product between the following vectors

$$< c, x_1^2, x_2^2, \sqrt{2c x_1}, \sqrt{2c x_2}, \sqrt{2c x_1 x_2} >$$
$$< c, y_1^2, y_2^2, \sqrt{2c y_1}, \sqrt{2c y_2}, \sqrt{2c y_1 y_2} >$$

since the result is the product of these two vectors. But it never explicitly created these vectors. The whole point of this *kernel trick* is that, hopefully, in the higher-dimensional space that is the playground of the kernel, things become easier to separate than in the entangled input space. Kernels do not explicitly represent this space; they implicitly work in it. You can imagine that for long vectors and large exponents of the polynomial, this kernel trick quickly becomes a practical advantage!

In the transformed space created by the kernel trick, two classes are at best separated with maximally wide boundaries (called *maximum margins*). The data points determining the slope of these boundaries are called *support vectors*. See figure 1.8.

Learning weights that optimize the margins with the least error (as measured on some held-out test data) is the job an SVM has to solve during training. After training, the support vectors and various weights plus biases constitute the model. New input is projected onto the support vectors and, depending which side it lands on, receives a positive or negative label (recall that SVMs are binary classifiers). So, SVMs throw away a lot of their training data and keep only some of it: the support vectors. They can be called *eager* forms of machine learning.

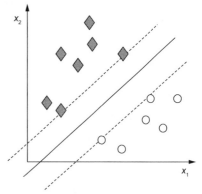

Figure 1.8   Maximum margins of an SVM. The support vectors are the points on the dashed lines.

The connection between kernel-based machine learning and neural network–based learning is briefly discussed in the book *Deep Learning with Python* (Chollet 2017). It is based on the intuition that hidden layers in neural networks act like kernels in disentangling linearly inseparable input data layer by layer, step by step.

1.1.3   *Memory-based learning*

Unlike the *eager* types of machine learning that build compact and representative models of their training data, memory-based learning (MBL; Daelemans and van den Bosch 2005) is a form of *lazy* learning. It does not compress training data into generalizations but instead keeps all training data available in memory. During classification, the actual processing of the training takes place: input data is matched with training data by the application of similarity or distance measures. Similar to SVMs, distance functions between vectors compute similarities. But here, we work on explicit vectors, and we do not perform any dimensionality tricks.

A well-known distance function is the IB1 metric, a simplified version of which is shown in the following listing.

Listing 1.2   IB1 distance metric

```
def IB1(a,b):
  return sum( [delta(a[i],b[i]) for i in range(len(a))])

def delta(x,y):
    if x==y:
      return 0
    if x!=y:
      return 1
```

This metric computes the distance between two feature vectors based on *feature value overlap*: exact similarity for symbolic (non-numerical) values. Most MBL algorithms extend these distance metrics with feature weighting (such as information-gain-based weighting) or exemplar weighting (Daelemans and van den Bosch 2005). They partition the search space for matching in sets consisting of training items with the same distance to the current test item. For instance, sets of distances $d_1, d_2, \ldots$ can be found first, after which the algorithm computes the most frequent class in those sets. It then votes over all classes to determine the most probable label for the test item. The k parameter addresses the number of distance sets to take into account, which is why MBL often is k-nearest *distances* classification rather than k-nearest *neighbor* classification.

MBL has interesting advantages for NLP. Keeping all original training data available for classification allows handling exceptions in language. For instance, in certain languages, morphological operations on words, such as diminutive formation, can be arranged in *pockets of exceptions*: small families of subregularities. In Dutch, for instance, we encounter these:

- *gat* => *gaatje* ("small hole")
- *pad* => *paadje* ("small path")
- *blad* => *blaadje* ("small leaf")

Notice the extra vowel in the diminutive form, and the diminutive suffix *-je*. We also have a subfamily of patterns like these:

- *kat => katje* ("small cat")
- *rat => ratje* ("small rat")
- *schat => schatje* ("(my) dear")
- *schot => schotje* ("small fence")
- *schip => scheepje* ("small ship")
- *schaap => schaapje* ("small sheep")
- *guit => guitje* ("little maverick")

While *schat* is phonetically quite similar to *gat* (*-ch-* is pronounced similarly to *-g-*), it is inflected analogous to other words prefixed with *sch-*. But *schip* does not follow this pattern.

The benefit of using a memory-based learner for highly exceptional data is that exceptions can, in principle, always be retrieved for labeling a similar exceptional input case. Memory-based learners have perfect memory: they store everything. But *eager* machine learning models tend to "compile away" these exceptions. They are after string regularities rather than exceptions. Editing away these exceptions from training data has been found detrimental to generalization accuracy (the ability to handle new, unseen cases outside of the training data) of the resulting classifier (Daelemans et al., 1999). Apparently, it is beneficial to keep the subregularities of pockets of exceptions. One of the challenges for deep learning, an "eager" form of machine learning, will be to handle these subregularities in a similar vein.

1.2 Deep learning

Deep learning is one of the most vibrant buzz phrases of the past 5 years. Deep learning by itself is nothing new: in the strictest sense, it is a neural network with lots of internal or hidden layers and specific filtering operations. Deep learning deploys constructive ways of dealing with large quantities of information organized in many layers of representations. While deep learning in its essential form was invented in the 1960s of the previous century, it took three decades before it was finally ready to use. In this section, we shed some light on why this happened (see figure 1.9 for the setup).

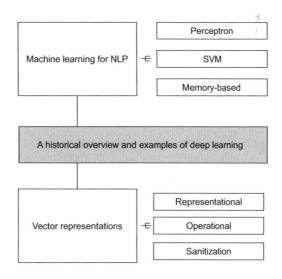

Figure 1.9   Deep learning: some historical background

But first: which problem does deep learning solve for NLP? Deep learning can be seen as a very effective statistical technique for working with (very) many parameters. It can effectively handle millions of parameters, each one encoding an aspect of input data. Layers in deep learning act as transformations that—step by step—accommodate input data with the labels we assign to that data; they *disentangle* the spaghetti of input data so that labels can be assigned more easily. The fact that we can stack many such declutter steps on top of each other is a major *forte* of deep learning. For language, deep learning provides two types of advantages:

- The repeated application of data decluttering steps proves good for NLP, but this is not specific for language; it applies to virtually every modality deep learning is applied to.
- Deep learning has facilities for handling sequential information with memory operators and buffers. This is important for language, and in this respect, deep learning is a form of *stateful* machine learning, as opposed to the other, usually *stateless* types of machine learning models. These models also usually perform just a single disentanglement step (like SVMs).

Central to deep learning is the learning of hierarchical representations of data. Under a vertical interpretation of a multilayer neural network, every "lower" layer feeds into a "higher" layer. Layers can be seen as complex functions processing a set of inputs and weights. These weights encode the importance of the information stored in the network. Networks receive their inputs in a dedicated input layer and process that input layer by layer, sending it upward into the network.

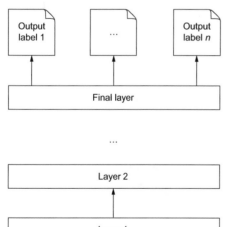

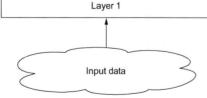

Output layers, finally, produce an outcome: the label the model assigns to its input. Usually, the network produces probabilities for a set of possible outcomes. The outcome with the highest probability then constitutes the final output label. All layers except input and output layers are *hidden layers*, as they cannot be readily observed. As mentioned, hidden layers in neural networks disentangle linearly inseparable input data layer by layer, step by step. Figure 1.10 shows a generic deep learning network.

During training, weights are estimated and fine-tuned between *neurons*, which are the basic processing units of a neural network. Every layer keeps a record of the weights for the neurons that feed into that layer. Estimating weights is the essential business of neural networks.

Figure 1.10   Deep learning networks: general architecture

Since the layers in a neural network are hierarchically organized (stacked), the representations they produce can be interpreted as hierarchical representations as well, going from specific (close to the input layer) to more abstract (close to the output layer). In general, it is hard to come up with human-understandable interpretations of these representations. Yet, in the field of image analysis, the weights associated with the layers of deep learning networks have been shown to encode interpretable concepts. They can be visualized, and the lower layers appear to encode pixels, whereas higher layers represent edges, corners, and even concepts like facial objects (see Lee 2010).

In 1965, presumably the first reference to such hierarchical representation learning was published by Ivakhnenko and Lapa (see Ivakhnenko and Lapa 1965). Their work describes a *group method of data handling* (GMDH)—a method for producing outputs by layers feeding into each other, based on the following formula:

$$Y(x_1, \ldots, x_n) = a_0 + \sum_{i=1}^{n} a_i x_i + \sum_{i=1}^{n} \sum_{j=1}^{n} a_{ij} x_i x_j + \sum_{i=1}^{n} \sum_{j=1}^{n} \sum_{k=1}^{n} a_{ijk} x_i x_j x_k + \ldots$$

This intimidating formula describes nothing but a function Y that computes a complex sum of weighted combinations (groups) of input values x_i, with every factor a being a weight or *coefficient*. This value can be compared with a desired value (an output), and then the weights can be adjusted to closely approximate this "true" value. Notice that we have a one-dimensional weight or coefficient matrix a_i, a two-dimensional one a_{ij}, a three-dimensional one a_{ijk}, and so on. The weight matrices are usually referred to as *polynomial models*. The complex function can be represented by a sequence of quadratic terms (polynomials) addressing just two values, like this:

$$Y(x_i, x_j) = a_0 + a_1 x_i + a_2 x_j + a_3 x_i^2 + a_4 x_j^2 + a_5 x_i x_j + \ldots$$

(In GMDH networks, every neuron has two inputs and produces a polynomial value from these two values.) The coefficients a can be learned from training data through simple methods such as *least squares* (https://en.wikipedia.org/wiki/Least_squares). GMDH networks optimize themselves by minimizing an external quality criterion: they select subsets of polynomial functions and estimate their coefficients. In 1971, Ivakhnenko presented the first deep eight-layer network based on GMDH (see Ivakhnenko 1971).

Yet this memorable fact did not coincide with the official launch of deep learning. The simplistic methods for weight tuning by GMDH were not scalable to large-scale training. It took a while before more scalable weight-tuning methods like backpropagation came into being: while invented around 1970, they found their way into neural nets not before the late 1980s. (See section 2.4 of *Deep Learning with Python* [Chollet 2017] for an introduction to backpropagation.)

But even with backpropagation, neural networks suffered from various practical problems, including the notorious *vanishing gradient* issue. This problem arises during the training of a network. The crucial ingredient of backpropagation is the stepwise minimization of the error function of a neural network by taking partial derivatives of the error function of the network, differentiating for all weights, and moving stepwise toward its minimum. Gradients are a generalization of the one-variable partial derivative of a function. Setting a partial derivative to zero finds a local maximum or minimum of a function. If this function is an error function that computes the error a network makes for predicting certain output based on weights, we can look for weight adjustments that push the error function ever closer to its minimum. This procedure is called *gradient descent*, and it's the driving force behind backpropagation. Backpropagation has built up an impressive track record and underlies the majority of neural network results.

However, for deep and complex networks with millions of weights, weight adjustments can easily become too tiny to be useful: they vanish, and gradient descent is no longer effective. Backpropagation deploys the so-called *chain rule* from calculus to compute the weight adaptations per layer. The chain rule is an algorithm for computing derivatives of functions that are applied to functions. Essentially, this is what happens when we apply activation functions to the output of layers (which themselves apply activation functions to the output of the layers that feed into them, and so on).

As mentioned, gradient descent uses composed derivatives by working across layers and their respective activation functions and, accordingly, makes weight updates that move the network closer to perfection. Activation functions with gradients in intervals capped by small numbers (say, between 0 and 1) result in weight adaptations that are small by nature, and repeated multiplication of these small numbers with the chain rule leads to thinning and, eventually, evaporation of values. This means the weight adaptations (which are computed from the topmost layer of the network, just under the output layer) never reach the layers close to the input layer, which subsequently do not get trained.

So, how did deep learning escape this conundrum? There are at least a couple of solutions that have alleviated the problem. The most prominent is the use of a feature selection/data reconstruction cycle, as put forward by restricted Boltzmann machines (RBMs). RBMs are complete networks that learn probability distributions from data. They can be stacked on top of each other, as layers, where every layer is a separate RBM sending its hidden layer data as input to the next layer and not through interlayer connections between hidden layers. This setup allows for layer-wise training of networks and eliminates much of the vanishing gradient problem since gradients don't need to travel far down the network: they are confined to separate layers. A similar idea—multilevel hierarchies of recurrent neural networks—was coined earlier by Jürgen Schmidhuber (1992). Sequential, recurrent models like LSTMs have also been found to be relatively insusceptible to vanishing gradients.

In addition to all this, a new type of activation function has become popular in deep learning: the rectified linear unit (ReLU). A ReLU is a very simple non-linear function that computes a maximum of two values, one of which is the input to a neuron. Specifically,

```
ReLU(x)  = max(0,x)
```

So, ReLU(x) just returns which is bigger: zero or *x*. It eliminates all values of *x* less than zero.

Now, if we apply this function to every neuron in our network, only those with positive values promote their values:

$$y = \text{ReLU}(\Sigma_i\,(\text{weight}_i \times \text{input}_i) + \text{bias})$$

This formula expresses the effect of ReLU applied to a sum (Σ) of inputs multiplied by weights, augmented with a bias term. Figure 1.11 shows how this works.

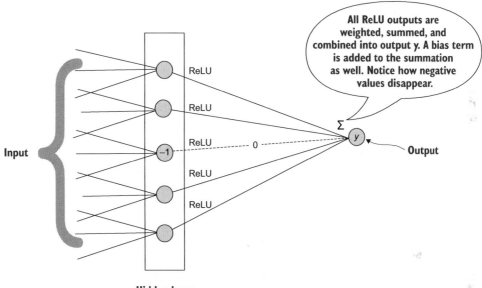

Figure 1.11 **ReLU operations at work on the final hidden layer output of a neural net. Negative values are squashed to zero by the ReLU operations.**

The ReLU function is differentiable almost everywhere except exactly 0, and its derivative is quite simple,

$$\text{ReLU}'(x) = 1 \text{ if } x > 0 \text{ and } 0 \text{ else}$$

which has beneficial effects on the speed and scalability of the network computations during backpropagation.

A traditional activation function is the sigmoid function:

$$\text{sigmoid}(x) = 1\ /\ (1 + e^x)$$

To witness the dramatic effect the choice of an activation has on the performance of your neural network, let's try out an overly deep network on a small snippet of sentiment data.

Scenario: Sentiment labeling

You want to train a deep network on a sentiment labeling task. The task consists of labeling texts with sentiment labels: 1 for positive sentiment and 0 for negative. You are unsure about which activation function you should choose. Can you find out experimentally the best option?

Our processing pipeline is depicted in figure 1.12.

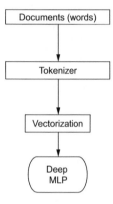

Figure 1.12 **Labeling sentiments with a deep multilayer perceptron. Documents are tokenized, vectorized, and fed to a deep MLP, together with their sentiment labels.**

Our data, taken from Pang and Lee (2004), is a set of sentences, each labeled with either a zero (negative sentiment) or a one (positive sentiment).

Review	Sentiment score
smart and alert , thirteen conversations about one thing is a small gem	1
color , musical bounce and warm seas lapping on island shores and just enough science to send you home thinking	1
it is not a mass-market entertainment but an uncompromising attempt by one artist to think about another	1
a love affair with a veterinarian who is a non-practicing jew	1
initially reluctant to help , daniel's conscience eventually gets the better of him	0
his plans go awry , however , when his older brother , keith , returns from prison	0
inspired and motivated , the kids save the day , showing bravery and nobility	0

In raw format, our data looks like the following. It is tab-delimited data with a header containing the names of two columns:

```
"text"<tab>"label"
smart and alert , thirteen conversations about one thing is a small gem <tab>1
...
```

Our model is a network 10 layers deep, as shown in the following listing. The model is trained on 90% of our training data, and we keep 10% separate for validation purposes.

Listing 1.3   10-layer MLP sentiment classifier

The pandas library has many handy functions for processing comma-separated (csv) and tab-delimited (tsv) data.

Our data is tab-delimited: sentences separated from their labels by tabs. We read the data into a dataframe (a primitive of pandas) and extract the "text" field (the column labeled with "text" in our data) as our document set.

```python
from keras.models import Sequential
from keras.utils import np_utils
from keras.preprocessing.text import Tokenizer
from keras.layers.core import Dense, Activation

import pandas as pd
import sys

data = pd.read_csv(sys.argv[1],sep='\t')
docs=data["text"]

tokenizer = Tokenizer()
tokenizer.fit_on_texts(docs)

X_train = tokenizer.texts_to_matrix(docs, mode='binary')
y_train=np_utils.to_categorical(data["label"])

input_dim = X_train.shape[1]
nb_classes = y_train.shape[1]

model = Sequential()
model.add(Dense(128, input_dim=input_dim))
model.add(Activation('sigmoid'))
model.add(Dense(128))
model.add(Activation('sigmoid'))
model.add(Dense(128))
model.add(Activation('sigmoid'))
model.add(Dense(128))
model.add(Activation('sigmoid'))
model.add(Dense(128))
model.add(Activation('sigmoid'))
model.add(Dense(128))
model.add(Activation('sigmoid'))
model.add(Dense(128))
model.add(Activation('sigmoid'))
model.add(Dense(128))
model.add(Activation('sigmoid'))
model.add(Dense(128))
model.add(Activation('sigmoid'))
model.add(Dense(nb_classes))
model.add(Activation('softmax'))
model.compile(loss='binary_crossentropy',
```

We obtain the text field contents of our dataframe (the document texts).

Keras has a tokenizer facility for converting text into numerical vectors, consisting of unique integers referring to the original words.

We apply the tokenizer to our documents.

We infer the input size (dimension) from our vectorized data and the number of classes.

The network contains 10 Dense layers (standard, fully connected layers) and deploys sigmoid activation functions that pass the incoming connections into each neuron through the sigmoid function.

Next we generate vector representations of our documents. Together, they form a matrix. The tokenizer builds up a lexicon mapping words to integers and generates binary vectors of a fixed dimension with a 1 for every word in the input document, counting from zero. So, a 1 on position 3 means that word 2 in the lexicon is in the document.

The output layer is a Dense layer with as many neurons as the number of classes.

The softmax activation function generates output probabilities.

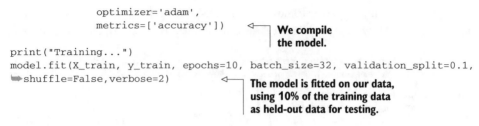

```
              optimizer='adam',
              metrics=['accuracy'])          We compile
                                             the model.
print("Training...")
model.fit(X_train, y_train, epochs=10, batch_size=32, validation_split=0.1,
    shuffle=False,verbose=2)                 The model is fitted on our data,
                                             using 10% of the training data
                                             as held-out data for testing.
```

Here is an example of a Keras tokenizer vectorizing text data:

```
>>> docs = ['smart and alert , thirteen conversations about one thing is a
    small gem','not very smart movie']
>>> tok=Tokenizer()
>>> tok.fit_on_texts(docs)
>>> tok.texts_to_matrix(doc, mode='binary')
array([[0., 1., 1., 1., 1., 1., 1., 1., 1., 1., 1., 1., 1., 0., 0., 0.,
        0.],
       [0., 0., 0., 0., 0., 0., 0., 0., 0., 0., 0., 0., 1., 0., 1., 1.,
        1.]])
>>> tok.word_index
{'and': 1, 'a': 9, 'about': 5, 'very': 15, 'not': 14, 'conversations': 4,
    'is': 8, 'one': 6, 'mart': 13, 'thing': 7, 'thirteen': 3, 'movie': 16,
    'small': 10, 'alert': 2, 'gem': 11, 'smart': 12}
```

On our data, the model produces the following output:

```
Train on 1800 samples, validate on 200 samples
Epoch 1/10
2s - loss: 0.7079 - acc: 0.5078 - val_loss: 0.6937 - val_acc: 0.5200
Epoch 2/10
1s - loss: 0.6983 - acc: 0.5144 - val_loss: 0.6938 - val_acc: 0.5200
Epoch 3/10
1s - loss: 0.6984 - acc: 0.5100 - val_loss: 0.6955 - val_acc: 0.5200
Epoch 4/10
1s - loss: 0.6988 - acc: 0.5000 - val_loss: 0.6979 - val_acc: 0.5200
Epoch 5/10
1s - loss: 0.6994 - acc: 0.4922 - val_loss: 0.6994 - val_acc: 0.5200
Epoch 6/10
1s - loss: 0.6999 - acc: 0.4989 - val_loss: 0.6986 - val_acc: 0.5200
Epoch 7/10
1s - loss: 0.6999 - acc: 0.4978 - val_loss: 0.6966 - val_acc: 0.5200
Epoch 8/10
1s - loss: 0.6993 - acc: 0.4956 - val_loss: 0.6953 - val_acc: 0.5200
Epoch 9/10
1s - loss: 0.6986 - acc: 0.5000 - val_loss: 0.6946 - val_acc: 0.5200
Epoch 10/10
1s - loss: 0.6982 - acc: 0.5111 - val_loss: 0.6944 - val_acc: 0.5200
```

We observe that the network doesn't seem to learn at all: its validation accuracy (the accuracy it attains on a held-out test portion of its training data during training) does not increase. You can see this in the output listing: the val_acc value remains fixed at 0.52 throughout training. Further, the accuracy of the classifier (acc), as computed on its own training data, fluctuates around 50% and doesn't seem to get any better.

Now, let's compare this to a network that has exactly the same structure but is equipped with ReLU activation functions.

Listing 1.4   Deep MLP sentiment classifier with ReLU activation functions

```
...
model = Sequential()
model.add(Dense(128, input_dim=input_dim))
model.add(Activation('relu'))
model.add(Dense(128))
model.add(Activation('relu'))
model.add(Dense(128))
...
```

This produces the following:

```
Epoch 1/10
2s - loss: 0.6042 - acc: 0.6128 - val_loss: 0.3713 - val_acc: 0.8350
Epoch 2/10
1s - loss: 0.1335 - acc: 0.9478 - val_loss: 0.5356 - val_acc: 0.8250
Epoch 3/10
1s - loss: 0.0073 - acc: 0.9983 - val_loss: 0.9263 - val_acc: 0.8500
Epoch 4/10
1s - loss: 1.3958e-05 - acc: 1.0000 - val_loss: 0.9707 - val_acc: 0.8550
Epoch 5/10
1s - loss: 6.7025e-06 - acc: 1.0000 - val_loss: 1.0057 - val_acc: 0.8550
Epoch 6/10
1s - loss: 4.2353e-06 - acc: 1.0000 - val_loss: 1.0420 - val_acc: 0.8550
Epoch 7/10
1s - loss: 2.8474e-06 - acc: 1.0000 - val_loss: 1.0798 - val_acc: 0.8500
Epoch 8/10
1s - loss: 2.0100e-06 - acc: 1.0000 - val_loss: 1.1124 - val_acc: 0.8500
Epoch 9/10
1s - loss: 1.4673e-06 - acc: 1.0000 - val_loss: 1.1427 - val_acc: 0.8500
Epoch 10/10
1s - loss: 1.1042e-06 - acc: 1.0000 - val_loss: 1.1698 - val_acc: 0.8500
```

Much better! We now obtain a score of 85% on the 10% held-out portion of our data during training and even a 100% accuracy score on our training data (which actually may mean we're overfitting our model). (Check that the results of the ReLU network are consistently better than those of the sigmoid network by running both networks a number of times.)

In the next chapter, we will explore the technology of deep learning further. Deep learning needs data in vectorized formats. How do we turn textual data into such representations?

1.3   *Vector representations of language*

Most machine learning algorithms work with *vectors*: fixed-size containers (sequences) of (usually) numerical values. In this section, we address procedures for generating these vectors from text. From a mathematical point of view, these vectors correspond to points in multidimensional spaces. Machine learning is all about measuring distances between objects (points) in these spaces, which, for typical machine learning applications like text mining, are very high-dimensional and, as such, escape our human intuition in terms of geometry. To convert texts to vectors, quite a number of approaches are possible (figure 1.13). There are roughly two types of vector representations of language:

- *Representational vectors*—Vectors that are directly computed
- *Operational (or procedural) vectors*—Vectors estimated from data, either with statistics or with machine learning

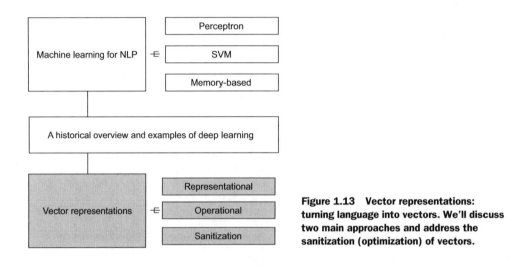

Figure 1.13   Vector representations: turning language into vectors. We'll discuss two main approaches and address the sanitization (optimization) of vectors.

As mentioned, we focus mainly on representational vectors in this section. These are vector representations that are not learned (estimated) from data; they can be computed directly (and exactly) from data.

1.3.1   *Representational vectors*

Representational vectors represent texts by describing them across a number of human-interpretable *feature dimensions*. For text, trivially, representing words with characters is the simplest form of such a vector. An example would be 10-dimensional character-valued vectors:

$$v\ e\ c\ t\ o\ r ----$$

But usually, we deploy more elaborate representations. Consider again Dutch diminutive formation in lexical morphology. Dutch uses diminutive suffixes:

hospitaal => hospitaal+tje ("small hospital") woning => wonin+kje ("small house")

These suffixes are conditioned on a fixed number of phonetic (sound), morphological (word formation), and orthographic (spelling) features of the suffix (ending) of a word, plus similar features of the preceding context. An imaginable feature vector with 12 dimensions (separated with commas) plus a class label for *hospitaal* would be

$$+,h,O,s,-,p,i,=,-,t,a,l,T$$

with the "+,-" indicating phonetic stress or no stress on the syllables *hos*, *pi*, and *taal*, and the other features denoting phonemic representations of the characters in the word. The T label indicates the type of diminutive suffix (here: *-tje*).

In our representation, words that are shorter than 12 characters obtain dummy values for absent dimensions:

$$=,=,=,=,=,=,=,=,+,v,A,xt,J \; (\,'vacht',\,fur)$$

And words that exceed 12 characters are truncated:

$$+,G,e,t,-,m,@,=,-,n,i,t,J \; (\,'\ldots geetmenietje',\,from\,'vergeetmenietje'\,(forget\text{-}me\text{-}not))$$

Bag-of-words representations are also representational in the sense that every dimension can be interpreted as representing a clear feature dimension: the presence (binary-valued, yes/no) of a certain word in an index lexicon. As an example, the following sentences

> *Natural language is hard for computers. Computers are capable of learning natural language.*

can be represented by binary vectors as follows. First we create a lexicon consisting of the set of different words, with each word linked to a unique identifier.

are	1
capable	2
computers	3
for	4
hard	5
is	6
language	7
learning	8
natural	9
of	10

Based on this lexicon, we index the two sentences like this.

are	capable	computer	for	hard	is	language	learning	natural	of
0	0	1	1	1	1	1	0	1	0

and

are	capable	computer	for	hard	is	language	learning	natural	of
1	1	1	0	0	0	1	1	1	0

with every 0 or 1 at a certain position i indicating the absence or presence of the ith word in the lexicon in the sentence.

A simple Python example to compute such binary bag-of-words representations is shown in listing 1.5. This example creates a count vector for documents in a tab-separated text file, with a structure like this

```
text    label
"Natural language is hard for computers."    0
"Computers are capable of learning natural language."    1
```

where the labels are the different classes in which the different texts reside. Every document is represented by a vector of fixed size; and at every position, a count for a specific word is bound to that position. The algorithm fits a dictionary function called a CountVectorizer (a construct native to the SciKit library sklearn: see chapter 2) to the documents, capped at the 1,000 most recent words. Effectively, these 1,000 words form the lexicon by which texts are indexed, leading to vectors of maximum size 1,000 (if the number of different words in the underlying documents is $N < 1,000$, the vector size will be N).

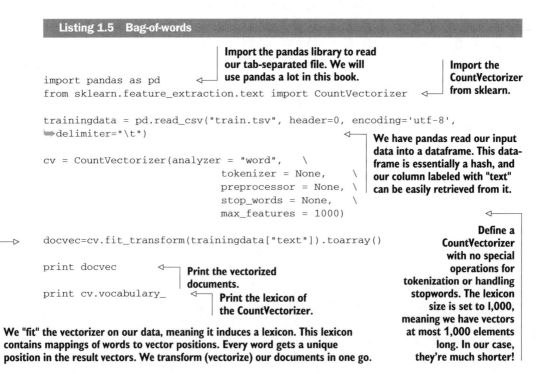

Listing 1.5   Bag-of-words

```
import pandas as pd
from sklearn.feature_extraction.text import CountVectorizer

trainingdata = pd.read_csv("train.tsv", header=0, encoding='utf-8',
⇒delimiter="\t")

cv = CountVectorizer(analyzer = "word",      \
                     tokenizer = None,       \
                     preprocessor = None,    \
                     stop_words = None,      \
                     max_features = 1000)

docvec=cv.fit_transform(trainingdata["text"]).toarray()

print docvec

print cv.vocabulary_
```

Import the pandas library to read our tab-separated file. We will use pandas a lot in this book.

Import the CountVectorizer from sklearn.

We have pandas read our input data into a dataframe. This dataframe is essentially a hash, and our column labeled with "text" can be easily retrieved from it.

Define a CountVectorizer with no special operations for tokenization or handling stopwords. The lexicon size is set to 1,000, meaning we have vectors at most 1,000 elements long. In our case, they're much shorter!

Print the vectorized documents.

Print the lexicon of the CountVectorizer.

We "fit" the vectorizer on our data, meaning it induces a lexicon. This lexicon contains mappings of words to vector positions. Every word gets a unique position in the result vectors. We transform (vectorize) our documents in one go.

This produces the following:

```
[ [0 0 1 1 1 1 1 0 1 0]
  [1 1 1 0 0 0 1 1 1 1]
  ]

{u'hard': 4, u'natural': 8, u'for': 3, u'language': 6, u'capable': 1,
 u'of': 9, u'is': 5, u'computers': 2, u'are': 0, u'learning': 7}
```

This result includes two vectorized documents and a dictionary linking positions (starting at zero) in each vector to words. For instance, word position zero is for *are*; only the second document has a 1 in this position. (If there were two instances of *are* in the second document, we would have a value of 2 here.)

> **One-hot vectors**
>
> *One-hot* vector representations of words consist of a sparsely populated *N*-dimensional vector, with *N* the size of a lexicon. Only one of the dimensions has a value of 1, the dimension corresponding to a given word. For instance, given a lexicon of 100,000 words, every word in a document is represented by an unwieldy 100,000-dimensional vector with just one digit "on."

1.3.2 Operational vectors

Operational vector representations reflect a derived representation of data, as produced by some algorithm. Typically, these vectors are not human-interpretable, as they are produced by irreversible computations producing numerical vectors.

An example is the TF.IDF vector representation. With this representation, words are weighted with numerical scores consisting of a product of *term frequency* and *inverse document frequency*. These scores express a degree of *salience*: lower-weighted words like stopwords are less salient (that is, less "special").

Document representations based on TF.IDF weighting help machine learning algorithms zoom in on important words. Virtually every machine learning algorithm computes (often implicitly) similarities between vectors, and stressing important dimensions (like salient words) while downplaying others (like stopwords) can contribute to fine-grained similarity estimates.

The *term frequency* quantity expresses the frequency of a given word in the document to be represented:

$$tf(w \mid d) = \mid w \in d \mid$$

This simply defines the term frequency of a word w given a document d as the number of times the word w occurs in d.

The *inverse document frequency* describes the frequency of the word in other documents in a given document collection D consisting of documents d:

$$idf(w \mid d, D) = \log \frac{\mid D \mid}{\mid d \in D : w \in d \mid}$$

The product of these two quantities, TF.IDF, is a number that balances the frequency of a word with the number of documents it appears in:

$$tf.idf(w \mid d, D) = tf(w \mid d) \times idf(w \mid d, D)$$

Whenever the latter number is high (meaning a given word is common), the *idf* quantity will approach zero, since $\log(1) = 0$ and the ratio of the log will reach 1 when d occurs in all documents in the collection D. The idf factor thus effectively suppresses the contribution of the frequency of the word to the TF.IDF weight. This implies that stop words like *the*, *is* and *what* usually (depending on the document collection D) have low TF.IDF scores, whereas peculiar words typically produce high scores.

Binary bag-of-words vectors can be augmented with frequencies

$$BOW(d = w_1, \ldots, w_n \mid L) = \vec{v}[i] \mapsto tf(w_i \mid d) \; if \; w_i \in L$$

or with tf-idf:

$$BOW(d = w_1, \ldots, w_n \mid L, D) = \vec{v}[i] \mapsto tf.idf(w_i \mid d, D) \; if \; w_i \in L$$

where L is a lexicon.

Another type of operational vector for texts is produced by neural networks: neural word embeddings.

NEURAL WORD EMBEDDINGS

Neural word embeddings are easily one of the most important inventions in text mining in the last decade. These embeddings, commonly known as Word2Vec embeddings (Mikolov 2013), generate operational vector representations of words. Embeddings are produced by neural networks that predict words given a certain context or, vice versa, a lexical context (words likely to occur in the context) given a certain word. The inputs and outputs to these networks usually consist of one-hot vectors. For instance, the latter variant (predicting contexts for words) has the structure shown in figure 1.14.

In the figure, input vectors represent a single word of dimension V, a hidden layer (H) of dimension N, and a composed output layer (O) of dimension M, with subvectors corresponding to predicted context words. Two weight matrices W and W' encode the learned weights. Once the network is

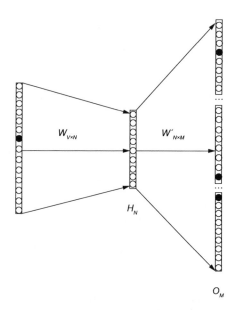

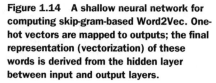

Figure 1.14   A shallow neural network for computing skip-gram-based Word2Vec. One-hot vectors are mapped to outputs; the final representation (vectorization) of these words is derived from the hidden layer between input and output layers.

trained on large numbers of words mapping to contexts, the hidden layer serves as a vector representation of each input word. We discuss this in much more detail in chapter 3.

During training, the network fine-tunes hidden-layer representations that can represent words in a compact and semantically meaningful way: two words that share similar contexts are associated with vectors that are relatively similar. This is a form of *distributional semantic similarity*. Neural networks that create word embeddings are by no means *deep*: they are, in fact, *shallow*, typically consisting of one hidden layer and one input layer. However, word embeddings have become very popular as input to deep neural networks.

Scenario: Vector combination

Let's assume we are building a sentiment classifier. The classifier needs to work with fixed-size vectors, and every vector represents a short document such as a tweet.

We can generate neural word embeddings for every word in our tweets by using a freely available large set of 300-dimensional vectors produced by Google on a 1-billion-word corpus of news texts. One way of combining the separate word embeddings is by *averaging*: we sum all N-dimensional vectors, again producing an N-dimensional result vector, and divide every component of that vector by K, with K being the number of words in our tweet. So, the tweet is represented with an average word embedding, which, geometrically, corresponds to the centroid of the vector space spanned by the various word embeddings vectors of its words. The process is depicted in figure 1.15.

The code in listing 1.6 does all that. It starts by defining an array of tweets: in this case, a few tweets by Donald Trump. Subsequently, using the Gensim open source library (https://radimrehurek.com/gensim), it loads the Google news-based Word2Vec model storing three-dimensional word vectors (it's huge, so this takes a while). After that, it creates a vector container, to which it adds an averaged Word2Vec vector for every

Figure 1.15   Averaged Word2Vec vectors as document representations. Words are mapped to vectors through lookup, after which these word vectors are added and averaged for entire documents.

tweet. These vectors could serve as training data by linking them to adequate labels such as topics or sentiments.

Listing 1.6   Average Word2Vec vectors

```
import gensim
import numpy as np
```

```
tweets=["With the great vote on Cutting Taxes, this could be a big day for
➥the Stock Market - and YOU","Putting Pelosi/Schumer Liberal Puppet
➥Jones into office in Alabama would hurt our great Republican Agenda
➥of low on taxes, tough on crime, strong on military and borders...
➥& so much more. Look at your 401-k's since Election. Highest Stock
➥Market EVER! Jobs are roaring back!",
...]                                          ◄──┤ A list of tweets

model = gensim.models.Word2Vec.load_word2vec_format(
➥'GoogleNews-vectors-negative300.bin', binary=True)               ◄─────┐

vectA=[]                                                    Load a pre-trained Word2Vec
                                                            model from Google consisting
for tweet in tweets:            Create a result vector      of 300-dimensional vectors
    vect=np.zeros(300)    ◄──┘  consisting of zeros.        derived from news data.
    n=0                                ◄─┐
    for word in tweet.split(" "):        │  Declare a counter for the number of words in
        if word in model.wv:             │  a tweet that we find in our Word2Vec model.
            vect=np.add(vect, model.wv[word])   ◄─┐
            n+=1                                   │  To the result vector, we add the
    vect=np.divide(vect,n)        ◄─┐              │  Word2Vec vectors of the words in
    vectA.append(vect)             │              │  the tweet, if those words are in
                       Normalize the vector by    │  the Word2Vec model. The gensim
return vectA           dividing the aggregated Word2Vec  method wv defined on Word2Vec
                       contributions by the number of    models performs that check.
                       words found in the model.
```

This produces normalized Word2Vec vectors for tweets. It turns out these representations are adequate for performing all kinds of analyses, like sentiment classification. More on that later: in chapter 3, we will build Word2Vec embeddings ourselves rather than using pre-built embeddings.

1.4   *Vector sanitization*

Whether representational or operational, vectors can be sanitized or optimized using many postprocessing procedures. We discuss two of them next: dimensionality reduction by hashing, and normalization.

1.4.1   *The hashing trick*

Large vectors are unwieldy to handle. They take up lots of memory and may consist of many irrelevant, sparsely populated dimensions. Imagine indexing documents based on a very large lexicon, say, 100,000 words. Even for the shortest text, this would lead to a vector representation of 100,000 dimensions. Representing every binary digit (0,1) with one bit, every vector claims 12,500 bytes, or 12 KB. Now imagine your training data for, say, a topic classifier contains 100,000 labeled example documents. This produces a dataset that is roughly 1.2 GB, which is a hefty size even for current hardware. As it turns out, there is a handy option available for reducing dimensionality through algorithmic processing: the *hashing trick*, also known as *feature hashing*.

The hashing trick is an algorithm for reducing the dimensionality of large feature vectors by applying a hashing function to the features in the vectors. The hashing function maps every feature to an index, and the algorithm updates the information at those indices only.

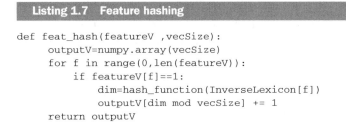

```
def feat_hash(featureV ,vecSize):
    outputV=numpy.array(vecSize)
    for f in range(0,len(featureV)):
        if featureV[f]==1:
            dim=hash_function(InverseLexicon[f])
            outputV[dim mod vecSize] += 1
    return outputV
```

In this code, assume we have an inverted lexicon `InverseLexicon`, which maps an integer to a word (rather than mapping words to indices). This inverse lexicon restores the positive indices in the binary-valued input vector `featureV`, a hash value given some hashing function. The value is capped to fall in the range 0…`vecSize` (where `vecSize` is the desired size of the output vector). In this way, the hashing function performs the indexing: similar input values will lead to similar numerical indices being incremented. The amount of similarity is handled by the specific hash function chosen.

Collisions may occur where different features share the same indices due to the use of the `modulo` function:

$$5 \bmod 4 = 1 \; 9 \bmod 4 = 1$$

But these can be handled gracefully with an extra hashing function (for example, see https://en.wikipedia.org/wiki/Feature_hashing).

1.4.2   *Vector normalization*

Vectors represent quantities in vector space. It is intuitive to think about vectors as arrows with both magnitude (the length of an arrow) and direction (the angle of an arrow with respect to the origin of the space it lives in). See figure 1.16.

The magnitude of a vector v can be computed using Pythagoras' theorem:

$$\| v \| = \sqrt{\sum_{i}^{n} v_i^2}$$

Dividing every component of the vector v by its magnitude forces the magnitude of the vector to be exactly 1.

Vectors containing numeric information (like the TF.IDF vectors we came across) can be *normalized*. This means they are squeezed into a subspace, reducing the variance across

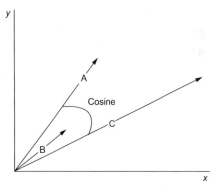

Figure 1.16   Vectors represented in 2D space. Vectors with the same direction can be added (A and B) and can have different lengths. The cosine can be computed between vectors as a measure for similarity. In document space, where documents are represented as vectors, the x-axis is essentially meaningless and corresponds to a certain word. The y-axis corresponds to, for example, the frequency of that specific word in a document.

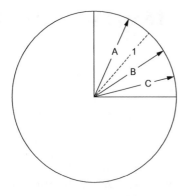

Figure 1.17   Normalized vectors: the unit norm

their dimensions. In figure 1.17, all vectors have been normalized to a magnitude of 1.

In this case, all vectors A, B, and C have been normalized by dividing all components of every vector by their magnitude. A vector v's normalized version can be expressed as

$$\hat{v} = \frac{v}{\| v \|}$$

Any such normalized vector is called a *unit vector*. Why bother with normalization? Because it forces vectors to lie in the same data range, aiding any machine learning algorithm that is sensitive to outlier data.

Now that we've gotten all that out of our way, it is time to turn to deep learning. The next chapter discusses the fundamental architectures of deep learning for NLP. We return to the topic of vector representations in chapter 3, where we discuss operational vector representations (embeddings) of texts.

Summary

- Many different forms of NLP are rooted in machine learning and statistics.
- Deep learning traces back to the 1960s, but it only became operational a few decades later.
- Text needs to be vectorized in order for machine learning to perform natural language processing.
- While many options are open for vectorization, inferring and optimizing vectorization from data with machine learning (like Word2Vec) is preferable.

Deep learning and language: The basics

This chapter covers

- Highlighting the fundamental architectures of deep learning: multilayer perceptrons and spatial and temporal filtering
- Introducing deep learning models for natural language processing

After reading this chapter, you will have a clear idea of how deep learning works in general, why it is different from other machine learning approaches, and what it brings to the field of natural language processing. This chapter introduces you to some Keras concepts and their implementation details through examples.

2.1 Basic architectures of deep learning

Let's investigate the basic architectures of deep learning: multilayer perceptrons and different forms of filtering input, spatial and temporal (see figure 2.1).

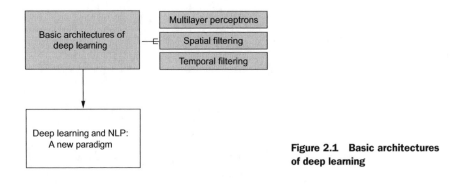

Figure 2.1   **Basic architectures of deep learning**

2.1.1   *Deep multilayer perceptrons*

The prototypical deep learning network is a *multilayer perceptron* (MLP). We came across these in chapter 1, and we repeat the architecture in figure 2.2 for a simple multilayer perceptron that has only a single hidden layer.

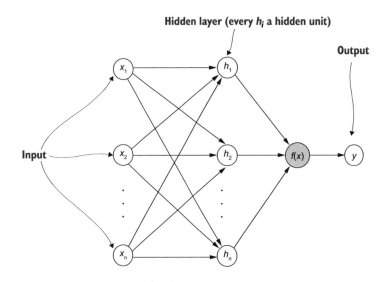

Figure 2.2   **A multilayer perceptron with an input layer, one hidden layer ($h_1...h_n$), and an output layer. Multidimensional input is processed by neurons $x_1...x_n$. These neurons are like singular perceptrons, the difference being that they do not threshold their activation and produce a label, but instead send their activations to neurons in the hidden layer. Finally, the threshold function $f(x)$ gathers all input, and an output y is predicted. Every connection between input and neurons, and between neurons, is weighted; and weights are learned during the training of the perceptron.**

MLPs consist of layers containing *artificial neurons*, which are basically mathematical functions that receive input from weighted connections to other neurons. They produce output values through a variety of mathematical operations. Deep neural networks have many neurons and lots of weights to manipulate. A typical deep network usually has many hidden layers. But how many? Is there a magic threshold that demarcates the boundary between shallow and deep learning? As you may guess, there is no such magic number; but informally, networks with more than two layers between their input and output layer may be deemed *deep*.

Let's go through a Keras implementation of a five-layer-deep architecture of such an MLP step by step, sidestepping the processing of training data. Figure 2.3 illustrates how the model is built up.

Listing 2.1   A deep MLP: creating the model

```
from keras.models import Sequential
from keras.utils import np_utils
from keras.preprocessing.text import Tokenizer
from keras.layers.core import Dense, Activation, Dropout
# ... process data
model = Sequential()
model.add(Dense(128, input_dim=input_dim))
model.add(Activation('relu'))
```

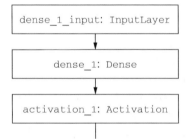

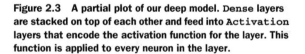

Figure 2.3   **A partial plot of our deep model.** `Dense` **layers are stacked on top of each other and feed into** `Activation` **layers that encode the activation function for the layer. This function is applied to every neuron in the layer.**

Our definition of the network starts by importing the relevant Keras facilities: a `Sequential` model, which defines a container for a stacked set of layers, and facilities for defining layers. We initialize such a container called `model`. To this container, we add a `Dense` layer with an input dimension of `input_dim` (a self-defined variable) and an output dimension of 128. `Dense` layers connect all incoming neurons from a previous layer to neurons in the next layer; they are *fully connected*. In our case, the first `Dense` layer consumes input with dimension (`batch_size`, `input_dim`), which is a tensor (a container for numerical data). The `batch_size` determines the grouping of data points in batches that are handled collectively during network training. Leaving the `batch_size` implicit is permitted; it then defaults to 1. Every layer is followed by an `Activation` layer, encoding the activation function for that layer. This can be done through a separate layer (as we did) or by specifying an attribute for the `Dense` layer in Keras. This `Dense` layer feeds into a layer of dimension 128, producing a tensor (`batch_size`, 128).

Every input unit (that is, every component of the input_dim-sized input vector) feeds into every one of those 128 next Dense layer components. Notice that you only need to specify the size of the data feeding into a Dense layer once: upon initialization.

Let's add a couple of those layers to our network. Each deploys a rectified linear unit (ReLU) activation function by feeding into a ReLU layer.

Listing 2.2   A deep MLP: adding layers

```
# ...
model.add(Dense(128))
model.add(Activation('relu'))

model.add(Dense(128))
model.add(Activation('relu'))

model.add(Dense(128))
model.add(Activation('relu'))

model.add(Dense(128))
model.add(Activation('relu'))

model.add(Dense(nb_classes))
model.add(Activation('softmax'))
```

After devising our model, we "compile" it. This means we prepare the model for training by specifying a *loss function* (a real-valued function that computes the mismatch between predictions the model makes and the labels it should assign according to the training data) plus a numerical optimizer algorithm carrying out the gradient descent process and an evaluation metric, which is used to perform an intermediate evaluation of the model during training and which specifies the loss of the loss function (like accuracy, or mean squared error). Refer back to chapter 1 if you need a refresher on gradient descent, or pick up the book *Deep Learning with Python* by François Chollet (Manning, 2017). The evaluation metric evaluates the model performance during training on held-out test data taken from the training dataset. In the "fit" step, we can determine the size of this held-out portion of the training data (validation_split=0.1: use 10% of the training data for testing), the number of training epochs (epochs=10), and the size of the batches of training data that are taken into account at every training step (batch_size=32).

Listing 2.3   A deep MLP: compiling and fitting the model to data

```
model.compile(loss='binary_crossentropy',
              optimizer='adam',
              metrics=['accuracy'])

model.fit(X_train, y_train, epochs=10, batch_size=32,
➡validation_split=0.1, shuffle=True,verbose=2)
```

This network is deep according to our informal definition of depth; it has five layers. Its structure is quite simplistic: it connects five similar-sized `Dense` layers in a standard feedforward manner. Our deep learning toolkit has more to offer, though. Let's look at two basic operators we have at our disposal: *spatial* and *temporal* filters.

2.1.2   Two basic operators: Spatial and temporal

Deep learning networks often display the interplay between two types of information filtering: spatial filtering and temporal filtering. Spatial filters address properties of the structure of input data, weeding out irrelevant patches and letting the valuable ones pass. Temporal filters do something similar but work on sequences of memory states that store information from the past. They are typically used for processing sequences.

SPATIAL FILTERING: CONVOLUTIONAL NEURAL NETWORKS

The *convolutional neural network* (CNN) is the driving force behind many of the big successes in image processing. It can be applied to text analysis as well. A CNN applies a set of weighted filters (called *convolutions*) to input data and learns the weights of these filters based on training data. The filters scan the data in multiple locations and gradually become specialized feature detectors, extracting (or rather, *emphasizing*) important pieces of information. Stacking layers of these detectors recreates the marvel of deep learning, where we focus on increasingly abstract representations of our data. We will see how this works in the context of text, but the use of convolutional filters is easiest to understand when applied to images. So let's look at those first. Images can be represented as three-dimensional objects (height, width, color depth), as shown in figure 2.4.

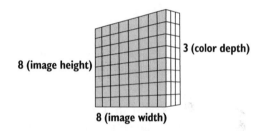

Figure 2.4   A 3D representation of an image. The image has 8 × 8 = 64 pixels, each of which has three RGB (red-green-blue) values for its color. This produces 64 × 3 = 192 numerical values.

A CNN applies a prespecified number of filters to the grid of pixels that constitutes an image. These filters are actually nothing more than weight matrices. Together, they emphasize certain parts of the input image with respect to the classification task at hand. Picture such a filter as a piece of paper smaller than the image, shifted over the image from left to right, top to bottom, visiting all possible arrangements one at a time and continuously shifting a certain fixed number of pixels. This step size is called a *stride*. In the case of processing images, every filter performs a weighted aggregation (a sum of products) on the $N \times N \times 3$ grid of pixel (RGB) values it is visiting.

Every time the filter slides over the image, a separate value is computed based on all the pixels in the image it visits. This value is entered into a new result matrix, which has the dimension $H \times V$, where N is the number of horizontal moves the filter makes and V is the number of vertical moves.

Figure 2.5 shows a 2×2 filter being applied to the top-left corner of our $8 \times 8 \times 3$ image. To explain what's going on, let's assume we're dealing with black-and-white images with just one channel rather than the three RGB channels in color images. Figure 2.6 displays such an image representation.

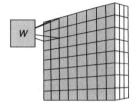

Figure 2.5   Filtering an image with a convolutional filter. The filter W is applied to the selected portion of the image.

1	0	1	1
1	1	1	0
1	0	0	0
1	0	1	1

Figure 2.6   An image represented as a binary grid of numbers; 0 is for black, and 1 is for white.

Assume we have a filter like the one in figure 2.7. Figure 2.8 shows the top-left corner of the grayscale image. Suppose we apply the filter to that portion. Doing so produces the following sum of products:

$$1 \times 1 + 0 \times 0 + 0 \times 1 + 1 \times 1 = 2$$

1	0	…	…
1	1	…	…
…	…	…	…
…	…	…	…

Figure 2.8   Applying a filter to an image. It is applied to the upper-left corner.

1	0
0	1

Figure 2.7   A convolutional filter. This binary filter is applied to the black/white values of the image.

Since we can shift a maximum of three times in the horizontal direction and three times in the vertical direction in the source image, the filter creates a 3×3 output matrix with the sum product of the filter output in every cell, as figure 2.9 shows.

2	…	…
…	…	…
…	…	…

Figure 2.9   Filter output: the result of applying the binary filter to the upper-left corner of the input image

The crucial trick CNNs perform is learning their filters from training data. So, rather than prespecifying the filter matrices by hand, we let CNNs start with random initializations of these filters. Of course, we have to make a few specifications: the number of filters, the stride, and the filter size. But after that, during training, CNNs figure out better weights for their filters and learn to emphasize or de-emphasize certain parts of their data. While these weights will never be optimal in a theoretical sense, they are optimized using the training data and the parameters of the training procedure and are certainly better than the initial random weights.

In separate *max pooling* layers, so-called *max* filters perform a maximum selection over the grids they visit. For instance, if a filter visits a 4×4 image, addressing 2×2 patches with the following values

- [1,1;5,6]
- [2,4;7,8]
- [3,2;1,2]
- [1,0;3,4]

then max pooling will take out the maximum value (6,8,3,4) from this array and send it through to the next layer in the network.

Max pooling can be interpreted as a form of downsampling. Notice how patches of images in this example are converted into separate numbers by just picking out maximum values. This process performs *dimensionality reduction of feature representations*: it converts representations of a certain dimension into lower-dimensional representations. In our example, a 4 × 4 matrix is turned into a 2 × 2 matrix.

CNNs FOR TEXT

CNNs can be applied to text as well. Textual objects like strings are typically 1D objects: streams of characters extending into one dimension, which, for strings, is a horizontal dimension. (It makes no real sense to also discern a vertical dimension of strings; it might make sense for documents, though.) See figure 2.10.

| This | will | be | a | big | week | for | infrastructure | .... |

Figure 2.10   A one-dimensional sequence of words

What is the meaning of the spatial sampling CNNs perform on text? Recall that a regular filter is nothing but a weight matrix that emphasizes or de-emphasizes its input. So, applied to text, a CNN can detect interesting words or other features that are relevant for a certain NLP task. This is (metaphorically) similar to a human scanning a document and marking certain fragments as relevant.

Let's construct a sentiment analysis network, as we did in chapter 1. This time, instead of Dense layers, we'll use convolutional layers. Let's introduce the code first and then go through it step by step. The model is depicted in the diagram in figure 2.11, which was generated by the Keras built-in plot_model function.

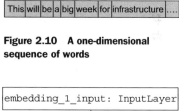

Figure 2.11   Our CNN model. Three 1D convolutional layers are stacked on top of an embedding.

Listing 2.4   CNN for sentiment analysis

```
from keras.models import Sequential
from keras.layers import Dense
from keras.preprocessing.text import Tokenizer
from keras.preprocessing.sequence import pad_sequences
```

Import the necessary modules.

```
from keras.layers import Convolution1D, Flatten, Dropout
from keras.layers.embeddings import Embedding
from sklearn.model_selection import train_test_split
from keras.preprocessing import sequence
import pandas as pd
import sys
from keras.utils.vis_utils import plot_model
```

Read out tab-delimited input data and process it to become a pair of numerical vectors (X) and associated labels (Y).

```
data = pd.read_csv(sys.argv[1],sep='\t')     ◁─┘
max_words = 1000
tokenizer = Tokenizer(num_words=max_words, split=' ')
tokenizer.fit_on_texts(data['text'].values)

X = tokenizer.texts_to_sequences(data['text'].values)
X = pad_sequences(X)
Y = pd.get_dummies(data['label']).values

X_train, X_test, y_train, y_test = train_test_split(
➥X,Y, test_size = 0.2, random_state = 36)
```

Split X and Y into training and test partitions.

```
embedding_vector_length = 100
```

Declare and define our model.

```
model = Sequential()     ◁─┘
model.add(Embedding(
➥max_words, embedding_vector_length,
➥input_length=X.shape[1]))
```

The first (input) layer is an embedding.

```
model.add(Convolution1D(64, 3, padding="same"))     ◁─┐
model.add(Convolution1D(32, 3, padding="same"))
model.add(Convolution1D(16, 3, padding="same"))
```

Three convolutional layers are stacked onto each other.

```
model.add(Flatten())
model.add(Dropout(0.2))
model.add(Dense(2,activation='sigmoid'))
```

They are followed by a flattening operation and a Dropout() action that randomly deselects neurons to prevent overfitting: a too-tight fit to the training data, preventing the model from coping successfully with new, unseen cases.

```
model.summary()     ◁─┘
plot_model(model, to_file='model.png')

model.compile(loss='binary_crossentropy', optimizer='adam',
➥metrics=['accuracy'])     ◁─┐

model.fit(X_train, y_train, epochs=3, batch_size=64)

scores = model.evaluate(X_test, y_test, verbose=0)
print("Accuracy: %.2f%%" % (scores[1]*100))
```

Compile the model and prepare it for fitting the data. It consumes its training data in batches of size 64 during training.

First we read and split our data, our tab-separated file with sentiment-labeled texts:

```
data = pd.read_csv(sys.argv[1],sep='\t')
max_words = 1000
tokenizer = Tokenizer(num_words=max_words, split=' ')
tokenizer.fit_on_texts(data['text'].values)

X = tokenizer.texts_to_sequences(data['text'].values)
X = pad_sequences(X)
Y = pd.get_dummies(data['label']).values

X_train, X_test, y_train, y_test = train_test_split(
➥X,Y, test_size = 0.2, random_state = 36)
```

X and Y together constitute our training data, with X the set of documents and Y the labels. Each document is represented by an array of integers referring to its words, padded to a uniform length with the Keras function pad_sequences. This uniform length is the maximum length of the documents in X, which in our case happens to be 65. We split our data into 80% for training and 20% for testing.

Subsequently, we produce an embedding of the words in our data based on 100-dimensional vector embeddings for every word (embeddings are discussed in chapter 3; they are used for turning text into vector representations):

```
embedding_vector_length = 100

model = Sequential()
model.add(Embedding(
⟿max_words, embedding_vector_length,
⟿input_length=X.shape[1]))
```

We go on to define our model. It contains three convolutional layers:

```
model.add(Convolution1D(64, 3, padding="same"))
model.add(Convolution1D(32, 3, padding="same"))
model.add(Convolution1D(16, 3, padding="same"))
model.add(Flatten())
model.add(Dropout(0.2))
model.add(Dense(2,activation='sigmoid'))
```

Every layer specifies the dimensionality of the output space (64,32,16) and the size of every filter (3), also known as the *kernel size*. The values (64,32,16) were chosen arbitrarily; good practice would be to estimate these values (*hyperparameters*) on some held-out validation data. The stride (step size) is set to 1 by default, but this can be overridden.

The Dropout layer randomly resets a specified fraction (0.2, in our case) of its input units to 0 during training time, at every update step, in order to prevent over-fitting. The longest document in our texts contains 65 words.

Keras has a function model.summary() that generates the layout of a model. The architecture of our model is as follows:

Layer (type)	Output Shape	Param #
embedding_1 (Embedding)	(None, 65, 100)	100000
conv1d_1 (Conv1D)	(None, 65, 64)	19264
conv1d_2 (Conv1D)	(None, 65, 32)	6176
conv1d_3 (Conv1D)	(None, 65, 16)	1552
flatten_1 (Flatten)	(None, 1040)	0
dropout_1 (Dropout)	(None, 1040)	0

```
dense_1 (Dense)                 (None, 2)                    2082
=================================================================
Total params: 129,074
Trainable params: 129,074
Non-trainable params: 0
```

The `Flatten` layer coerces the 65×16 output of the final convolutional layer into a 1040-dimensional array, which is fed into `Dropout`, and a final two-dimensional `Dense` layer containing the binary representation of the output labels (subjective or objective sentiment).

Training the classifier for three iterations and running it on the 20% held-out data gives the following:

```
8000/8000 [==============================] - 4s - loss: 0.4339 - acc: 0.7729
Epoch 2/3
8000/8000 [==============================] - 3s - loss: 0.2558 - acc: 0.8948
Epoch 3/3
8000/8000 [==============================] - 3s - loss: 0.2324 - acc: 0.9052
Accuracy: 87.80%
```

Each line represents the output from an epoch (three epochs total). An epoch represents a full sweep through the training data. The *s indicates the amount of time spent on this epoch (which, of course, is machine and dataset dependent). The loss reported is the error obtained on the training data, which, in our case, is measured with *binary cross-entropy*. Cross-entropy-based loss expresses how well a classification model performs when producing probabilities (values between 0 and 1). This loss function produces larger values when the predictions deviate from the correct labels, so we want to keep the value as low as possible. The `acc` scores express the accuracy of the model, obtained on the training data during training.

Let's see how this works up close. The diagram in figure 2.12 describes the process of stacking the three CNN layers. The words in our data are squeezed through an embedding of size 100, with $1000 \times 100 \times 1$ (100,000) parameters. Its output matrix, padded for the maximum length of our input documents (65), has a size of 65×100. So, every input document is represented by a matrix of size 65×100. The 65 rows correspond to the original word order in the input document, which implements some form of temporal structure. All this is fed to the first convolutional layer, which applies 64 convolution operations with kernel size 3 to the 65 100-dimensional entries of the input vector.

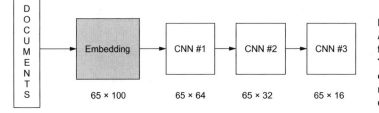

Figure 2.12
A convolutional network for sentiment analysis. Three CNNs are stacked on top of an embedding representing input documents.

Since the filter length (the kernel size) is 3, we start with the first three words (or rows in the matrix). The first filter is applied to the three vector representations of these words. Then we shift one word (`stride=1`) and apply the filter to the vectors of words 2, 3, 4, and so on until we reach the final group (words 63, 64, and 65).

So, for an example like

The quick brown fox jumps over the lazy dog

the filter would proceed like this:

- the quick brown
- quick brown fox
- brown fox jumps
- . . .

For every step, the filter creates a single value. The final list of values is padded to become the same length as the input (in our case, we have 65 − 3 = 62 shifts, so we pad the result vector to 65). This produces one sequence of 65 numbers. Repeating this 64 times with different filters, we end up with a matrix with 65 × 64 values.

The second convolutional layer receives this 2D matrix as input. Since it is a 1D convolutional layer, it applies its 32-fold convolution to the 65 64-dimensional entries. As the first layer, it works on groups of three-word vectors at a time. This again produces 2D output, now with dimensions 65 × 32, and so on.

TEMPORAL FILTERING: RECURRENT NETWORKS

Recurrent neural networks (RNNs) are another type of deep network, with depth extending across the horizontal direction of a timeline: once unfolded, an RNN becomes a sequence of many dependent layers, and the dependencies between weights across these layers are exactly what makes such a network deep.

Similar to CNNs, RNNs emphasize or de-emphasize certain aspects of the information they process, in an end-to-end fashion, working in a temporal dimension rather than a spatial dimension. As with CNNs, this selection process boils down to learning weight matrices. Crucially, RNNs can memorize their previous cognitive states and the decisions they made in the past. This provides a facility for implementing a certain *bias* in a neural net, allowing it to carry out classifications that are in line with what it has done in the recent past. There are two main brands of these networks: simple RNNs and *long short-term memory* (LSTM) networks. Let's start with simple RNNs.

A simple RNN is a neural network with a limited amount of memory. At every time tick, it deploys the hidden memory state of a previous time tick to produce a current output. At any time, an RNN memory state is determined by three factors:

- The memory state at the previous time tick (we assume time passes in a discrete fashion, one tick at a time)
- A weight matrix weighting the previous memory state
- A weight matrix weighting the current input to the RNN

This is illustrated in figure 2.13.

The memory state *S* is updated iteratively, for every time tick *t*, as follows:

$$S_t = S_{t-1} \times W_t + x_t \times W_x$$

Importantly, weights (W_t and W_x) are shared by all updates. Notice how this network has a recurrent loop. It can be expanded (*unrolled*) as shown in figure 2.14.

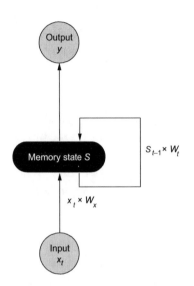

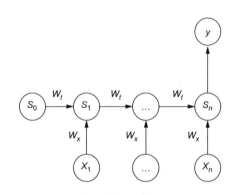

Figure 2.13   A simple RNN. A shared memory state is available in every time step (such as processing a word), and it encodes information from the left context.

Figure 2.14   A simple unrolled RNN. The input $X_1...X_n$ is processed left to right, and at every time step (processing X_i), hidden state information from the left context is available. The unrolled presentation makes this explicit.

Notice that there are as many states as inputs. Every new input transforms the RNN into a new "cognitive" state.

The number of time steps arising from this unrolling constitutes the depth of the network across the temporal dimension. By sharing and updating weights across all inputs (x_t) the network is exposed to, we obtain a system that learns from previous experience and optimizes its weights globally to minimize its training error.

Let's dive into an example. We will build a simple RNN that learns to predict the next character in a string based on the characters that precede that character. Figure 2.15 describes the network.

In this diagram, we start with a one-hot encoding of characters. The one-hot vectors are fed into the hidden units of the RNN that form a temporal chain, with every hidden unit feeding into the next unit through time. Every time tick processes one

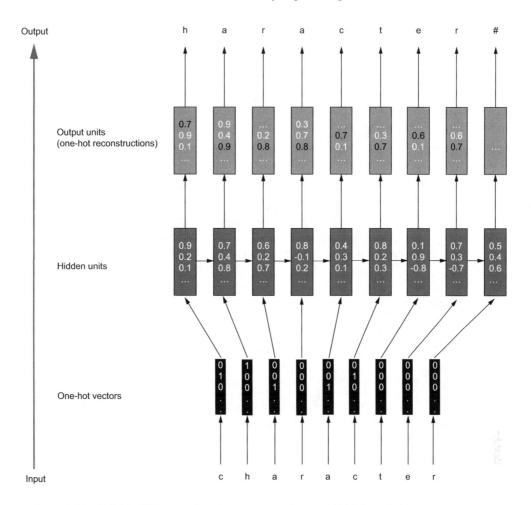

Figure 2.15   A simple RNN to predict characters (see Karpathy 2015 for a similar, less complex example). Normally we would show this diagram top-down, but such diagrams are usually presented bottom-up in the literature. The network predicts characters based on the preceding context.

character. We end with a reconstruction step, where one-hot vectors are reconstructed from the hidden unit outputs. The following listing shows the code.

Listing 2.5   Predicting one character at a time with a simple RNN

```
from keras.models import Sequential
from keras.layers import SimpleRNN, TimeDistributed, Dense
from sklearn.preprocessing import LabelEncoder
```

We use sklearn's LabelEncoder and OneHotEncoder to vectorize our data (one-hot vectors for every character.

Keras offers a dedicated RNN layer (SimpleRNN) and a facility for passing weight information through time (TimeDistributed).

```
from sklearn.preprocessing import OneHotEncoder
import numpy as np
```

Our data is just the string "character."

```
data = ['character']
enc = LabelEncoder()
alphabet = np.array(list(set([c for w in data for c in w]))) #
enc.fit(alphabet)
int_enc=enc.fit_transform(alphabet)
onehot_encoder = OneHotEncoder(sparse=False)
int_enc=int_enc.reshape(len(int_enc), 1)
onehot_encoded = onehot_encoder.fit_transform(int_enc)
```

We derive an alphabet from our data.

```
X_train=[]
y_train=[]
```

We create our training data.

```
for w in data:
    for i in range(len(w)-1):
        X_train.extend(onehot_encoder.transform([enc.transform([w[i]])]))
        y_train.extend(onehot_encoder.transform([enc.transform([w[i+1]])]))
```

```
X_test=[]
y_test=[]
```

```
test_data = ['character']
```

We create our test data.

```
for w in test_data:
    for i in range(len(w)-1):
        X_test.extend(onehot_encoder.transform([enc.transform([w[i]])]))
        y_test.extend(onehot_encoder.transform([enc.transform([w[i+1]])]))
```

```
sample_size=256
sample_len=len(X_train)
```

We generate 256 samples of our training data to arrive at a sizable training set for this toy problem.

```
X_train = np.array([X_train*sample_size]).reshape(
➥sample_size,sample_len,len(alphabet))
y_train = np.array([y_train*sample_size]).reshape(
➥sample_size,sample_len,len(alphabet))
test_len=len(X_test)
X_test= np.array([X_test]).reshape(1,test_len,len(alphabet))
y_test= np.array([y_test]).reshape(1,test_len,len(alphabet))
```

```
model=Sequential()
model.add(SimpleRNN(input_dim  = len(alphabet), output_dim = 100,
➥return_sequences = True))
model.add(TimeDistributed(Dense(output_dim = len(alphabet),
➥activation  = "sigmoid")))
model.compile(loss="binary_crossentropy",metrics=["accuracy"],
➥optimizer = "adam")
model.fit(X_train, y_train, nb_epoch = 10, batch_size = 32)
```

We define and fit the model on the training data. It has a SimpleRNN layer feeding into a so-called TimeDistributed layer wrapper. This is a Keras facility for applying a layer (in our case, a Dense layer) to every sample (corresponding to a time step) in a received set of samples (in this case, produced by the SimpleRNN layer). The return_sequences=True setting in the SimpleRNN layer ensures that the SimpleRNN layer sends out predictions as characters.

```
preds=model.predict(X_test)[0]
for p in preds:
    m=np.argmax(p)
    print(enc.inverse_transform(m)),
```

We apply the model to our test data.

```
print(model.evaluate(X_test,y_test,batch_size=32))
```

This produces the following output:

```
Epoch 1/10
256/256 [==============================] - 0s - loss: 0.5248 - acc: 0.8125
Epoch 2/10
256/256 [==============================] - 0s - loss: 0.2658 - acc: 0.9375
Epoch 3/10
256/256 [==============================] - 0s - loss: 0.1633 - acc: 0.9661
Epoch 4/10
256/256 [==============================] - 0s - loss: 0.1169 - acc: 0.9792
Epoch 5/10
256/256 [==============================] - 0s - loss: 0.0913 - acc: 0.9922
Epoch 6/10
256/256 [==============================] - 0s - loss: 0.0752 - acc: 1.0000
Epoch 7/10
256/256 [==============================] - 0s - loss: 0.0637 - acc: 1.0000
Epoch 8/10
256/256 [==============================] - 0s - loss: 0.0548 - acc: 1.0000
Epoch 9/10
256/256 [==============================] - 0s - loss: 0.0474 - acc: 1.0000
Epoch 10/10
256/256 [==============================] - 0s - loss: 0.0411 - acc: 1.0000

h
a
r
a
c
t
e
r

[0.037899412214756012, 1.0]
```

The network starts its work right after it sees the initial "c" and predicts every next character in turn. The output shows that the network has generated the correct characters for its (only) training sample. The two final numerical scores express the loss and accuracy of the classifier for the test data; the 1.0 indicates a 100% accuracy score.

Despite this modest success, simple RNNs are rather crude temporal networks. They fail on long sequences (meaning they have small, limited-capacity memories) and blindly reuse hidden states in their entirety without discriminating between information that is rubbish and information that has value.

LSTM networks attempt to remedy the defects of simple RNNs by adding gating operations to the passage of historical network information into the present. Every LSTM consists of a number of cells chained in sequence, each consuming the same input: time steps consisting of discrete linguistic units like words. The number of cells is a hyperparameter: a value you must estimate yourself as an NLP engineer, based on validation data. The internal information of these cells can be read out per time step (such as a word) or for the entire sequence (by using the last cell). Processing the cell information on a time-step basis allows for subsequent so-called *time-distributed* processing; an example would be part-of-speech tagging. It is important to note that LSTM cells encode contextual information: they make this information available on local positions in the time-distributed case and globally (for example, for an entire sequence of words) in the non-time-distributed case.

Now, what do these magical cells look like? Figure 2.16 shows their generic structure.

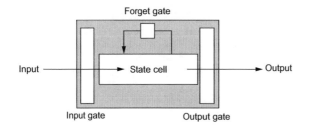

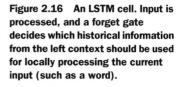

Figure 2.16   **An LSTM cell. Input is processed, and a forget gate decides which historical information from the left context should be used for locally processing the current input (such as a word).**

So, we have the following ingredients:

- Input data
- An input gate, weighting new input by applying a weight matrix to it.
- A State cell, the "hidden state" of the network, which consumes the weighted input data and applies a forget gate that weights information from the previous State cell.
- A forget gate, selectively letting through old information from the previous State cell. This gate also weights the input with a separate weight matrix.
- An output gate, selectively sending out the information from the current State cell.
- Output, computed from what the output gate lets through.

The careful gating of information through an LSTM cell takes place based on nine weight matrices. These weight matrices play a role in an ingenious computation. We'll step through the equations describing it. While the details of these equations need not concern us now, if you read the equations carefully, you'll get a feel for how historical information percolates through the network.

The nine weight matrices are as follows:

- W_i—Weights on the input gate, applied to the input
- W_o—Weights on the output gate, applied to the input

- W_f—Weights on the forget gate, applied to the input
- W_c—Weights on the input for computing the activity of the entire cell
- H_i—Input gate weights applied to the previous hidden state of the net h_{t-1} (which is defined in terms of its output at a previous time step and its previous hidden state)
- H_c—Weights applied to the hidden state of the net for computing the activity of the entire cell
- H_f—Forget gate weights applied to the previous hidden state of the net
- H_o—Output gate weights applied to the previous hidden state of the net
- V_c—Weights applied to the cell activity

How are all these weight matrices used to compute the simple output of an LSTM cell? Let's work through the various gates at a given time step t with an associated input x_t and every b_i a vector of bias values. The network computes a candidate cell activation C', which is turned into an actual cell activation based on the output of the input and forget gates. This cell activation is then used for the final output computation:

1 Input gate: $i_t = \text{sigmoid}(W_i\, x_t + H_i\, h_{t-1} + b_i)$

   Apply a sigmoid activation function to the weighted input plus the weighted hidden state and a bias term.

2 Forget gate: $f_t = \text{sigmoid}(W_f\, x_t + H_f\, h_{t-1} + b_f)$

   Apply a sigmoid function to the input weighted with the forget gate weights plus the forget gate weighted hidden state and a bias term.

3 $C'_t = \tanh(W_c\, x_t + H_c\, h_{t-1} + b_c)$

   This auxiliary state cell variable (the candidate cell activation) is a tanh function of weighted input, weighted hidden states, and a bias term.

4 $C_t = i_t \times C'_t + f_t \times C_{t-1}$

   The current cell activation is computed from the input weighted auxiliary state C' and the forget gate weighted previous cell activation.

5 $o_t = \text{sigmoid}(W_o\, x_t + H_o\, h_{t-1} + V_c\, C_t + b_o)$

   The output gate produces the output of the sigmoid function applied to the output gate weighted input plus the output gate weighted hidden state plus the weighted cell activation plus a bias term.

6 $h_t = o_t \tanh(C_t)$

   The hidden state at time t is a tanh function of the current state cell C_t.

Notice the heavy use of addition in these equations. Avoiding multiplication is one way of tackling the vanishing gradient problem. Using tanh ensures that values will be in the interval [-1,1]. Similarly, the sigmoid function recasts values to the interval [0,1].

The current cell activation C_t combines incoming data (passed through the input gate) with the forget gate applied to the previous state of the cell, which is a ledger of old information kept alive. Notice how much weighting and bias application is going on in this tiny memory structure. In Keras, an LSTM layer incorporates exactly one such cell or memory state for every batch. So, given a dataset of 1,000 sequences, if we have a batch size of 100, with 20 sequences of length 10, we obtain 10 batches, each containing one memory state or instantiation of the LSTM cell we presented in figure 2.16. Parameter updates are shared across batches during the training phase. After each sequence has been processed during training or testing, the memory states are reset. The memory states can be collected for all sequences and preserved across batches, if desired, with so-called *stateful* LSTMs (more on that in chapter 5).

Let's rework our previous example, migrating from a simple RNN to a full-fledged LSTM network. After that, we will put both the RNN and the LSTM network to the test: memorizing parts of a string.

In Keras, an LSTM needs 3D input of the form *(samples, timesteps, features)* and consumes its input data in batches. The *samples* dimension is the number of data blocks we feed to the LSTM, the *timesteps* dimension refers to the number of observations in each batch, and the *features* dimension is the number of features in each observation. Keras LSTMs are not specified for cell units; every timestep corresponds implicitly to one unit, meaning that if you unrolled the LSTM, it would have as many units as timesteps. Here is the code.

> **Listing 2.6 Predicting one character at a time with an LSTM**

```
from keras.models import Sequential
from keras.layers import LSTM, TimeDistributed, Dense        Keras has a separate
from sklearn.preprocessing import LabelEncoder               Layer for LSTMs.
from sklearn.preprocessing import OneHotEncoder
import numpy as np

np.random.seed(1234)

data = ['xyzaaaaaaaaaaaaaaaaaaaaaaaaaaaaaaaaaaaaaaaaaaaaaaaaaxyz',
        'pqraaaaaaaaaaaaaaaaaaaaaaaaaaaaaaaaaaaaaaaaaaaaaaaapqr']

test_data = ['xyzaaaaaaaaaaaaaaaaaaaaaaaaaaaaaaaaaaaaaaaaaaaaaaaaaxyz',
             'pqraaaaaaaaaaaaaaaaaaaaaaaaaaaaaaaaaaaaaaaaaaaaaaaapqr']

enc = LabelEncoder()
alphabet = np.array(list(set([c for w in data for c in w])))      Our data:
enc.fit(alphabet)                                                 long strings
int_enc=enc.fit_transform(alphabet)
onehot_encoder = OneHotEncoder(sparse=False)
int_enc=int_enc.reshape(len(int_enc), 1)
onehot_encoded = onehot_encoder.fit_transform(int_enc)

X_train=[]
y_train=[]

for w in data:
    for i in range(len(w)-1):
        X_train.extend(onehot_encoder.transform([enc.transform([w[i]])]))
        y_train.extend(onehot_encoder.transform([enc.transform([w[i+1]])]))
```

```
X_test=[]
y_test=[]

for w in test_data:
    for i in range(len(w)-1):
        X_test.extend(onehot_encoder.transform([enc.transform([w[i]])]))
        print i,w[i],onehot_encoder.transform([enc.transform([w[i]])])
        y_test.extend(onehot_encoder.transform([enc.transform([w[i+1]])]))

sample_size=512
sample_len=len(X_train)

X_train = np.array([X_train*sample_size]).reshape(
➥sample_size,sample_len,len(alphabet))
y_train = np.array([y_train*sample_size]).reshape(
➥sample_size,sample_len,len(alphabet))

test_len=len(X_test)
X_test= np.array([X_test]).reshape(1,test_len,len(alphabet))
y_test= np.array([y_test]).reshape(1,test_len,len(alphabet))

model=Sequential()
model.add(LSTM(input_dim  = len(alphabet), output_dim = 100,
➥return_sequences = True))
model.add(TimeDistributed(Dense(output_dim = len(alphabet),
➥activation  = "sigmoid")))
model.compile(loss="binary_crossentropy",metrics=["accuracy"],
➥optimizer = "adam")
```

◁─┐ **The model setup is similar to the RNN.**

```
n=1
while True:
        score = model.evaluate(X_test, y_test, batch_size=32)
        print "[Iteration %d] score=%f"%(n,score[1])
        if score[1] == 1.0:
            break
        n+=1
        model.fit(X_train, y_train, nb_epoch = 1, batch_size = 32)

preds=model.predict(X_test)[0]
for p in preds:
    m=np.argmax(p)
    print(enc.inverse_transform(m))

print(model.evaluate(X_test,y_test,batch_size=32))
```

┃ **Fit the model as long as it does not
◁─┘ produce a 100% correct result.**

This LSTM is performing a tricky task. As in the RNN example, it is reconstructing a piece of training data, in this case these 52-character strings:

xyzaaaaaaaaaaaaaaaaaaaaaaaaaaaaaaaaaaaaaaaaaaaaaaaxyz
pqraaaaaaaaaaaaaaaaaaaaaaaaaaaaaaaaaaaaaaaaaaaaaaapqr

Take a close look at these strings. The final characters (*suffixes*, in NLP lingo) xyz and pqr are conditioned on the start of the strings (*prefixes*): xyz and pqr. Notice that the suffixes are not directly conditioned on the preceding a...a sequence; normally, an a is followed by an a in these strings. So, the task is to keep the remote prefixes (xyz,pqr) in mind and do some counting of the intervening a characters to decide when to generate the suffixes (which are exact copies of the prefixes). While such a task could be implemented much more easily with an explicit counter, the important takeaway here is that the network figures out by itself when to produce the suffixes and can condition the suffixes on old information (the prefixes). This shows that the network has some memory capacity.

This seemingly simple task is actually quite complex in terms of bookkeeping. We feed the training and test strings to our original RNN, increasing the number of samples (batch size) from 256 to 512. This means we're creating 512 batches of (in our case) 102 sequences (the size of our training samples, based on two strings of 52 characters, minus the first character of each).

Running the RNN for 100 iterations does not yield a good result. The RNN produces the following output (the generation starts after the first character, which is skipped in the output as indicated with [ ]):

```
[x]yzaaaaaaaaaaaaaaaaaaaaaaaaaaaaaaaaaaaaaaaaaaaaaaaaaaaaaaaaaaaaaaayz
[p]qraaaaaaaaaaaaaaaaaaaaaaaaaaaaaaaaaaaaaaaaaaaaaaaaaaaaaaaaaaaaaaaaqr
```

It misses the first character of both suffixes (the x in xyz and the p in pqr).

But with an otherwise identical setup (100 iterations, 512 samples), the LSTM succeeds in reconstructing both strings flawlessly in less than 100 iterations:

```
[x]yzaaaaaaaaaaaaaaaaaaaaaaaaaaaaaaaaaaaaaaaaaaaaaaaaaaaaaaaaaaaaaxyz
[p]qraaaaaaaaaaaaaaaaaaaaaaaaaaaaaaaaaaaaaaaaaaaaaaaaaaaaaaaaaaaaaapqr
```

2.2   *Deep learning and NLP: A new paradigm*

From a superficial point of view, deep learning appears to be a revamped, highly performant type of machine learning. When applied to language, however, deep learning brings two novel and useful ingredients to the table: temporal and spatial filtering. Language consists of words arranged in sequences, flowing from the past into the present; the combination of spatial and temporal filtering opens up a range of new, interesting possibilities for NLP (figure 2.17). The important thing to realize is that we are working on abstract representations. Spatial processing of an abstract, intermediate

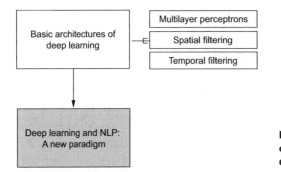

Figure 2.17   **The new paradigm of deep learning–based NLP. What does deep learning bring to NLP?**

layer representation is difficult to imagine. But it is just another way of emphasizing or de-emphasizing parts of a complex data representation. In a similar fashion, the temporal dimension allows us to gate historical data into this process of abstraction, learning to forget or keep certain parts of these complex representations.

We demonstrated how to apply convolutional operations to vector representations of words, pretending there was some spatial structure in the juxtaposition of those vectors. The RNN and LSTM layers gate historical information into the present. There is nothing preventing us from applying CNN layers to the output of LSTM layers, which would result in spatial filtering of temporal, gated information. We could also do the opposite: LSTM operations to CNN outputs. The combinations for composing layers seem unbounded. In the image domain, some best practices for layer composition have been proposed in the literature-based myriad experiments. Can we come up with similar best practices for NLP? We will discover many such practices in the remainder of this book.

Finally, language is not only sequential but also *recursive*:

John says that Mary says that Bill told Richard he was on his way.

The ability to handle these recursive structures with deep learning is an active topic of research and can be seen as one of the approaches to establish long-distance relations across words.

Equipped with the background of this chapter, we are now ready to get our hands dirty on a number of real-life NLP problems. We will start in the next chapter by getting text into a deep learning model using text embeddings.

Summary

- Basic deep learning architectures are multilayer perceptrons, spatial (convolutional), and temporal (RNN and LSTM-based) filters.
- Convolutional and recurrent neural networks, as well as long short-term memory-based networks, can be easily coded in Keras.
- Deep learning examples applied to language analysis in this chapter include sentiment analysis and character prediction.

Text embeddings

3

This chapter covers
- Preparing texts for deep learning using word and document embeddings
- Using self-developed vs. pretrained embeddings
- Implementing word similarity with Word2Vec
- Retrieving documents using Doc2Vec

After reading this chapter, you will have a practical command of basic and popular text embedding algorithms, and you will have developed insight into how to use embeddings for NLP. We will go through a number of concrete scenarios to reach that goal. But first, let's review the basics of *embeddings*.

3.1 Embeddings

Embeddings are procedures for converting input data into vector representations. As mentioned in chapter 1, a vector is like a container (such as an array) containing numbers. Every vector lives in a multidimensional vector space, as a single point, with every value interpreted as a value across a specific dimension. Embeddings result from systematic, well-crafted procedures for projecting (embedding) input data into such a space.

We have seen ample vector representations of texts in chapters 1 and 2, such as one-hot vectors (binary-valued vectors with one bit "on" for a specific word), used for bag-of-word representations and frequency- or TF.IDF-based vectors. All these vector representations were created by embeddings.

Let's work our way up from the simplest of embeddings to the more complex ones. Recall from chapter 1 that there are two major types of vector encodings, depending on how they are created: representational and procedural (figure 3.1). Representational vector encodings are designed by hand: they can be directly computed from data, for instance, by using statistical operations like simple counting. On the other hand, procedural encodings are inferred (learned or estimated) from data with machine learning or statistics. Let's take a quick look at the representational type, now from the perspective of embeddings.

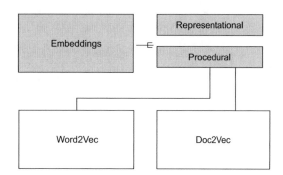

Figure 3.1 There are different types of embeddings: representational and procedural. We will discuss two types of procedural embeddings in detail: Word2Vec and Doc2Vec.

3.1.1 Embedding by direct computation: Representational embeddings

The simplest representational embedding for mapping text to vectors is *one-hot embedding*. Given a lexicon of N entries (such as characters or words), we represent every word as a vector of $N-1$ zeros and a single, distinct numeral 1.

the	cat	sat	on	a	mat
1	0	0	0	0	0
0	1	0	0	0	0
0	0	1	0	0	0
0	0	0	1	0	0
0	0	0	0	1	0
0	0	0	0	0	1

This primitive embedding maps words to a binary, six-dimensional vector space. Every word is represented with a binary vector, like this:

- cat: 010000
- a: 000010

Ideally, words that are related should lie close to each other in such a vector space. "Close" here means near each other, as measured by a distance function. One such function is the *Euclidean distance*. This distance measure computes the length of a straight line between two points in a Euclidean space using the Pythagorean algorithm. Euclidean space is a space with a finite number of dimensions. Points in Euclidean space are specified by coordinates for every dimension. So, a vector such as (0,1,0) is a unique coordinate of a point in three dimensions. Figure 3.2 displays a three-dimensional Euclidean space. Notice how the 2^3 (8) different coordinates correspond to the corners of the cube.

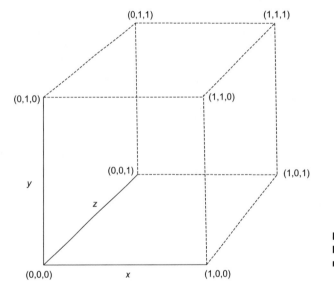

Figure 3.2   A three-dimensional Euclidean space. The coordinates represent a 3D cube.

Distances between vectors in our contrived six-dimensional space do not make any sense from a linguistic point of view: every vector is the same distance from every other vector, since they all differ in just one bit. So, there is no apparent spatial relation between "the" and "a," even though such words are related from a linguistic point of view (they are both articles). This does not necessarily mean these representations are too simple to be used. In fact, they are used a lot as encodings of text where distance-based similarity does not come into play. For example, in chapter 2, they served as representations for our characters in the recurrent neural network (RNN) and long short-term memory (LSTM) examples. Now, let's turn to more advanced embeddings: embeddings that are learned from data.

3.1.2 *Learning to embed: Procedural embeddings*

Let's look at machine learning–based (operational, procedural) embeddings. We will start with Keras. It has its own facility, a layer-type called `Embedding`, for producing embeddings. Keras `Embeddings` are trainable layers and deploy a matrix of weights that is optimized during training. As such, they are shallow (one hidden layer) mininetworks. `Embeddings` implicitly minimize a loss function. That is, they optimize the representations they create given a certain criterion. The implicit default criterion is to maximize the distinctiveness of the vector representations such that the confusability of any two vectors is kept to a minimum. As we will see shortly, we can also drive them with other criteria.

The standard Keras `Embedding` example from the Keras documentation is the following. It creates an embedding of random integers in an eight-dimensional vector space. So, every integer in a random input sample becomes represented by an eight-dimensional numerical vector.

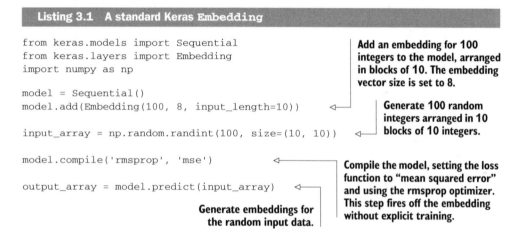

Listing 3.1 A standard Keras `Embedding`

```
from keras.models import Sequential
from keras.layers import Embedding
import numpy as np

model = Sequential()
model.add(Embedding(100, 8, input_length=10))

input_array = np.random.randint(100, size=(10, 10))

model.compile('rmsprop', 'mse')

output_array = model.predict(input_array)
```

Add an embedding for 100 integers to the model, arranged in blocks of 10. The embedding vector size is set to 8.

Generate 100 random integers arranged in 10 blocks of 10 integers.

Compile the model, setting the loss function to "mean squared error" and using the rmsprop optimizer. This step fires off the embedding without explicit training.

Generate embeddings for the random input data.

This embedding consumes a matrix of 10 × 10 integers with a maximum integer value of 100 (10 batches of 10 integers). In this example, this matrix was generated by the call to the `randint` function of numpy. It looks like this:

```
array([[17, 92, 74, 87, 60, 34,  8, 77, 16, 98],
       [99, 12, 83, 33, 98, 47, 55, 56, 28, 19],
       [97, 62, 88, 18, 13, 25, 39, 99, 62,  5],
       [38, 96, 11, 79, 67, 90, 66, 39, 52, 76],
       [12, 24, 79, 78, 15, 88,  1, 11, 43, 73],
       [45, 60, 26, 71, 44, 63, 69, 55, 28, 10],
       [89, 64, 63,  0, 13, 74, 96, 99, 10, 25],
       [90,  5, 98, 92, 11, 77,  4, 57, 61, 93],
       [ 7, 41, 80, 31, 74, 33,  3, 33, 55, 20],
       [83, 79, 28, 40, 65, 87, 60, 71, 44, 41]])
```

For every array of 10 integers (a row in the matrix), the embedding generates a 10 × 8 matrix consisting of eight-dimensional values, one for every integer in the integer array. These values correspond to the trained weights of the `Embedding` layer and are the embeddings of the input integers. For example, the values for the final row of the input matrix are as follows:

```
[[  1.28672235e-02    8.03406164e-03   -2.44486574e-02   -2.50550359e-03
    -1.29224174e-02    2.64333598e-02   -2.68703699e-02   -4.35554162e-02]

  ...

  [
      3.53093855e-02   -1.42144933e-02    3.14533599e-02   -5.73614985e-03]]
```

So, in this row

```
[83, 79, 28, 40, 65, 87, 60, 71, 44, 41]
```

integer 83 is embedded as an eight-dimensional vector:

```
[1.28672235e-02    8.03406164e-03   -2.44486574e-02   -2.50550359e-03
-1.29224174e-02    2.64333598e-02   -2.68703699e-02   -4.35554162e-02]
```

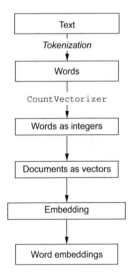

Let's apply this to text. Representing a set of documents as vectors of integers, we can create a standard embedding of these documents similar to the embedding for random integers. We will use the schema in figure 3.3.

Figure 3.3 Embedding words with a standard Keras embedding. Text is tokenized (divided into words), words are represented as integers, and documents become represented as sequences of numbers. After this document preprocessing, the numbers representing words are finally turned into embeddings.

The following code handles document preprocessing.

Listing 3.2 Document preprocessing

```
docs=["Chuck Berry rolled over everyone who came before him ? and turned up
      everyone who came after. We'll miss you",
      "Help protect the progress we've made in helping millions of
      Americans get covered.",
      "Let's leave our children and grandchildren a planet that's healthier
      than the one we have today.",
      "The American people are waiting for Senate leaders to do their jobs.",
```

```
"We must take bold steps now ? climate change is already impacting
➡millions of people.",
"Don't forget to watch Larry King tonight",
"Ivanka is now on Twitter - You can follow her",
"Last night Melania and I attended the Skating with the Stars Gala at
➡Wollman Rink in Central Park",
"People who have the ability to work should. But with the government
➡happy to send checks",
"I will be signing copies of my new book"
]
```

```
docs=[d.lower() for d in docs]
```
⟵ **We lowercase our documents stored in the docs array.**

```
count_vect = CountVectorizer().fit(docs)
tokenizer = count_vect.build_tokenizer()
```

⟵ **Fit a CountVectorizer on the lowercased documents. The CountVectorizer (a facility from sklearn) maps every word in a set of documents to a unique and arbitrary integer. For example, "children" is represented by 20, "our" by 66, and "we" by 96. These integer values have no special meaning.**

Associate a tokenizer with the CountVectorizer: a function that tokenizes documents (strings) by splitting (by default) on whitespace.

```
input_array=[]
for doc in docs:
    x=[]
    for token in tokenizer(doc):
        x.append(count_vect.vocabulary_.get(token))
    input_array.append(x)

max_len=max([len(d) for d in input_array])

input_array=pad_sequences(input_array, maxlen=max_len,
åpadding='post')
```

Create an input array for our embedding similar to the integer example presented earlier, but now consisting of arrays with integers referring to words (as created by the CountVectorizer).

Pad all documents to the same length using the Keras function pad_sequences. This function pads an array of arrays up to a specified maximum length by adding zeroes at the end of each array (padding='post').

Now we are ready to feed these arrays into the Embedding so that every integer in each array becomes represented by an eight-dimensional vector. We can visualize the vector embeddings with the well-known visualization algorithm T-SNE (van der Maaten and Hinton, 2008). The following algorithm maps high-dimensional vectors to lower-dimensional planes, like 2D.

Listing 3.3 Visualizing Keras embeddings with T-SNE

```
from keras.models import Sequential
from keras.layers import Embedding
import numpy as np
from sklearn.manifold import TSNE
import matplotlib.pyplot as plt

def tsne_plot(model,max_words=100):
    labels = []
    tokens = []
```

```
        n=0
        for word in model:
            if n<max_words:
                tokens.append(model[word])
                labels.append(word)
                n+=1

            tsne_model = TSNE(perplexity=40, n_components=2, init='pca',

n_iter=10000, random_state=23)
            new_values = tsne_model.fit_transform(tokens)

        x = []
        y = []
        for value in new_values:
            x.append(value[0])
            y.append(value[1])

        plt.figure(figsize=(8, 8))
        for i in range(len(x)):
            plt.scatter(x[i],y[i])
            plt.annotate(labels[i],
                        xy=(x[i], y[i]),
                        xytext=(5, 2),
                        textcoords='offset points',
                        ha='right',
                        va='bottom')
        plt.show()

# ... The document preprocessing from the previous listing

model = Sequential()
model.add(Embedding(100, 8, input_length=10))
input_array = np.random.randint(100, size=(10, 10))
model.compile('rmsprop', 'mse')
output_array = model.predict(input_array)

M={}
for i in range(len(input_array)):
    for j in range(len(input_array[i])):
        M[input_array[i][j]]=output_array[i][j]

tsne_plot(M)
```

Create a T-SNE model for dimensionality reduction and run it for 10,000 iterations on our data.

The T-SNE algorithm generates 2D-shaped data, which we can plot as (x,y) coordinates.

Embedding for random integers

This produces pictures like figure 3.4, where the multidimensional vectors are cast into a 2D space reflecting their distances. The embedding produces even-spaced vector representations of the various words (represented by integers, each of which is embedded as an eight-dimensional vector), but the topology doesn't make sense: for example, word 96 ("we") is closer to word 55 ("Melania") than to word 66 ("our") in this 2D space. That's understandable: we did not constrain the Embedding by any loss function specific to this data that computes the distances between our data points in a sensible way.

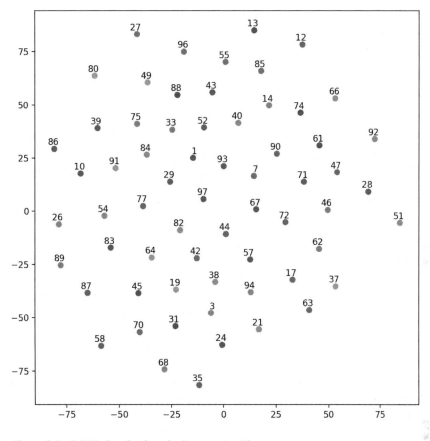

Figure 3.4 T-SNE visualization of a Keras embedding

Now, let's add a more interpretable criterion to creating an embedding: let's train a word embedding as part of adding sentiment labels to restaurant reviews. This means we are after a word embedding that is trained as part of a sentiment-labeling task: words should be embedded so that they contribute maximally to discerning documents with positive sentiment from documents with negative sentiment. Notice that standard Keras embeddings start as random embeddings: they segregate words maximally from each other without worrying about lexical or semantic relationships between words. But luckily, these embeddings are *malleable*: they can be trained to encode such relationships, to some extent, by being fine-tuned in the context of a learning task.

NOTE An external task for fine-tuning an embedding is called a *downstream task*.

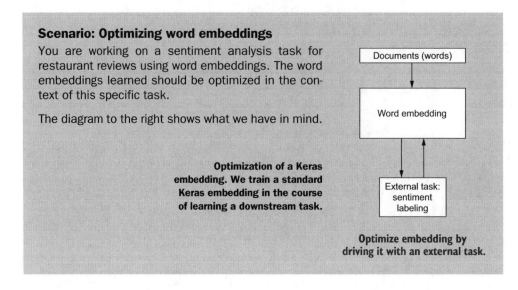

Scenario: Optimizing word embeddings

You are working on a sentiment analysis task for restaurant reviews using word embeddings. The word embeddings learned should be optimized in the context of this specific task.

The diagram to the right shows what we have in mind.

Optimization of a Keras embedding. We train a standard Keras embedding in the course of learning a downstream task.

Optimize embedding by driving it with an external task.

Suppose we have a set of documents (restaurant reviews) represented by vectors of integers, with each integer corresponding to a specific word identifier (an entry in a lexicon). Technically, this is exactly the same representation as our earlier random integer example. Let's add document labels to the documents, like a 1 for positive sentiment and a 0 for negative sentiment. We can now train a word embedding constrained by a loss function that aims for maximum separation of the documents. So, the word embedding must learn this task: find optimal embeddings for the words such that the provided document labeling is learned with maximum accuracy (figure 3.5).

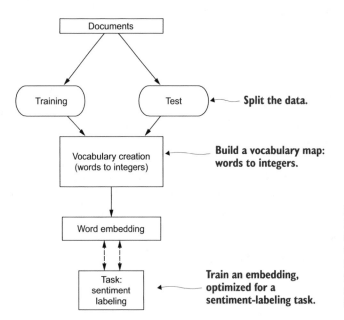

Figure 3.5   Optimization of a Keras embedding: procedure. Split the data into training and test data, map words to integers, embed words, and fine-tune the embedding to optimize a downstream task, optimizing for results on the test data.

How do we proceed? First we need to read in training and test data, which in our case consists of sentiment-labeled text data. We will use a public domain dataset of 1,000 Yelp restaurant reviews (https://www.ics.uci.edu/~vpsaini/).

Review	Sentiment score
Wow... Loved this place.	1
Crust is not good.	0
Not tasty and the texture was just nasty.	0
Stopped by during the late May bank holiday off Rick Steve recommendation and loved it.	1
The selection on the menu was great and so were the prices.	1
Now I am getting angry and I want my damn pho.	0
Honestly it didn't taste THAT fresh.	0
The potatoes were like rubber and you could tell they had been made up ahead of time being kept under a warmer.	0
The fries were great too.	1
A great touch.	1
Service was very prompt.	1
Would not go back.	0

Every sentence is flagged as either positive (1) or negative (0) for sentiment. We split this data into a training set of 700 cases (the first 700) and a test set with the remaining 300 sentences. The dataset contains 11,894 words (tokens) in total. When applied to this data, the network quickly achieves (in well under 100 iterations) a perfect score (100%) on the training data and a moderately good (given the small dataset and the simplistic network) score of 73.6% accuracy on the test data.

The following listing shows the code.

Listing 3.4   Learning an embedding as part of a sentiment-labeling task

```
from keras.models import Sequential
from keras.layers import Embedding,Dense,Flatten
import numpy as np
import random
import re
import sys
import codecs
from keras.preprocessing.sequence import pad_sequences

def save_embedding(outputFile, weights, vocabulary):
  rev = {v:k for k, v in vocabulary.iteritems()}
```

A function for saving an embedding to a file: every word is listed with its embedding vector.

```
        with codecs.open(outputFile, "w") as f:
          f.write(str(len(vocabulary)) + " " + str(weights.shape[1]) + "\n")
                      for index in sorted(rev.iterkeys()):
                              word=rev[index]
            f.write(word + " ")
                          for i in xrange(len(weights[index])):
                    f.write(str(weights[index][i]) + " ")
                      f.write("\n")


    def getLines(f):
        lines = [line.rstrip() for line in open(f)]
        return lines
```

A helper function for returning an array containing all the lines for a given text file, with trailing newlines stripped

```
    def create_vocabulary(vocabulary, sentences):
      vocabulary["<unk>"]=0
     for sentence in sentences:
      for word in sentence.strip().split():
            word=re.sub("[.,:;'\"!?()]+","",word.lower())
            if word not in vocabulary:
            vocabulary[word]=len(vocabulary)
```

This function fills a vocabulary based on the sentences (lines) of the input text file. The vocabulary maps every word to a unique integer. A special token for unknown words is also created.

```
    def process_training_data(textFile,max_len):
        data=[]
        sentences = getLines(textFile)
        vocab = dict()
        labels=[]
        create_vocabulary(vocab, sentences)
        for s in sentences:
            words=[]
            m=re.match("^([^\t]+)\t(.+)$",s.rstrip())
            if m:
                sentence=m.group(1)
                labels.append(int(m.group(2)))
            for w in sentence.split(" "):
                w=re.sub("[.,:;'\"!?()]+","",w.lower())
                if w!='':
                    words.append(vocab[w])
            data.append(words)
        data = pad_sequences(data, maxlen=max_len, padding='post')

        return data,labels, vocab
```

This function processes our training data, creating padded vectors of integers corresponding to words and arrays of labels (the sentiment labels, in our case). The vocabulary is filled in on the fly and is later supplemented by the words in the test data.

```
    def process_test_data(textFile,vocab,max_len):
        data=[]
        sentences = getLines(textFile)
        labels=[]
        create_vocabulary(vocab, sentences)
        for s in sentences:
            words=[]
            m=re.match("^([^\t]+)\t(.+)$",s.rstrip())
            if m:
                sentence=m.group(1)
                labels.append(int(m.group(2)))
            for w in sentence.split(" "):
                w=re.sub("[.,:;'\"!?()]+","",w.lower())
```

Similarly, this function processes our test data.

```
            if w!='':
                if w in vocab:
                    words.append(vocab[w])
                else:
                    words.append(vocab["<unk>"])
        data.append(words)
    data = pad_sequences(data, maxlen=max_len, padding='post')
    return data,labels

max_len=100
data,labels,vocab=process_training_data(sys.argv[1],max_len)
test_data,test_labels=process_test_data(sys.argv[2],vocab,max_len)

model = Sequential()
embedding=Embedding(len(vocab), 100, input_length=max_len)
model.add(embedding)
model.add(Flatten())
model.add(Dense(1,activation="sigmoid"))
model.compile(loss='binary_crossentropy', optimizer='adam',metrics=['acc'])
model.fit(data,labels,epochs=100, verbose=1)

loss, accuracy = model.evaluate(test_data, test_labels, verbose=0)
print accuracy

save_embedding("embedding_labeled.txt",embedding.get_weights()[0], vocab)
```

Notice how the training set vocabulary is passed on to the test data processing function.

We save our embedding to a text file for later processing and inspection.

We generate an embedding for the number of words in our vocabulary, with a vector length of 100.

What about the word embedding learned during this sentiment-labeling task? We can inspect the embedding that is learned by finding the nearest neighbors of the word vectors in the model output file (embedding_labeled.txt).

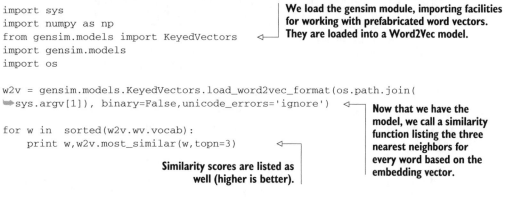

Listing 3.5 Inspecting embeddings: looking for nearest neighbors of vectors

```
import sys
import numpy as np
from gensim.models import KeyedVectors
import gensim.models
import os

w2v = gensim.models.KeyedVectors.load_word2vec_format(os.path.join(
➥sys.argv[1]), binary=False,unicode_errors='ignore')

for w in  sorted(w2v.wv.vocab):
    print w,w2v.most_similar(w,topn=3)
```

We load the gensim module, importing facilities for working with prefabricated word vectors. They are loaded into a Word2Vec model.

Now that we have the model, we call a similarity function listing the three nearest neighbors for every word based on the embedding vector.

Similarity scores are listed as well (higher is better).

NOTE We deploy the Gensim (https://radimrehurek.com/gensim) toolkit to find nearest neighbors. This highly optimized Python toolkit has facilities for working with (and deriving) Word2Vec models, and it has a speedy nearest neighbor search for analyzing models. The format of our exported embedding is compliant with that library, and we can deploy the Gensim nearest neighbor search to find matching word vectors.

Our program lists the three nearest neighbors for every word based on its derived vector representation. Some of the results are as follows:

```
waiter [(u'terrible', 0.8831709027290344), (u'2', 0.8141345381736755),
➥(u'rude', 0.8114627003669739)]
waitress [(u'breakfast', 0.8804935216903687),
➥(u'bartender', 0.8568718433380127), (u'server', 0.8293911218643188)]
```

For every word ("waiter," "waitress") the three nearest neighbors are sorted by (descending) similarity. So, for "waitress," "bartender" is more similar than "server."

While these examples seem to suggest a certain semantic relation between input words and their nearest neighbors, in general, the majority of the nearest neighbors are uninterpretable. Apparently this embedding was the best we could obtain for the choices (network structure, data) we made. But what if we want interpretable embeddings that show meaningful relations between words? Enter Word2Vec, the de facto algorithm for doing just that.

3.2   *From words to vectors: Word2Vec*

The Word2Vec algorithm, discussed in chapter 1, takes word context information into account for establishing relations between words and embedding words into vector space (figure 3.6). The algorithm we implemented in the previous section did not remotely do such a thing. It optimized the vector representation of words to maximize accuracy on the sentiment-labeling task, but it did not care about establishing relations between words that shared

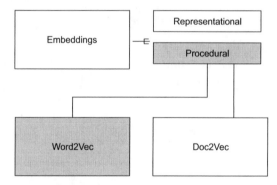

Figure 3.6   The Word2Vec algorithm: a procedural (learned) embedding

similar contexts. The vector representations we obtain with Word2Vec should, hopefully, express a more interpretable form of similarity between words based on shared contexts.

According to Word2Vec, two words are more similar if they share similar contexts, which is a modern incarnation of the tenet of the British linguist John Rupert Firth:

You shall know a word by the company it keeps.

—J. R. Firth

Scenario: Modeling meaningful relations between words

You want to establish meaningful, synonym-like relations between words based on a large text corpus (a set of restaurant reviews) you have at hand. The relations you are after should be based on the statistics of words co-occurring. Two words are more similar if they occur in the same contexts. You want to use these relations to implement an editor tool that suggests synonyms for words while you are editing a document, and you obviously do not want to write out these relations by hand. How can embeddings help you?

The following figure shows what we are after: establishing meaningful relations between words based on their vector embeddings.

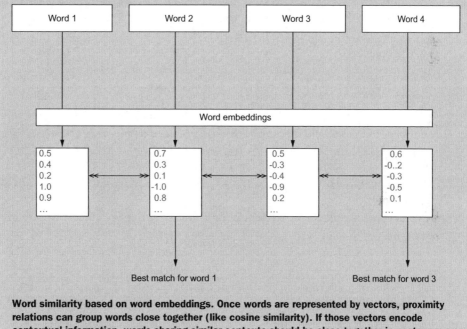

Word similarity based on word embeddings. Once words are represented by vectors, proximity relations can group words close together (like cosine similarity). If those vectors encode contextual information, words sharing similar contexts should be close together in vector space.

Here is how we plan to make this happen. The Word2Vec algorithm has two more or less equivalent implementations: predicting words from contexts (the CBOW variant) or contexts from words (the skipgram variant). We implement the latter approach: the skipgram version of Word2Vec with so-called *negative sampling*. Let's jump right in.

We will try to predict the validity of a certain context around a word, given that word. For instance, given a string like

the restaurant has a terrible ambiance and the food is awful

we want to predict if the words "terrible" for "restaurant" and "awful" for "food" are valid context words. Words with similar context predictions are judged to be similar by Word2Vec: they produce comparable vector representations.

To set up context prediction in a practical manner, we must create both positive and negative examples of contexts: valid contexts and invalid contexts. Doing this exhaustively is impractical because there are way too many negative possibilities to consider. This is where *negative sampling* comes in. Negative sampling means we do not gather just positive examples of valid contexts but also, randomly, negative examples of invalid contexts.

Here is what we do:

1 Create a dictionary for our data: a mapping from words to unique integers.
2 Using a random generator and a fixed context window size (which extends to both the left and right of an input word), collect the valid context words in this window.
3 Sample arbitrary words in the dictionary that are out of scope of the input word. Those words will generate negative contexts—hence the name *negative sampling*.

For instance, given the string

the restaurant has a terrible ambiance and the food is awful

with a window size of 3 and the input word "restaurant," the words in "has a terrible" are valid right context words for "restaurant," and the word "the" is a valid left context word. But the words "and the food is awful" are not valid context words for "restaurant" if they never occur in our dataset in the immediate left or right context of "restaurant."

As it turns out, Keras has a function that generates positive and negative context samples:

```
skipgrams(sequence, vocabulary_size, window_size=n, ...)
```

This function generates a set of word pairs (input word, context word) linked to a corresponding set of binary labels 0/1. These labels indicate whether in the data, for a certain word pair, the context word has been observed in the immediate context of the input word.

Figure 3.7 illustrates the process of negative sampling. Texts are encoded as integers, and valid contexts are determined. A few examples of (in)valid contexts appear in the rightmost box.

Figure 3.7   Skipgram labeling with negative sampling

Let's take a look again at our string:

the restaurant has a terrible ambiance and the food is awful

Assume we have created a dictionary containing the following:

- The → 1
- restaurant → 2
- has → 3
- a → 4
- terrible → 5
- ambiance → 6
- and → 7
- food → 8
- is → 9
- awful → 10

We set the `window_size` parameter of the `skipgrams` function to 3. For this example, we need to artificially set `vocab_size` to a large enough size (`100`) for drawing random samples; otherwise, we run the chance of labeling valid context words as non-context words. First we look up the input string in our dictionary, replacing words with integers. We split our sentence into words (based on spaces) and look up every word in our lexicon:

```
sequence=[vocab[w] for w in sentence.split(" ")]
```

This produces the bottom row of the following table.

The	restaurant	has	a	terrible	ambiance	and	the	food	is	awful
1	2	3	4	5	6	7	1	8	9	10

Setting the variable sequence to 1, 2, 3, 4, 5, 6, 7, 1, 8, 9, 10, we run

```
skipgrams(sequence, 100, window_size=3)
```

and obtain the following couples

```
[[7, 8], [2, 5], [3, 85], [3, 4], ...
]
```

and labels

```
[1, 1, 0, 1, ...]
```

For instance, for the couple [7,8], the label is a 1, since word 8 ("food") occurs in the context of word 7 ("and"). For couple [3,85], the randomly chosen word 85 is not in the context of our word 3 ("has"). Notice that our mini lexicon only has 10 words and that the `skipgrams` function randomly draws words from the lexicon for negative context words. For a large lexicon, the chances of drawing incorrectly valid context words as negative context words should be relatively small.

With this handy function at our disposal, let's build our Word2Vec script. We first define a function for processing our raw data consisting of plain sentences. These sentences are processed for skipgrams, and all skipgrams and their labels are collected for the entire dataset.

Listing 3.6   Processing data for Word2Vec

```
def process_data(textFile,window_size):
    couples=[]
    labels=[]
    sentences = getLines(textFile)
    vocab = dict()
    create_vocabulary(vocab, sentences)
    vocab_size=len(vocab)
    for s in sentences:
        words=[]
        for w in s.split(" "):
            w=re.sub("[.,:;'\"!?()]+","",w.lower())
            if w!='':
                words.append(vocab[w])
        c,l=skipgrams(words,vocab_size,window_size=window_size)
        couples.extend(c)
        labels.extend(l)
    return vocab,couples,labels
```

A special generator function loops over these samples during the training phase of the model, picking out random samples and labels and feeding them as batches to the model.

Listing 3.7   Function for generating batches

```
def generator(target,context, labels, batch_size):
    batch_target = np.zeros((batch_size, 1))
    batch_context = np.zeros((batch_size, 1))
    batch_labels = np.zeros((batch_size,1))

    while True:
        for i in range(batch_size):
            index= random.randint(0,len(target)-1)
            batch_target[i] = target[index]
            batch_context[i]=context[index]
            batch_labels[i] = labels[index]
        yield [batch_target,batch_context], [batch_labels]
```

Our network is a simple combination of two Embedding layers (one for the source words and one for their context words) feeding into a dense (regular, fully connected) layer to which the output labels are fed (0 if the context word is not a valid context for the source word or 1 if it is). Notice that we restrict contexts here to just one word, which is looked for in the immediate neighborhood of a source word, with a window size of 3 extending in either direction. The network learns to decide whether the chosen context words are valid contexts for the target words. This is illustrated in figure 3.8.

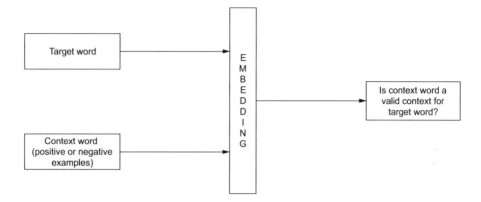

Figure 3.8   Word2Vec: predicting valid context words with negative sampling

Exercise

Can you come up with a stronger model by switching to a more advanced network architecture?

In our model, the input and target words share the same embedding for practical reasons (this limits the number of weights the model needs to estimate). The vector representations this embedding produces for inputs and target words are combined into one vector by means of a dot product. Finally, the weights of the trained embeddings produce the Word2Vec vectors for the input words.

Here is the full code listing.

Listing 3.8   Word2Vec with negative sampling

```
from keras.models import Model
from keras.layers import Input, Dense, Reshape, merge
from keras.layers.embeddings import Embedding
from keras.preprocessing.sequence import skipgrams
from keras.preprocessing import sequence

import numpy as np
import sys

import random
import re
import codecs
```

```
def save_embedding(outputFile, weights, vocabulary):
  rev = {v:k for k, v in vocabulary.iteritems()}
 with codecs.open(outputFile, "w") as f:
  f.write(str(len(vocabulary)) + " " + str(weights.shape[1]) + "\n")
    for index in sorted(rev.iterkeys()):
            word=rev[index]
          f.write(word + " ")
            for i in range(len(weights[index])):
              f.write(str(weights[index][i]) + " ")
            f.write("\n")


def getLines(f):
    lines = [line.rstrip() for line in open(f)]
    return lines


def generator(target,context, labels, batch_size):
    batch_target = np.zeros((batch_size, 1))
    batch_context = np.zeros((batch_size, 1))
    batch_labels = np.zeros((batch_size,1))

    while True:
        for i in range(batch_size):
            index= random.randint(0,len(target)-1)
            batch_target[i] = target[index]
            batch_context[i]=context[index]
            batch_labels[i] = labels[index]
        yield [batch_target,batch_context], [batch_labels]


def process_data(textFile,window_size):
    couples=[]
    labels=[]
    sentences = getLines(textFile)
    vocab = dict()
    create_vocabulary(vocab, sentences)
    vocab_size=len(vocab)
    for s in sentences:
        words=[]
        for w in s.split(" "):
            w=re.sub("[.,:;'\"!?()]+","",w.lower())
            if w!='':
                words.append(vocab[w])
        c,l=skipgrams(words,vocab_size,window_size=window_size)
        couples.extend(c)
        labels.extend(l)
    return vocab,couples,labels


def create_vocabulary(vocabulary, sentences):
  vocabulary["<unk>"]=0
 for sentence in sentences:
  for word in sentence.strip().split():
        word=re.sub("[.,:;'\"!?()]+","",word.lower())
        if word not in vocabulary:
            vocabulary[word]=len(vocabulary)
```

This function processes our input dataset (a text corpus) and generates the context data (valid/invalid contexts) and corresponding labels.

```
window_size = 3
vector_dim = 100
epochs = 1000

vocab,couples,labels=process_data(sys.argv[1],window_size)

vocab_size=len(vocab)

word_target, word_context = zip(*couples)
```

We split the generated couples into the target words (the words for which we predict valid or invalid context words) and context words.

```
input_target = Input((1,))
input_context = Input((1,))
```

Both targets and contexts consist of one-dimensional Input layers.

```
embedding = Embedding(vocab_size, vector_dim,
➥input_length=1)
target = embedding(input_target)
target = Reshape((vector_dim, 1))(target)
context = embedding(input_context)
context = Reshape((vector_dim, 1))(context)
```

Our embedding accepts Inputs of size 1 and maps them to vectors of size vector_dim, for a total of vocab_size different words. We embed both Inputs (targets and contexts) in the same Embedding, reshaping them to the desired vector length.

```
dot_product = merge([target, context], mode='dot',
➥dot_axes=1)
dot_product = Reshape((1,))(dot_product)
output = Dense(1, activation='sigmoid')(dot_product)
model = Model(input=[input_target, input_context], output=output)
model.compile(loss='binary_crossentropy', optimizer='adam',metrics=['acc'])

print model.summary()

epochs=int(sys.argv[2])
```

The dot product of the target and context vectors is the intermediate representation on which the final classification (valid context word or not, for a given target word) is based.

```
model.fit_generator(generator(word_target, word_context,labels,100),
➥steps_per_epoch=100, epochs=epochs)
```

Our generator feeds random batches of target words, context words, and labels (each batch containing 100 cases) for 1,000 epochs. Every epoch carries out 100 optimization steps.

```
save_embedding("embedding.txt",
➥embedding.get_weights()[0], vocab)
```

We extract the per-word weights from the shared embedding. These weights constitute the Word2Vec embedding for the input words.

Running our Word2Vec implementation on the Yelp data with 100 samples per batch for 1,000 training epochs already produces more interesting results than our previous approach. Here are the nearest neighbors of some input words in the produced embedding file, computed with list_vectors.py:

- waitress → cashier
- seasonal → peach, fruit
- indian → naan
- café → crema
- baba → ganoush
- bone → marrow

But to obtain truly meaningful and convincing results, the model should be trained on much larger amounts of data, for many more iterations.

You may wonder whether the classification task we used to create our word embedding on the fly actually would benefit from a stronger embedding. From our small dataset, we could not derive a very interpretable embedding in terms of word relations. Fortunately, we can deploy models that have been compiled by others, and load them into our classifiers. Let's boost our Yelp review-labeling task with such a model.

Scenario: Pretrained embeddings

Rather than use an embedding that was trained for a certain task (like sentiment labeling), you want to use a pretrained Word2Vec model based on other (better, more) training data. Hopefully, doing so will improve the results of your specific task. How do you implement this?

This diagram describes the approach.

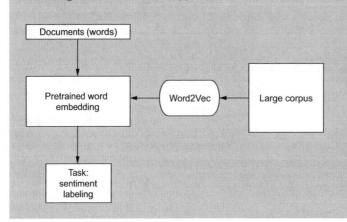

Using pretrained word embeddings for a sentiment labeling task. We derive a large Word2Vec model from external data and use that model to generate word embeddings for words in other data. Notice the one-way down arrow to the downstream task: in this setup, the off-the-shelf Word2Vec model is not trainable.

We will test this idea in two steps:

1 Replace the original embedding with the embedding we just produced with our Word2Vec implementation.
2 Use a really large off-the-shelf Word2Vec model compiled by Stanford University on 6 billion words (with a vocabulary of 400,000 words) and see how that pans out.

The Keras documentation has a good example for loading existing, pretrained embeddings into an `Embedding` layer. We will use this approach and first load our Word2Vec embedding into our sentiment classifier. We just read the saved embedding line by line into a dictionary, mapping words to vectors. Then we create a matrix of size

```
(number of words in vocabulary,embedding vector size)
```

and fill that matrix with the vectors for every word index (the integer value for a word) in the vocabulary.

Listing 3.9 Loading existing embeddings for a classification task

```
def load_embedding(f, vocab, embedding_dimension):
    embedding_index = {}
    f = open(f)
    n=0
    for line in f:
        values = line.split()
        word = values[0]
        if word in vocab: #only store words in current vocabulary
            coefs = np.asarray(values[1:], dtype='float32')
            if n: #skip header line
                embedding_index[word] = coefs
            n+=1
    f.close()

    embedding_matrix = np.zeros((len(vocab) + 1, embedding_dimension))
    for word, i in vocab.items():
        embedding_vector = embedding_index.get(word)
        if embedding_vector is not None:
            embedding_matrix[i] = embedding_vector
    return embedding_matrix
```

Notice that we do not train the `Embedding` after loading the pretrained embedding, since that process has been delegated to the external process generating our `Embedding`.

Listing 3.10 Initializing an Embedding with a pretrained model

```
embedding = Embedding(len(vocab) + 1,
                      embedding_dimension,
                      weights=[embedding_matrix],
                      input_length=max_len,
                      trainable=False)
```

Setting the `trainable` parameter to `True` may be helpful, though: it amounts to *seeding* an `Embedding` with a pretrained model and fine-tuning it for the specific task at hand.

Our code remains the same as listing 3.3, with the exception of importing an embedding from the file and loading it into our model.

Listing 3.11 Using existing embeddings for a classification task

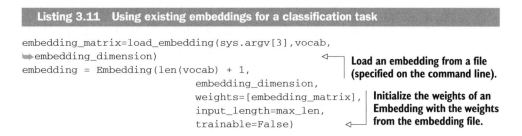

```
embedding_matrix=load_embedding(sys.argv[3],vocab,
    embedding_dimension)                        Load an embedding from a file
embedding = Embedding(len(vocab) + 1,           (specified on the command line).
                      embedding_dimension,
                      weights=[embedding_matrix],   Initialize the weights of an
                      input_length=max_len,         Embedding with the weights
                      trainable=False)              from the embedding file.
```

When we run this, feeding it the saved embedding produced by our Word2Vec implementation, we are unpleasantly surprised: the reported accuracy on the test data appears to drop significantly to a measly 62%. How come? The most likely explanation is that the embedding created by our first classifier was geared toward its classification task, apparently superseding the weak Word2Vec model we induced from the smallish data sample.

So, let's move to a much stronger model. We will load a model consisting of 100-dimensional word embeddings of 400,000 words, based on a 2014 version of English Wikipedia. The embeddings were created by GloVe, a word embedding tactic based on statistical word co-occurrences. This time, we will use a different loading function, specialized for processing large zip files (the GloVe vector file is over 820 MB).

Listing 3.12   Loading a pretrained, zipped embedding

```
def load_embedding_zipped(f, vocab, embedding_dimension):
    embedding_index = {}
    with zipfile.ZipFile(f) as z:
        with z.open("glove.6B.100d.txt") as f:
            n=0
            for line in f:
                if n:
                    values = line.split()
                    word = values[0]
                    if word in vocab:
                        coefs = np.asarray(values[1:], dtype='float32')
                        embedding_index[word] = coefs
                n+=1
    z.close()
    embedding_matrix = np.zeros((len(vocab) + 1, embedding_dimension))
    for word, i in vocab.items():
        embedding_vector = embedding_index.get(word)
        if embedding_vector is not None:
            embedding_matrix[i] = embedding_vector
    return embedding_matrix
```

We restrict the import of the model to the words that are in our training and test data. A quick inspection of a fragment of the model with T-SNE shows interpretable clusterings of words (figure 3.9). Word vectors are mapped to 2D through a dimensionality reduction algorithm in T-SNE.

T-SNE casts the various GloVe vectors into a 2D space as points with two coordinates. The scale of the x-axis and y-axis was determined automatically by T-SNE (the x-axis ranges from −1 to 8 and the y-axis from −3 to 4) and need not concern us. Notice how words like "championship," "race," and "round" or "international" and "global" are put close to each other. This makes sense since these words are near-synonyms.

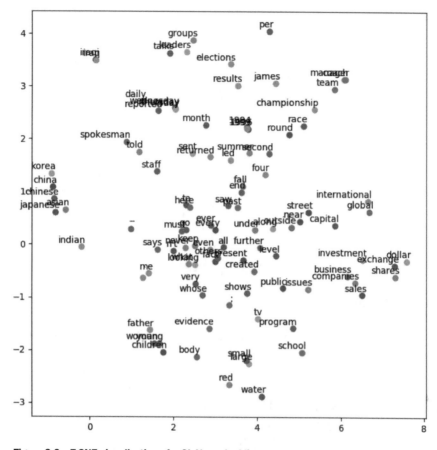

Figure 3.9   T-SNE visualization of a GloVe embedding

But also notice how "small" and "large" are lumped together. This demonstrates that the type of synonymy vector-based models like GloVe (and, for that matter, Word2Vec) deduce is basically *distributional similarity*: two words obtain vector representations that are more similar if those words share more contexts in the training data. As it turns out, the GloVe model also does not fare well, although the result is slightly better. It produces an accuracy of 66%.

What happens when we retrain the pretrained embeddings by setting the `train-able` parameter of `Embedding` to `True`? Figure 3.10 shows how we retrain a pretrained word embedding as part of a sentiment-labeling task.

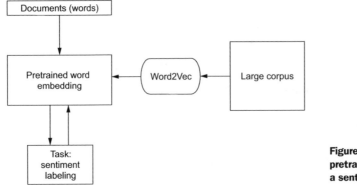

Figure 3.10   **Retraining a
pretrained word embedding for
a sentiment-labeling task**

Both our Word2Vec embedding and the GloVe model produce accuracies in the range of 72% on the test data, which is close to the original result (73.6%) produced by our first classifier. (These accuracies were obtained by running the code a couple of times consecutively. Adding a `numpy.random.seed(1234)` statement to the beginning of the code will reproduce consistent results.)

Apparently there is not a lot to be gained here. The general, external Word2Vec models do not bring any advantages to our task. This could be because our data is from a fairly specific domain compared to the much broader Wikipedia domain of the GloVe model. Regardless, a lesson we can take away from this small experiment is that task-specific embeddings, optimized for a certain task, may under specific circumstances be superior to pretrained word embeddings. Testing the benefits or drawbacks of external word embeddings is fortunately quite easy with the pattern we implemented.

Exercise

Validate the differences between task-specific and pretrained external embeddings a bit more. Take a look at word embedding repositories on the web, such as http://vectors.nlpl.eu/repository and https://github.com/3Top/word2vec-api#where-to-get-a-pretrained-models.

3.3   *From documents to vectors: Doc2Vec*

Embeddings are not restricted to the word level. We can embed (vectorize) larger linguistic units like sentences, paragraphs, or even entire documents. (Here we'll refer to all of them as documents.) Why would we do such a thing? Some useful applications are matching questions with answers, and document retrieval (looking for similar documents for an input document). By representing documents with vectors, we can look for similarity in the derived vector space, just like semantic similarity between words.

Scenario: Document similarity

Given a certain document like a restaurant review complaining about the food (such as the fish), you want to find reviews with similar complaints (for example, about seafood). Can you establish similarity using document embeddings?

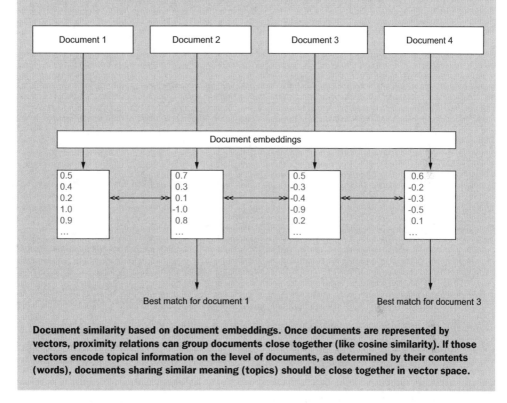

Document similarity based on document embeddings. Once documents are represented by vectors, proximity relations can group documents close together (like cosine similarity). If those vectors encode topical information on the level of documents, as determined by their contents (words), documents sharing similar meaning (topics) should be close together in vector space.

The original paper on paragraph vectors by Le and Mikolov (2014) proposes an elegant extension of Word2Vec to entire documents. Their approach has become known as Doc2Vec (figure 3.11).

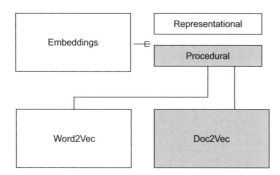

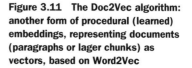

Figure 3.11 The Doc2Vec algorithm: another form of procedural (learned) embeddings, representing documents (paragraphs or lager chunks) as vectors, based on Word2Vec

The idea is simple. First, we assign every document a unique identifier like a filename or an integer. Then, the idea is to jointly embed these document identifiers in a separate embedding, together with a word-based embedding of their content. Figure 3.12 illustrates the process (for the original diagram, see Le and Mikolov 2014).

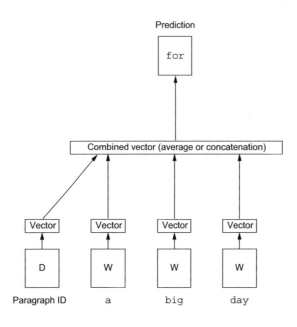

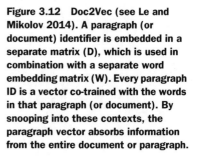

Figure 3.12   Doc2Vec (see Le and Mikolov 2014). A paragraph (or document) identifier is embedded in a separate matrix (D), which is used in combination with a separate word embedding matrix (W). Every paragraph ID is a vector co-trained with the words in that paragraph (or document). By snooping into these contexts, the paragraph vector absorbs information from the entire document or paragraph.

We create a sliding window over the words in the documents and generate word n-grams of a prespecified size (such as 3), with a separate embedding for every word in the n-grams. For every combination of an n-gram and a document identifier, we generate a target to be predicted. These targets consist of the first word beyond the current n-gram. The document identifiers become associated with many n-grams during training (but, importantly, only the n-grams in their text). The identifiers form a type of memory, encoding the missing information from the local n-grams to predict the next word. They receive a vector, just like an arbitrary word. This vector becomes co-trained with the words in the document or paragraph. Once trained, the document identifiers become associated with vectors that describe the aggregation of the missing information for predicting the next words for all sequences. This missing information is an approximation of the topic of a document.

For instance, given the following document 127

127 My first visit to Hiro was a delight!

we generate the following n-grams, where we arbitrarily set *n* to 3 (so we are generating *trigrams*):

- my first visit
- first visit to

- visit to Hiro
- to Hiro was
- Hiro was a
- was a delight

These are the respective target words:

- to
- Hiro
- was
- a

So, for the trigram "my first visit," the target word is "to" since "to" is the first word to the right of this trigram in document 127.

For the last n-gram, "was a delight," we may opt to generate an "end of sentence" pseudo-token (in our code, we just ignore it).

Exercise

Practice a bit with trigrams and target words for a few short sentences.

Our data is the set of Yelp reviews we used earlier. Every line consists of a sentence containing a review statement:

```
Took an hour to get our food only 4 tables in restaurant my food was Luke
warm, Our server was running around like he was totally overwhelmed.
There is not a deal good enough that would drag me into that establishment
again.
Hard to judge whether these sides were good because we were grossed out by
the melted styrofoam and didn't want to eat it for fear of getting sick.
On a positive note, our server was very attentive and provided great service.
Frozen pucks of disgust, with some of the worst people behind the register.
The only thing I did like was the prime rib and dessert section.
```

First, let's define a function for turning our data (consisting of a file with one document per line) into integer-valued arrays for the document identifiers, context arrays of word n-grams, and target words.

Listing 3.13 Processing data for Doc2Vec

```
def process_data(textFile,window_size):
    docs = getLines(textFile)
    vocab = dict()
    create_vocabulary(vocab, docs)
    docid=0
    contexts=[]
    docids=[]
    targets=[]
```

```
f=open("docs.legend","w")
for s in docs:
    f.write("%d %s\n"%(docid,s))
    docids.append(docid)
    ngs=list(ngrams(s.split(), window_size))
    for i in range(len(ngs)-1):
        cs=[docid]
        ng=ngs[i]
        for w in ng:
            w=re.sub("[.,:;'\"!?()]+","",w.lower())
            cs.append(vocab[w])
        contexts.append(cs)
        target_word=re.sub("[.,:;'\"!?()]+","",ngs[i+1][0].lower())
        targets.append(vocab[target_word])
    docid+=1
f.close()
return np.array(contexts),np.array(docids),np.array(targets),vocab
```

This function uses the ngrams function of sklearn to generate word n-grams, where *n* is set to the parameter value window_size. For every line in our data file, a unique, ascending document identifier is generated. A context array is built up, containing the document identifier and the numerical representations (integers) of the words in every n-gram. The function also generates a legend file consisting of combinations of document identifiers (integers) and raw document content (in our case, our documents are single-line text files). We will use the legend file later to interpret the results. Figure 3.13 illustrates the gist of the process.

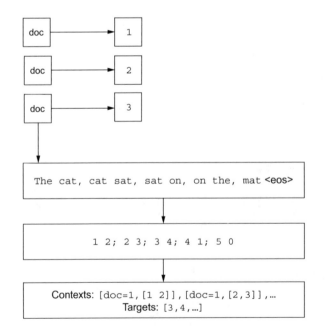

Figure 3.13 Document processing for Doc2Vec. Word contexts are now linked to document (or paragraph) identifiers, which are *pseudo-words*. These identifiers are repeated across contexts and become trained as regular word vectors. They absorb the contextual information of the various words they combine with in this process and afterward encode properties (topics) of entire documents or paragraphs.

We next define a *generator function* that deploys these arrays to generate batches of training data based on random selections.

YP 511 4191

Listing 3.14   Generating training batches for Doc2Vec

```
def generator(contexts, targets, batch_size):
    w1 = np.zeros((batch_size, 1))
    w2 = np.zeros((batch_size, 1))
    w3 = np.zeros((batch_size, 1))
    docid = np.zeros((batch_size, 1))
    batch_targets = np.zeros((batch_size,1))

    while True:
        for i in range(batch_size):
            index= random.randint(0,len(targets)-1)
            batch_targets[i] = targets[index]
            docid[i]=contexts[index][0]
            w1[i] = contexts[index][1]
            w2[i] = contexts[index][2]
            w3[i] = contexts[index][3]
        yield [w1,w2,w3,docid], [batch_targets]
```

This function is called during training and generates random batches consisting of 2D arrays (with size `(batch size,1)`) harboring the words in the contexts generated by `collect_data`, the corresponding document identifiers, and the target words.

With all this in place, let's look at our model.

Listing 3.15   Model definition for Doc2Vec

```
input_w1 = Input((1,))
input_w2 = Input((1,))
input_w3 = Input((1,))
input_docid=Input((1,))

# Embeddings
embedding = Embedding(vocab_size, vector_dim, input_length=1,
➥name='embedding')

vector_dim_doc=vector_dim
embedding_doc=Embedding(len(docids)+1,vector_dim_doc)

docid=embedding_doc(input_docid)
docid = Reshape((vector_dim_doc,1))(docid)

w1 = embedding(input_w1)
w1 = Reshape((vector_dim, 1))(w1)

w2 = embedding(input_w2)
w2 = Reshape((vector_dim, 1))(w2)

w3 = embedding(input_w3)
w3 = Reshape((vector_dim, 1))(w3)
```

```
context_docid=concatenate([w1,w2,w3,docid])
context_docid=Flatten()(context_docid)
output = Dense(vocab_size,activation='softmax')(context_docid)
model = Model(input=[input_w1, input_w2, input_w3, input_docid],
➥output=output)
model.compile(loss='sparse_categorical_crossentropy',
➥optimizer='adam',metrics=['acc'])

print model.summary()

epochs=int(sys.argv[2])

model.fit_generator(generator(contexts,targets,100),
➥steps_per_epoch=100, epochs=epochs)
```

We have four inputs in our model: three words and one document identifier. Targets for the next word prediction task that drives our model are computed by our pro- cess_data function. The words and document identifiers all share the same embed- ding, the outputs of which are combined by concatenation into one context vector.

This concatenation of vector representations is flattened and fed into a Dense out- put layer. Notice how we predict a numerical value for a target word (the word follow- ing a trigram in our data). Using Keras's sparse_categorical_crossentropy as a loss function caters to this type of output. Our generator function provides our model with fresh, random samples of contexts and corresponding targets during training. The document identifier embedding gets trained on the fly during the process of training the word embeddings with this next-word prediction objective.

When trained on the Yelp data, this system displays a number of interesting results. Following are some of the matches produced by the nearest neighbor search with Gensim (we use the legend file generated by our data processing function to reason back from nearest neighbors [document identifiers] to texts). These texts are quite similar in terms of content (without taking into account their sentiment polarity):

```
In the summer, you can dine in a charming outdoor patio - so very delightful.
I liked the patio and the service was outstanding.

Will never, ever go back.
Won't ever go here again.

The nachos are a MUST HAVE!
It sure does beat the nachos at the movies but I would expect a little bit
➥more coming from a restaurant

The Greek dressing was very creamy and flavorful.
My side Greek salad with the Greek dressing was so tasty, and the pita and
➥hummus was very refreshing.

This place is two thumbs up....way up.
2 Thumbs Up!!

Service was slow and not attentive
Waitress was a little slow in service.
```

The following listing shows the full code.

Listing 3.16 Doc2Vec

```
from keras.models import Model
from keras.layers import Input, Dense, Reshape, merge, concatenate,
➥average, Flatten
from keras.layers.embeddings import Embedding
from keras.preprocessing import sequence
import numpy as np
import sys
import random
import re
from keras.utils import to_categorical
from nltk.util import ngrams
import codecs


def save_embedding(outputFile, weights, nb_docs):
    with codecs.open(outputFile, "w", "utf-8") as f:
        f.write(str(nb_docs) + " " + str(weights.shape[1]) + "\n")
                for index in range(nb_docs):
            f.write("doc_"+str(index) + " ")
                        for i in xrange(len(weights[index])):
                    f.write(str(weights[index][i]) + " ")
                    f.write("\n")

def getLines(f):
    lines = [line.rstrip() for line in open(f)]
    return lines


def create_vocabulary(vocabulary, docs):
        vocabulary["<unk>"]=0
    for doc in docs:
        for word in doc.strip().split():
                        word=re.sub("[.,:;'\"!?()]+","",word.lower())
                        if word not in vocabulary:
                    vocabulary[word]=len(vocabulary)


def generator(contexts, targets, batch_size):
    w1 = np.zeros((batch_size, 1))
    w2 = np.zeros((batch_size, 1))
    w3 = np.zeros((batch_size, 1))
    docid = np.zeros((batch_size, 1))
    batch_targets = np.zeros((batch_size,1))

    while True:
        for i in range(batch_size):
            index= random.randint(0,len(targets)-1)
            batch_targets[i] = targets[index]
            docid[i]=contexts[index][0]
```

```
                w1[i] = contexts[index][1]
                w2[i] = contexts[index][2]
                w3[i] = contexts[index][3]
            yield [w1,w2,w3,docid], [batch_targets]


def process_data(textFile,window_size):
    docs = getLines(textFile)
    vocab = dict()
    create_vocabulary(vocab, docs)
    docid=0
    contexts=[]
    docids=[]
    targets=[]

    f=open("docs.legenda","w")
    for s in docs:
        f.write("%d %s\n"%(docid,s))
        docids.append(docid)
        ngs=list(ngrams(s.split(), window_size))
        for i in range(len(ngs)-1):
            cs=[docid]
            ng=ngs[i]
            for w in ng:
                w=re.sub("[.,:;'\"!?()]+","",w.lower())
                cs.append(vocab[w])
            contexts.append(cs)
            target_word=re.sub("[.,:;'\"!?()]+","",ngs[i+1][0].lower())
            targets.append(vocab[target_word])
        docid+=1
    f.close()
    return np.array(contexts),np.array(docids),np.array(targets),vocab



window_size = 3
vector_dim = 100
epochs = 1000

contexts,docids,targets,vocab=collect_data(sys.argv[1],3)
vocab_size=len(vocab)

input_w1 = Input((1,))
input_w2 = Input((1,))
input_w3 = Input((1,))
input_docid=Input((1,))

embedding = Embedding(vocab_size, vector_dim, input_length=1,
➥name='embedding')

vector_dim_doc=vector_dim
embedding_doc=Embedding(len(docids)+1,vector_dim_doc)
```

```
docid=embedding_doc(input_docid)
docid = Reshape((vector_dim_doc,1))(docid)

w1 = embedding(input_w1)
w1 = Reshape((vector_dim, 1))(w1)

w2 = embedding(input_w2)
w2 = Reshape((vector_dim, 1))(w2)

w3 = embedding(input_w3)
w3 = Reshape((vector_dim, 1))(w3)

context_docid=concatenate([w1,w2,w3,docid])
context_docid=Flatten()(context_docid)
output = Dense(vocab_size,activation='softmax')(context_docid)
model = Model(input=[input_w1, input_w2, input_w3, input_docid],
➥output=output)
model.compile(loss='sparse_categorical_crossentropy', optimizer='adam',
➥metrics=['acc'])

print model.summary()

epochs=int(sys.argv[2])

model.fit_generator(generator(contexts,targets,100), steps_per_epoch=100,
➥epochs=epochs)

save_embeddings("embedding_doc2vec.txt", embedding_doc.get_weights()[0],
➥len(docids))

exit(0)
```

We have gone through quite a lot in this chapter. Starting from random word embeddings, we went into on-the-fly embeddings that were trained while learning a specific NLP task, in our case, sentiment labeling of restaurant reviews. We contrasted these embeddings with special-purpose embeddings like Word2Vec and GloVe and went into the details of Word2Vec and Doc2Vec. Interestingly, the internal representations of LSTMs have been used for word embeddings as well. In particular, bidirectional LSTMS (biLSTMs) have been used to pack contextual word information (looking backward and forward in sequences of words) into vector representations of separate words (see Peters 2018).

Now, let's move from these representational issues to linguistic analysis: textual similarity, the topic of the next chapter. Chapter 9 discusses one other ingredient of embeddings: *positional encoding*, which helps keep track of the original positions of input elements like words.

> **NOTE** The code written in this chapter was partially inspired by the Keras GitHub examples repository and open source derivatives of those examples.

Summary

- Embeddings themselves can be optimized during optimization for an objective, like training a sentiment classifier.
- Pretrained embeddings are not always beneficiary.
- Sometimes it makes sense to use an on-the-fly embedding that is specific to (and optimized for) the NLP task at hand.
- Two examples of embedding algorithms are Word2Vec and Doc2Vec.

Part 2

Deep NLP

Part 2 focuses on assessing textual similarity (chapter 4) with deep learning. Applications involve authorship attribution ("Who wrote this?") and authorship verification ("Did this author write this?"). In chapter 5, we switch to processing long sequences with memory-equipped models for Question Answering. We apply such memory models to other NLP tasks in chapter 6.

Textual similarity

One of the most common applications in natural language processing (NLP) is determining whether two texts are similar. Common applications include

- *Document retrieval*—Determining query-result similarity
- *Topic labeling*—Assigning a topic to an unlabeled text based on similarity with a set of labeled texts
- *Authorship analysis*—Determining whether a text is written by a certain author, based on texts attributed to that author

We will approach the topic of text similarity from the perspective of authorship analysis. There are two main topics in authorship analysis:

- *Authorship attribution*—The problem of assigning a text to one of many authors
- *Authorship verification*—The problem of deciding whether a certain text of unknown origin is written by the known author of another text

In this chapter, we will go through a few practical scenarios and investigate techniques for assessing authorship of documents.

4.1   The problem

We start with a general scenario: who, of many potential authors, wrote a particular document?

Scenario: Authorship analysis—who wrote this document?

Suppose you are tasked with detecting textual plagiarism. Maybe you are working at a publishing house, judging incoming manuscripts. You are on the lookout for copied work. Skimming through texts, you focus on characteristic features such as writing style, choice of words, and so on. This task quickly becomes impractical. Luckily, you have in your possession a dataset with texts written by verified authors. Create a system that automatically detects whether a text presented by one author was actually written by another author.

We will decompose this scenario into two sub-scenarios.

Sub-scenario: Authorship attribution

You want to find out which of your authors wrote a specific anonymous document. This entails creating author profiles from named documents that express writing style. You will do the same for the unnamed document at hand, and the best match of the document profile with one of your author profiles will reveal who wrote the document.

Sub-scenario: Authorship verification

You receive a document with an author's name on it, but you are doubtful whether this author wrote the document. Create a system that decides whether the author wrote this specific piece of text.

Let's first take a look at our data.

4.2   The data

For both types of authorship analysis, we will use public domain data from the well-known academic PAN network for digital text forensics (see figure 4.1). This network fosters the analysis of texts by organizing challenges: scientific competitions aimed at advancing the state of the art for a certain application of NLP. The data we will use can be found at https://pan.webis.de/data.html. Specifically, we will use the PAN12 dataset for both authorship attribution and verification; it consists of zipped training and test datasets.

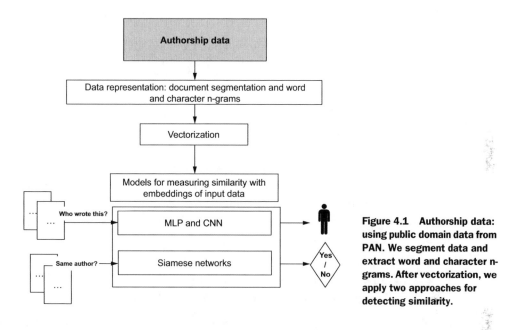

Figure 4.1   **Authorship data: using public domain data from PAN. We segment data and extract word and character n-grams. After vectorization, we apply two approaches for detecting similarity.**

4.2.1   *Authorship attribution and verification data*

Unzipping the authorship attribution data creates separate folders holding 74 training and 78 test documents, including a ground truth file for the test data. The ground truth file contains the real author labels for the unlabeled test documents:

```
file 12Atest01 = B  #(author=B)
file 12Atest02 = A  # (etc)
file 12Atest03 = A
file 12Atest04 = C
file 12Atest05 = C
file 12Atest06 = B


....
```

For training documents, the ground truth author label is part of the filename:

```
12CtrainC1.txt
12CtrainC2.txt
```

These two documents represent one author, C. There are 14 different authors in the training data.

Each document contains text snippets representing one specific author, and the task is to label the test documents with the correct author names. In our authorship experiments (both attribution and verification), we will use only the training data from PAN and split it into training/test partitions. For authorship verification, we will create pairs of documents belonging to either the same author or two authors and train a network on predicting whether the two documents belong to the same author.

With our data in place, let's get to work. We will start by creating vector representations of our data: word-based features, character n-gram features and linguistic features (representational features), and Word2Vec representations (operational vectors).

4.3 *Data representation*

There are roughly two approaches to representing text for authorship analysis. Both approaches aim at deriving textual profiles for authors, in order to compare new texts with unknown authorship to author-labeled documents. As you can imagine, style is determined by both lexical choices and stylistic parameters dealing with word combinations. Further, there are subtle parameters at play, such as choices of grammatical categories like parts of speech, regular typos, abbreviations, and other peculiarities. Summarizing, style is expressed by

- Word choice
- Word order and other grammatical choices
- Low-level characteristics like typos and abbreviations

Linguistic features such as parts of speech and other stylistic markers can also be used. For instance, the use of adjectives and adverbs is indicative of certain sentiments, which can be author-specific:

I am totally crazy about this cool phone

We can represent this information in different types of vectors (for instance, one-hot or numerical vectors), which subsequently can be used in embeddings within the networks (see figure 4.2). In this chapter, we will limit ourselves to embeddings of words and subwords (character n-grams), and we will not address other linguistic features.

Figure 4.3 shows what we have in mind. Let's flesh out the necessary data preprocessing tools we need.

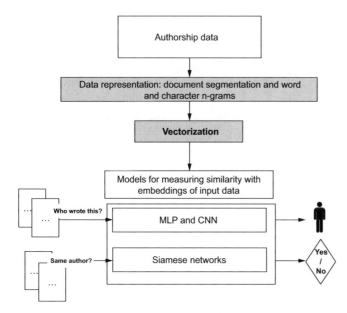

Figure 4.2 Turning data into vectors after preprocessing

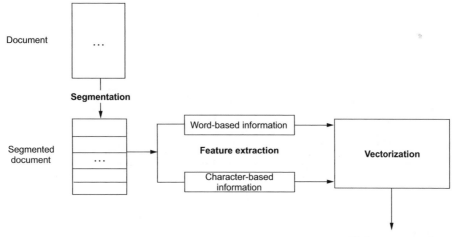

Figure 4.3 Turning document segments into vectors for author analysis. Segmentation is followed by either word-based or character-based information extraction, leading to vectorization.

4.3.1 Segmenting documents

First, it makes sense to chop up documents into fixed-size blocks of a number of words and represent each of those blocks with a vector, rather than generating one vector for each document: it is unlikely that a single vector can express a stylistic profile of an author. For instance, while a Doc2Vec-based vector of 300 dimensions may represent the contents of the underlying document in a global (*semantic*) manner, it will not represent word order or other personal style indicators.

Here is how to segment documents based on a specified block size (the desired number of words per block).

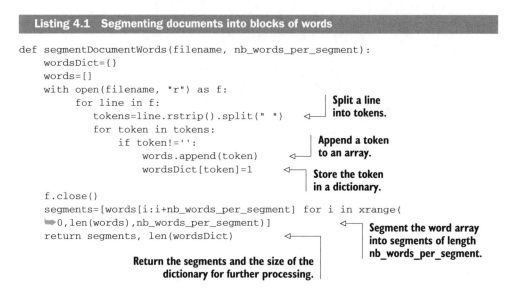

Listing 4.1   **Segmenting documents into blocks of words**

```
def segmentDocumentWords(filename, nb_words_per_segment):
    wordsDict={}
    words=[]
    with open(filename, "r") as f:
        for line in f:
            tokens=line.rstrip().split(" ")          ⟵  Split a line into tokens.
            for token in tokens:
                if token!='':
                    words.append(token)               ⟵  Append a token to an array.
                    wordsDict[token]=1                 ⟵  Store the token in a dictionary.
        f.close()
        segments=[words[i:i+nb_words_per_segment] for i in xrange(
        ⇒0,len(words),nb_words_per_segment)]          ⟵  Segment the word array into segments of length nb_words_per_segment.
        return segments, len(wordsDict)                ⟵
```

Return the segments and the size of the dictionary for further processing.

Calling this function on file 12AtrainA1.txt in our dataset with a segment size of 20 words produces a list of word-based segments, the first of which is as follows:

```
['Victor', 'Dolor', 'went', 'to', 'the', 'diner', 'because', 'two',
⇒'months', 'ago', 'a', 'man', 'killed', 'five', 'people', 'there.',
⇒'The', 'man', 'was', 'Hugo']
```

4.3.2   *Word-level information*

Document representations based on a single word (unigram) go only so far for determining authorship. Lexical choice may be an important stylistic trait, but the combination of words seems even more important. But we will give unigram-based (word-based) vectors a fair try. Let's dig up a Keras procedure from chapter 2 for generating such vectors: a bag-of-words representation with the hashing trick, now applied to our document segments. Remember that the hashing trick creates vectors of a specified length by hashing its vector input data and using the hashed values as indices of the result vector. This gives us exact control over the length of our vectors.

First let's extract a dictionary of labels from our data. Recall that our training data resides in files with names like 12AtrainB.txt. The *B* is the unique single-character identifier of the author. We will use a dictionary to hold all labels. We convert every author identifier into a number by subtracting 65 (the ASCII value of *A*) from the ASCII value of the identifier. This creates a 0 for *A*, a 1 for *B*, and so on. Since we do not know if labels are missing in our data, we store these values in the dictionary, which maps every subtraction result to a unique index. This is done by the following `createLabelDict` procedure that inspects both training and test data for labels.

Listing 4.2 Creating a label dictionary

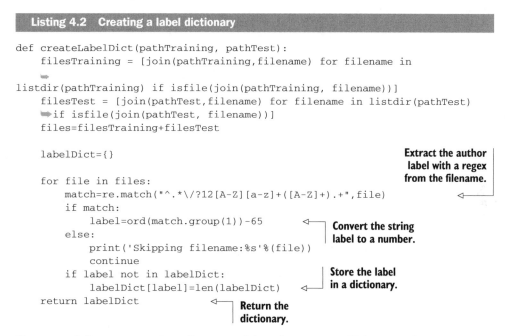

```
def createLabelDict(pathTraining, pathTest):
    filesTraining = [join(pathTraining,filename) for filename in
⮑
listdir(pathTraining) if isfile(join(pathTraining, filename))]
    filesTest = [join(pathTest,filename) for filename in listdir(pathTest)
⮑if isfile(join(pathTest, filename))]
    files=filesTraining+filesTest

    labelDict={}                                          Extract the author
                                                          label with a regex
    for file in files:                                    from the filename.
        match=re.match("^.*\/?12[A-Z][a-z]+([A-Z]+).+",file)   ◁
        if match:
            label=ord(match.group(1))-65    ◁⎺⎺  Convert the string
        else:                                    label to a number.
            print('Skipping filename:%s'%(file))
            continue
        if label not in labelDict:          ⎺⎺  Store the label
            labelDict[label]=len(labelDict)  ◁⎯  in a dictionary.
    return labelDict          ◁⎯  Return the
                                  dictionary.
```

Next, we define a procedure for vectorizing documents. This procedure generates word-based vectors for segmented documents.

Listing 4.3 Vectorizing documents using bag-of-words

```
def vectorizeDocumentsBOW(path, labelDict, nb_words_per_segment):
    files = [filename for filename in listdir(path) if isfile(
⮑join(path, filename))]
    segments=[]
    labels=[]            Define a global dictionary for storing the
    globalDict={}   ◁⎯  collected vocabulary of the various documents.

    for file in files:
        match=re.match("^.*12[A-Z][a-z]+([A-Z]+).+",file)
        if match:
            label=ord(match.group(1))-65    ◁⎺  Turn character-based author
        else:                                   identifiers into numbers:
            print('Skipping filename:%s'%(file))   they become the numeric
            continue                             labels we want to predict.

        (segmented_document,wordDict)=segmentDocumentWords(join(path,file),
⮑nb_words_per_segment)                                          ◁⎯⎯⎯

        globalDict=mergeDictionaries(globalDict,wordDict)   Segment the current
                                                                document into
```

Merge the document-based vocabulary with the   segments of length nb_words_per_segment,
global vocabulary (see listing 4.4 for the function).   and obtain the vocabulary for the document.

```
        segments.extend(segmented_document)          Store the
                                                      segments
        for segment in segmented_document:            just created.
            labels.append(label)

    vocab_len=len(globalDict)                         The vocabulary size is computed
                                                      from the global dictionary.
    labels=[labelDict[x] for x in labels]
    nb_classes=len(labelDict)

    X=[]
    y=[]

    for segment in segments:
        segment=' '.join(segment)
        X.append(pad_sequences([hashing_trick(        The hashing trick is applied to
          segment, round(vocab_len*1.3))],            create hashed vectors that are
          nb_words_per_segment)[0])                    the size of the segments.

    y=np_utils.to_categorical(labels, nb_classes)
                                                      Pick up the vocabulary
    return np.array(X), y, vocab_len                  length for later use.
```

Here is our helper function for merging two dictionaries.

Listing 4.4   Merging dictionaries

```
def mergeDictionaries(d1, d2):
    d = d1.copy()
    d.update(d2)
    return d
```

Similarly, a procedure for generating word n-gram (with $n) > 1$) vectors copies virtually all of listing 4.3, with a little change: we chop up sentences into word n-grams of a specified size (like 2 for bigrams or 3 for trigrams) using the nltk function ngrams(). First we segment documents based on word n-grams.

Listing 4.5   Segmenting documents using word n-grams

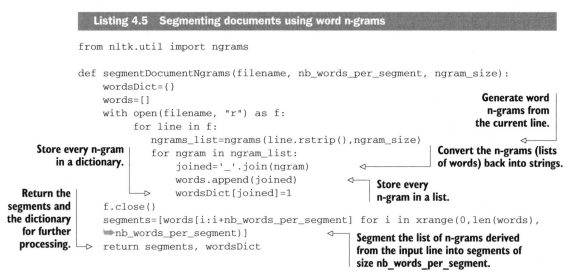

```
from nltk.util import ngrams

def segmentDocumentNgrams(filename, nb_words_per_segment, ngram_size):
    wordsDict={}                                                      Generate word
    words=[]                                                          n-grams from
    with open(filename, "r") as f:                                    the current line.
        for line in f:
            ngrams_list=ngrams(line.rstrip(),ngram_size)
            for ngram in ngram_list:                                 Convert the n-grams (lists
                joined='_'.join(ngram)                               of words) back into strings.
                words.append(joined)
                wordsDict[joined]=1                   Store every
    f.close()                                         n-gram in a list.
    segments=[words[i:i+nb_words_per_segment] for i in xrange(0,len(words),
      nb_words_per_segment)]
    return segments, wordsDict
```

Store every n-gram in a dictionary.

Return the segments and the dictionary for further processing.

Segment the list of n-grams derived from the input line into segments of size nb_words_per_segment.

The vectorization procedure for word n-grams is then exactly the same as for separate words (listing 4.3), with two small differences: we use segmentDocumentNgrams() rather than segmentDocumentWords(), and we specify an additional ngram_size parameter.

Listing 4.6 Vectorizing documents using character n-grams

```
def vectorizeDocumentsNgrams(path, ngram_size, labelDict,
 nb_words_per_segment):
    files = [filename for filename in listdir(path) if isfile(
    join(path, filename))]
    segments=[]
    labels=[]
    globalDict={}

    for file in files:
match=re.match("^.*12[A-Z][a-z]+([A-Z]+).+",file)
if match:
            label=ord(match.group(1))-65
else:
            print('Skipping filename:%s'%(file))
            continue
(segmented_document,wordDict)=segmentDocumentNgrams(join(path,file),
 nb_words_per_segment, ngram_size)

globalDict=mergeDictionaries(globalDict,wordDict)

segments.extend(segmented_document)
for segment in segmented_document:
            labels.append(label)

    vocab_len=len(globalDict)

    labels=[labelDict[x] for x in labels]
    nb_classes=len(labelDict)

    X=[]
    y=[]

    for segment in segments:
     segment=' '.join(segment)
     X.append(pad_sequences([hashing_trick(segment, round(vocab_len*1.5))],
     nb_words_per_segment)[0])

    y=np_utils.to_categorical(labels, nb_classes)

    return np.array(X),y, int(vocab_len*1.5)+1
```

Recall that convolutional neural networks (CNNs) apply filters to their input and that these filters usually address more than one piece of information at a time. Feeding plain words to a CNN results in the extraction of data-specific, weighted word n-grams. If we preprocess our data explicitly by generating word n-grams ourselves, a CNN can detect higher-order n-grams from these n-grams: n-grams of n-grams. Effectively, a CNN can combine (filter) n-grams into ordered lists of n-grams: it aims to detect interesting patches in the linear sequence of items it receives, and it does not care whether these items are words or word n-grams. Consider this example:

John+went, went+to,to+the,the+dinner => [John+went, went+to], [to+the, the+dinner]

The CNN detects the grouped word bigrams as interesting, informative patches. Alternatively, when fed plain words, the CNN might figure out that these are interesting patches:

John+went went+to

We will see in our experiments how that works out and whether it brings any advantages.

4.3.3   *Subword-level information*

Interestingly, a lot of research on authorship analysis (like Stamatatos 2009) has found that *subword information* like character n-grams also bears authorship-revealing information. A bag-of-characters n-gram representation can be computed pretty much the same as our word-based n-gram generator, with one difference: the use of the Python built-in function `list()`, which splits a string into characters rather than words. This example

```
list("Victor went to the diner")
```

produces the following:

```
['V', 'i', 'c', 't', 'o', 'r', ' ', 'D', 'o', 'l', 'o', 'r', ' ', 'w',
'e', 'n', 't', ' ', 't', 'o', ' ', 't', 'h', 'e', ' ', 'd', 'i',
'n', 'e', 'r']
```

This list comprehension builds character trigrams from the output of `list()`.

Listing 4.7   Generating character trigrams

```
[''.join(ngram) for ngram in ngrams(list("Victor Dolor went to the diner"),3)]
```

The results are as follows:

```
['Vic', 'ict', 'cto', 'tor', 'or ', 'r D', ' Do', 'Dol', 'olo', 'lor',
'or ', 'r w', ' we', 'wen', 'ent', 'nt ', 't t', ' to', 'to ', 'o t',
' th', 'the', 'he ', 'e d', ' di', 'din', 'ine', 'ner']
```

Here is a procedure for segmenting documents based on character n-grams. A suitable value for the parameter `ngram_size` would be 3 (trigrams), but the exact choice is open to experimentation (which also holds for the parameter `nb_words_per_segment`).

Listing 4.8   Segmenting documents based on character n-grams

```
def segmentDocumentCharNgrams(filename, nb_words_per_segment, ngram_size):
    wordsDict={}
    words=[]
    with open(filename, "r") as f:
        for line in f:
```

We define a dictionary for the words we encounter (in this case, character n-grams of size ngram_size).

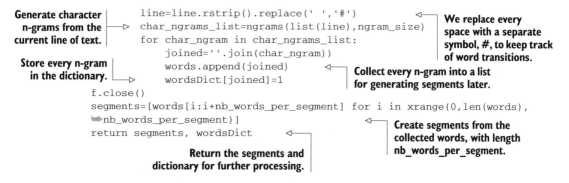

Generate character n-grams from the current line of text.

We replace every space with a separate symbol, #, to keep track of word transitions.

Store every n-gram in the dictionary.

Collect every n-gram into a list for generating segments later.

Create segments from the collected words, with length nb_words_per_segment.

Return the segments and dictionary for further processing.

```
line=line.rstrip().replace(' ','#')
char_ngrams_list=ngrams(list(line),ngram_size)
for char_ngram in char_ngrams_list:
    joined=''.join(char_ngram))
    words.append(joined)
    wordsDict[joined]=1
f.close()
segments=[words[i:i+nb_words_per_segment] for i in xrange(0,len(words),
    nb_words_per_segment)]
return segments, wordsDict
```

The vectorization procedure for character n-grams is the same as for separate words (listing 4.3), but we use `segmentDocumentCharNgrams()` rather than `segment-DocumentWords()`, and we specify the `ngram_size` parameter.

Listing 4.9   Vectorizing documents based on character n-grams

```
def vectorizeDocumentsCharNgrams(path, ngram_size, labelDict,
    nb_words_per_segment):
    files = [filename for filename in listdir(path) if isfile(
        join(path, filename))]
    segments=[]
    labels=[]
    globalDict={}

    for file in files:
        match=re.match("^.*12[A-Z][a-z]+([A-Z]+).+",file)
        if match:
            label=ord(match.group(1))-65
        else:
            print('Skipping filename:%s'%(file))
            continue

        (segmented_document,wordDict)=segmentDocumentCharNgrams(
            join(path,file),nb_words_per_segment, ngram_size)

    globalDict=mergeDictionaries(globalDict,wordDict)

    segments.extend(segmented_document)
    for segment in segmented_document:
        labels.append(label)

    vocab_len=len(globalDict)

    labels=[labelDict[x] for x in labels]
    nb_classes=len(labelDict)

    X=[]
    y=[]

    for segment in segments:
        segment=' '.join(segment)
        X.append(pad_sequences([hashing_trick(segment, round(vocab_len*1.5))],
            nb_words_per_segment)[0])
```

```
y=np_utils.to_categorical(labels, nb_classes)

return np.array(X),y, (vocab_len*1.5)+1
```

Let's conclude with an overview of our main data preprocessing routines.

Routine description	Reference
Segmenting documents based on words	Listing 4.1
Creating a table dictionary	Listing 4.2
Vectorizing documents using bag-of-words	Listing 4.3
Merging dictionaries	Listing 4.4
Segmenting documents using word n-grams	Listing 4.5
Vectorizing documents uxing character n-grams	Listing 4.6
Generating character trigrams	Listing 4.7
Segmenting documents based on character n-grams	Listing 4.8
Vectorizing documents based on character n-grams	Listing 4.9

Exercise
Recap for yourself the use of these routines and the order and dependencies between them.

4.4   *Models for measuring similarity*

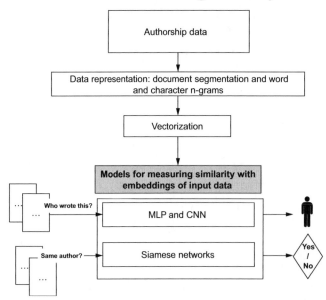

In this section, we develop a classification-based perspective on textual similarity. We investigate multilayer perceptrons (MLPs) and CNNs for authorship attribution and Siamese networks for authorship verification (figure 4.4).

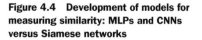

Figure 4.4   **Development of models for measuring similarity: MLPs and CNNs versus Siamese networks**

4.4.1   Authorship attribution

Let's return to our scenario for authorship attribution.

> **Scenario: Authorship attribution**
>
> You want to find out which of your authors wrote a specific anonymous document. This entails creating author profiles from named documents that express writing style. You will do the same for the unnamed document at hand, and the best match of the document profile with one of your author profiles will reveal who wrote the document.

Interpreting this as a multiclass problem, we set out to train a deep MLP and a CNN on the authorship attribution task (figure 4.5). The two models are evaluated for our three types of data representation—word unigrams, word n-grams, and character n-grams—on the PAN data.

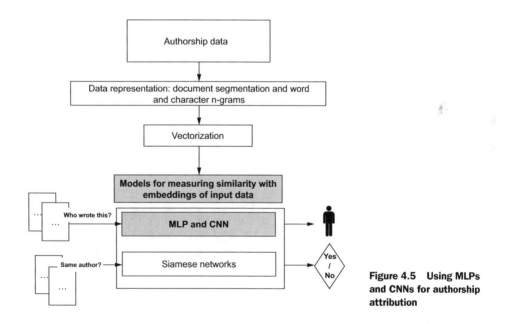

Figure 4.5   Using MLPs and CNNs for authorship attribution

MULTILAYER PERCEPTRONS

Under the multiclass approach to authorship attribution, we train a classifier on the authors in the PAN dataset for task A. Every author constitutes a class, so we have as many classes as authors, and we treat the problem as a regular classification problem. We assign every test document to exactly one author.

We start by processing our data. We will use just the training data from PAN and split it into 66% for training and 33% for testing. We therefore do not need a label dictionary based on both training and test data, which is why we use a `createLabel-DictOneFile()` variant of `createLabelDict()`.

Listing 4.10   Creating a single-file label dictionary

```
def createLabelDictOneFile(path):
    files = [join(path,filename) for filename in listdir(path) if isfile(
    join(path, filename))]
    labelDict={}                                    Extract the author label from
                                                    the filename with a regex.
    for file in files:
        match=re.match("^.*\/?12[A-Z][a-z]+([A-Z]+).+",file)  ◄───────┘
        if match:
            label=ord(match.group(1))-65    ◄──┐ Convert the string label
        else:                                  │ to a numerical value.
            print('Skipping filename:%s'%(file))
            continue
        if label not in labelDict:
            labelDict[label]=len(labelDict)    ◄──┐ Store the label
                                                  │ in a dictionary.
    return labelDict    ◄──│ Return the dictionary.
```

Our data processing then becomes the following:

```
train="/data/pan12-authorship-attribution-training-corpus-2012-03-28/"

labelDict=createLabelDictOneFile(train)

input_dim = 500

X, y, vocab_len = vectorizeDocumentsBOW(train,labelDict,input_dim)

X_train, X_test, y_train, y_test = train_test_split(X, y, test_size=0.33,
➥random_state=42)

nb_classes = len(labelDict)
```

Listing 4.11 shows our model. As you see, it is quite simple. It has a proprietary `Embedding` to represent the word indices of our 500-word blocks as 300-dimensional vectors. The `Embedding` connects to a `Dense` layer which feeds into a `Dropout` layer. `Dropout` layers randomly deactivate neurons in their (in this case, 300-dimensional) input in order to avoid overfitting. The 0.3 value is a parameter governing the random selection of neurons. Following this, we flatten our 500 × 300 layer and feed it into a `Dense` output layer with `nb_classes` dimensionality (the number of authors in our dataset).

Listing 4.11   MLP for authorship attribution

```
model = Sequential()
model.add(Embedding(vocab_len, 300, input_length=input_dim))
model.add(Dense(300, activation='relu'))
model.add(Dropout(0.3))
model.add(Flatten())
model.add(Dense(nb_classes, activation='sigmoid'))
```

```
model.compile(loss='categorical_crossentropy', optimizer='adam',
➥metrics=['acc'])

print model.summary()

nb_epochs=10

model.fit(X_train, y_train, epochs=nb_epochs, shuffle=True,batch_size=64,
➥validation_split=0.3, verbose=2)
loss, accuracy = model.evaluate(X_test, y_test, verbose=0)

print('Accuracy: %f' % (accuracy*100))
```

Running this MLP on the single-word-based representation of the PAN data results in around 65% accuracy. This is to be expected from a single-word-based approach that blissfully ignores word combinations.

Can we do better? First let's take a look at subword information. We apply the same model to five-character n-grams by generating X,y (vectors and labels) with

```
X, y, vocab_len = vectorizeDocumentsCharNgrams(train,5,labelDict,input_dim)
```

Unfortunately, performance drops significantly, to scores in the realm of 55% (54.17% in our run). Apparently we lose a lot of valuable lexical information in this word-based approach.

Suppose we want to apply the explicit word n-grams approach, where we restructure documents as sequences of n-grams, like bigrams:

   Victor_Dolor, 'Dolor_went, went_to, to_the, …

Using segmentDocumentNgrams() to do this, we run into another kind of trouble: our lexicon explodes to a much larger size because there is far less repetition with unique n-grams than with unigrams. For our data split, the vocabulary size for unigram words is 278,000 and for five-word n-grams is over 660,000. This has unpleasant ramifications for the size of our Embedding, which now has to cater to three times as many word indices. The model summary we have for unigrams is as follows:

```
Layer (type)                    Output Shape                 Param #
=====================================================================
embedding_1 (Embedding)         (None, 500, 100)             27801500
_____
dense_1 (Dense)                 (None, 500, 100)             10100
_____
dropout_1 (Dropout)             (None, 500, 100)             0
_____
dense_2 (Dense)                 (None, 500, 50)              5050
_____
flatten_1 (Flatten)             (None, 25000)                0
_____
dense_3 (Dense)                 (None, 14)                   350014
=====================================================================
Total params: 28,166,664
Trainable params: 28,166,664
Non-trainable params: 0
```

Comparing this to 5-grams, we observe an increase from 28 million parameters to over 66 million parameters:

```
Layer (type)                  Output Shape              Param #
=================================================================
embedding_1 (Embedding)       (None, 500, 100)          66251800

dense_1 (Dense)               (None, 500, 100)          10100

dropout_1 (Dropout)           (None, 500, 100)          0

dense_2 (Dense)               (None, 500, 50)           5050

flatten_1 (Flatten)           (None, 25000)             0

dense_3 (Dense)               (None, 14)                350014
=================================================================
Total params: 66,616,964
Trainable params: 66,616,964
Non-trainable params: 0
```

Let's see what happens when we switch to 10-grams (sequences of 10 words):

```
Layer (type)                  Output Shape              Param #
=================================================================
embedding_1 (Embedding)       (None, 500, 100)          1261507700

dense_1 (Dense)               (None, 500, 100)          10100

dropout_1 (Dropout)           (None, 500, 100)          0

dense_2 (Dense)               (None, 500, 50)           5050

flatten_1 (Flatten)           (None, 25000)             0

dense_3 (Dense)               (None, 14)                350014
=================================================================
Total params: 1,261,872,864
Trainable params: 1,261,872,864
Non-trainable params: 0
```

The parameter space derails to a dazzling 1.2 billion parameters. This is clearly not a fruitful approach: generating longer n-grams leads to dramatic increases in the number of lexical entries because there is less repetition. It is like going from 26 characters to words: if you split all the words in a document into their alphabetic characters, you end up with 26 different characters; and if you build a lexicon from them, it has only 26 entries. But if you split your words into character bigrams, the lexicon is much bigger, since there are in theory 26×26 different bigrams in your data. The same observation carries over to the word level.

How about a CNN that—by its nature—takes into account sequences of words or character n-grams without this parameter expansion?

CNNs FOR TEXT

CNNs have frequently been applied to authorship attribution. The motivation is simply that authorship is expressed by many features scattered across a document, and CNNs are good at picking up these features. Recall from chapter 2 that CNNs apply filtering to the data they process. In the textual domain, these filters address combinations of words. Just for comparison, let's keep the model as similar as possible to our previous MLP and apply it to word unigrams for a segment size of 500 words, as before. We'll insert an extra `Convolution1D` layer after the `Dense` layer, with 32 filters of size-30 words. These numbers were chosen arbitrarily and can (and should) be carefully tuned when optimizing a real-world application.

Exercise

Experiment with different settings for filters and filter sizes. Can you improve on the results reported here?

Here is the model (again, the preprocessing of the data remains the same as for the MLP).

Listing 4.12 CNN for authorship attribution

```
model = Sequential()
model.add(Embedding(vocab_size, 300, input_length=input_dim))
model.add(Dense(300, activation='relu'))
model.add(Convolution1D(32, 30, padding="same"))
model.add(Flatten())
model.add(Dense(nb_classes, activation='softmax'))

model.compile(loss='categorical_crossentropy', optimizer='adam',
➥metrics=['acc'])

print model.summary()

model.fit(X_train, y_train, epochs=nb_epochs, shuffle=True,batch_size=16,
➥validation_split=0.3, verbose=2)
```

Running this model produces accuracy results in the eighties (87.1% for our run), which is significantly better than our MLP. Apparently, and understandably, word sequences reveal a lot more about authorship and textual similarity than bare words do.

Likewise, running the model on character n-gram sequences (the 5-grams we used before) produces results that are better but still below the word-based sequences (74.7% in our run). Notice that in this case, the CNN spots combinations of character 5-grams.

The takeaway from these small experiments is, first, that lexical information alone is not sufficient for establishing textual similarity. Style is expressed both lexically and formally, in terms of word combinations. CNNs are the natural tools for emphasizing sequential information, which also carries lexical information, and they consistently outperformed a simple MLP in our experiments. Subword information (character n-grams) produced a reasonable baseline. We have seen that certain choices for feature representations (word n-grams for MLPs) have a direct bearing on model complexity and resource demands. These choices can be balanced with alternatives that implicitly use similar representations with fewer resources (like CNNs for word sequences). In general, models with fewer parameters are preferable to more complex models (Occam's razor). But the exact merits of alternatives have to be established through experimentation.

4.4.2 Verifying authorship

Let's now focus on implementing a method for determining authorship similarity using an LSTM-based Siamese network (figure 4.6). Recall our scenario for authorship verification.

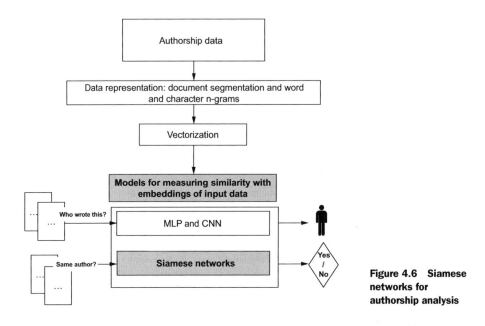

Figure 4.6   Siamese networks for authorship analysis

Scenario: Authorship verification
You receive a document with an author's name on it, but you are doubtful whether this author wrote the document. Create a system that decides whether the author wrote this specific piece of text.

Siamese networks are the natural choice for determining similarity between two pieces of data because they were specially designed to verify similarity between two data sources. Let's find out how they work and what they bring to authorship verification.

SIAMESE NETWORKS: NETWORK TWINS

Siamese networks are networks with (usually two) sister subnetworks and an arbiter. The two sister networks share the same weights. They are applied to pairs of inputs that are labeled for similarity: binary classes (0 or 1) that express whether the paired inputs are similar (according to some definition of similarity). Their latent representations (usually the weight activations of their final hidden layer) are used by the arbiter as follows: the arbiter computes a distance (called the *contrastive loss*) between these representations, and the overall network learns a threshold to decide whether the measured distance for two inputs indicates textual similarity or not. The two networks regulate each other by sharing weights.

Figure 4.7 depicts a typical Siamese network. To prepare our data for training such a network, which must be trained on pairs of similar (same author) or dissimilar (unrelated) texts, we take random samples (of a prespecified size) from the vectorized documents in our dataset. So, we start from the stage where we have already turned our documents into vectors labeled with one-hot class labels (we are using the output from `vectorizeDocumentsBOW()`):

```
...
labelDict=createLabelDictOneFile(train)

input_dim = 500

X, y, vocab_size=vectorizeDocumentsBOW(train,labelDict,input_dim)
```

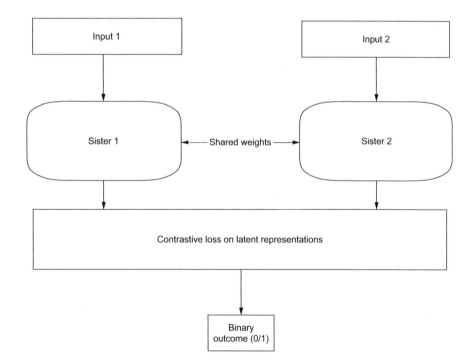

Figure 4.7   A Siamese network. Two sister networks share weights and regulate each other.

We next create a *data splitter* that randomly samples pairs of documents from the output from `vectorizeDocumentsBOW()`—X (vectors) and y (labels corresponding to authors)—and labels the pairs with a 1 if both members of the pair belong to the same author or 0 if not. Our data splitter is called `splitData()`, and the code is as follows.

Listing 4.13 A data splitter for authorship verification

```
def splitData(X,y, max_samples_per_author=10):
    X,y=shuffle(X,y,random_state=42)
    AuthorsX={}

    for (x,y) in zip(X,y):                      ◁─┐ Gather the documents written per author,
        y=np.where(y==1)[0][0]                    │ and store them as a list in a dictionary.
        if y in AuthorsX:
            AuthorsX[y].append(x)
        else:
            AuthorsX[y]=[x]

    X_left=[]
    X_right=[]
    y_lr=[]

    Done={}
    for author in AuthorsX:
        nb_texts=len(AuthorsX[author])
        nb_samples=min(nb_texts, max_samples_per_author)
        left_docs=np.array(AuthorsX[author])
        random_indexes=np.random.choice(left_docs.shape[0], nb_samples,
        ➥replace=False)
        left_sample=np.array(AuthorsX[author])[random_indexes]
        for other_author in AuthorsX:            ◁─┐ Sampling starts here. We draw two
            if  (other_author,author) in Done:     │ authors (they can be the same) and
                pass                               │ randomly sample documents from both.
            Done[(author,other_author)]=1

            right_docs=np.array(AuthorsX[other_author])

            nb_samples_other=min(len(AuthorsX[other_author]),
            ➥max_samples_per_author)
            random_indexes_other=np.random.choice(right_docs.shape[0],
            ➥nb_samples_other, replace=False)
            right_sample=right_docs[random_indexes_other]

            for (l,r) in zip(left_sample,right_sample):
                X_left.append(l)
                X_right.append(r)
                if author==other_author:
                    y_lr.append(1.0)
                else:
                    y_lr.append(0.0)
    return np.array(X_left),np.array(X_right),np.array(y_lr)
```

Label the drawn samples. If the two authors happen to be the same, we generate the label 1; otherwise, the label is 0.

Return the labeled data as two input arrays (X_left,X_right) and one array of associated labels.

To teach the network something about similarity, we need a distance function. We can use pretty much anything we like here, but an exponentiated negative sum of differences is a good choice since it produces values in the range [0,1]:

```
def exp_neg_manhattan_distance(x, y):
        return K.exp(-K.sum(K.abs(x-y), axis=1, keepdims=True))
```

This function measures the difference between two numerical vectors (in our case, the latent space embeddings of the two documents we're comparing). Differences close to zero produce values near to 1:

```
exp(-0.001)=0.999
```

And large differences produce outcomes close to zero:

```
exp(-100)=3.720075976020836e-44
```

This is exactly what we want, since we label similar document pairs with 1 and different pairs with 0.

To summarize, here is the code for processing our data:

```
train=...

labelDict=createLabelDict(train)

input_dim = 500 # word chunks

X, y, vocab_size=vectorizeDocumentsBOW(train,labelDict,input_dim)

nb_classes = len(labelDict)

X_train, X_test, y_train, y_test = train_test_split(X, y, test_size=0.33,
➥random_state=42)

X_train_left, X_train_right, y_train_lr=splitData(X_train,y_train,20)
X_test_left, X_test_right, y_test_lr=splitData(X_test,y_test,20)
```

Now, let's take a look at our network. We can use any architecture we like for the two sister networks, but in this case, we'll opt for a simple long short-term memory (LSTM) architecture. The structure is shown in figure 4.8.

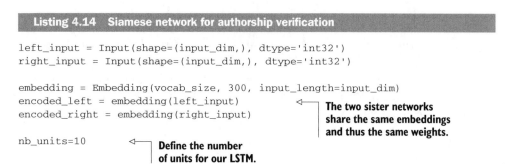

Listing 4.14 Siamese network for authorship verification

```
left_input = Input(shape=(input_dim,), dtype='int32')
right_input = Input(shape=(input_dim,), dtype='int32')

embedding = Embedding(vocab_size, 300, input_length=input_dim)
encoded_left = embedding(left_input)                    ◁──┐ The two sister networks
encoded_right = embedding(right_input)                     │ share the same embeddings
                                                           │ and thus the same weights.

nb_units=10      ◁──┐ Define the number
                    │ of units for our LSTM.
```

```
lstm = LSTM(nb_units)
left_output = lstm(encoded_left)
right_output = lstm(encoded_right)
```

The two networks also share the same LSTM layer, which is used as an encoder: it encodes the inputs into similar, latent representations.

```
model_distance = Lambda(function=lambda x: exp_neg_manhattan_distance(
➥x[0], x[1]),output_shape=lambda x: (x[0][0], 1))(
➥[left_output, right_output])

model = Model([left_input, right_input], [model_distance])

model.compile(loss='mean_squared_error', optimizer='adam',
➥metrics=['accuracy'])

model.fit([X_train_left, X_train_right], y_train_lr, batch_size=64,
➥nb_epoch=nb_epochs,
                          validation_split=0.3, verbose=2)
model.evaluate([X_test_left, X_test_right], y_test_lr)

loss, accuracy = model.evaluate([X_test_left, X_test_right], y_test_lr,
➥verbose=0)
print('Accuracy: %f' % (accuracy*100))
```

The model consumes two inputs and maps them to the distance between the latent representations of that input. It is constrained by our ground truth: a binary label stating whether the two inputs are from the same author.

A Lambda layer in Keras can be used to apply a function to an arbitrary layer and send the output to a following layer. In this case, that function is exp_neg_manhattan_distance().

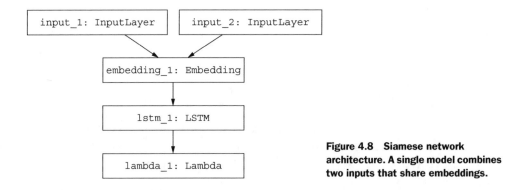

Figure 4.8 Siamese network architecture. A single model combines two inputs that share embeddings.

This Siamese network, when run on a training/test split similar to before (66/33%) with the training data based on 20 sample document segments per author (each consisting of 500 words), produces results with accuracy in the range of 86% (86.86% on our run). So for 33% of the data, consisting of paired 500-word segments (labeled 1 if two segments originate from the same author or 0 if not), the network makes an error in just under 14% of the cases.

> **Exercise**
> It is possible to adjoin multiple sister networks (not just two), and an interesting idea is to combine multiple feature representations of the same data. For instance, we could have two sister networks working on bag-of-words features, two on character n-grams, and so on, and combine all of them into one Siamese network. Can you implement such a setup for bag-of-words and character n-gram features?

In the next chapter, we turn to sequential NLP tasks and the use of memory.

Summary

- Textual similarity use cases include authorship attribution and authorship verification.
- Representational choices can have hefty ramifications for model complexity. Some models may bypass some of that burden by their intrinsic organization (like MLPs compared to CNNs).
- Lexical information only is not sufficient for establishing textual similarity. Style is expressed both lexically and formally, in terms of word combinations.
- CNNs are good for emphasizing sequential information. They outperformed a simple MLP in our authorship attribution experiments.
- Siamese networks can be used for textual similarity in authorship verification.

Sequential NLP

This chapter covers

- Using memory to analyze sequential NLP tasks
- Understanding how RNNs, LSTM networks, and end-to-end memory networks handle memory
- Applying these techniques to a shared task: Question Answering

The central task in this chapter is Question Answering: answering a question based on a number of facts. This task involves using memory: facts are stored in memory, and the question refers back to past information. How do the various models for sequential processing stack up to this task?

We will demonstrate the difference between *flat memory* approaches, like recurrent neural networks (RNNs), and long short-term memory (LSTM) networks and *responsive memory* approaches, like end-to-end memory networks, in the context of Question Answering, and we will assess the benefits of memory networks for Question Answering. In chapter 6, we will apply end-to-end networks to a number of other sequential NLP tasks.

5.1 *Memory and language*

Language is a sequential, contextual phenomenon and often addresses long-range dependencies that must be kept in memory when they emerge and must be available later for analysis. Examples are tagging parts of speech, parsing syntax, analyzing sentiments and topics, and labeling semantic roles. For instance, to assign the correct part of speech (verb, not noun) to *man* in the following confusing, so-called *garden path* sentence (see https://en.wikipedia.org/wiki/Garden-path_sentence), the use of context (both to the left and right of *man*) is crucial:

> *The old man the boat*

Another memory-intensive task is *Question Answering*: answering a question based on a preceding sequence of facts.

5.1.1 *The problem: Question Answering*

Question Answering involves matching answers (like factual statements) to questions (figure 5.1). In a machine learning context, this means teaching a machine to associate answers with questions. Especially in the case of having several independent pieces of information available that may or may not be relevant to answer a question, this task becomes dependent on memory: keeping information in memory and being able to revert to that stored information.

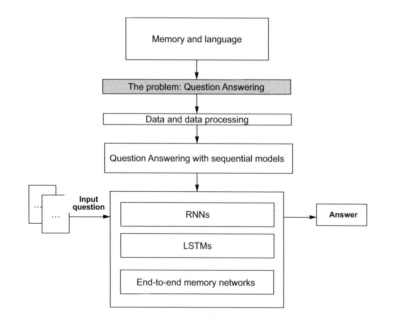

Figure 5.1   Background: Question Answering based on facts. We will investigate three types of sequential models for Question Answering: RNNs, LSTMs, and end-to-end memory networks.

Here is an example of such a case:

```
1 Mary moved to the bathroom.
2 John went to the hallway.
3 Where is Mary? bathroom
```

The answer to the question in sentence 3 depends on fact 1. Facts 1 and 2 together are called a *story* or a *context*. Fact 2 is irrelevant in respect to answering the question. A machine learning model learning these relations must have the capacity to store both facts, since when it encounters them, it does not know the upcoming question.

We will make Question Answering the central theme of this chapter and address it with a number of sequential, memory-based approaches:

- RNNs and LSTM networks
- End-to-end memory networks

Let's address the problem we are trying to solve by means of a scenario.

Scenario: A chatbot to answer questions

You are working on a language understanding module for a chatbot. The chatbot must be able to answer questions about historical facts you hand it through a chat window: it must be able to refer back to older information in order to answer a question. Specifically, every question can be answered by exactly one statement that occurred in the past. You have at hand a large dataset of hand-annotated questions linked to supporting facts and a set of candidate architectures that allow you to reason about memory. Using RNN, LSTM, and end-to-end memory networks, how can you implement this chatbot module?

The problem boils down to this: given a sequence of sentences and a question that can be answered by one (and only one) of the sentences, how can we retrieve the necessary information to answer the question? Clearly, we have no idea which specific fragment of which sentence holds the answer. So, we need to store all the information in these sentences (the *story*) and be able to get back to that information when the question pops up. The limitation of one sentence holding the answer to our question means we address *single-fact Question-Answering* as opposed to *multi-fact Question Answering*. The approaches we will work out also apply to multi-fact Question Answering, but we will not address that topic in this chapter.

5.2   *Data and data processing*

We will use data produced by Meta, called the bAbI dataset https://research.facebook.com/downloads/babi) (figure 5.2). This dataset consists of sequences of facts linked to questions. One or more of the facts hold the answer to the question. The dataset comprises a set of Question Answering tasks, and often, the link between the facts holding the answers and the question is remote: typically, many irrelevant facts intervene between question and answer.

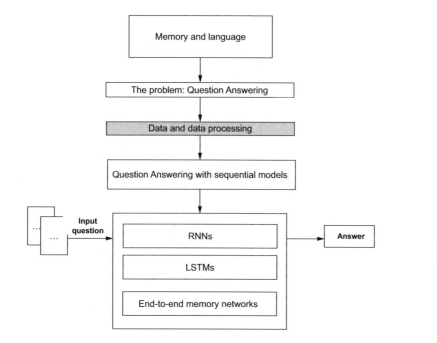

Figure 5.2 Processing the data

Here is some typical data. A list of facts (numbered sentences) is followed by a question, an answer to that question (just one word), and the identifier of the sentence holding the answer:

```
1  Mary moved to the bathroom.
2  John went to the hallway.
3  Where is Mary? bathroom 1
4  Daniel went back to the hallway.
5  Sandra moved to the garden.
6  Where is Daniel? hallway 4
7  John moved to the office.
8  Sandra journeyed to the bathroom.
9  Where is Daniel? hallway 4
10 Mary moved to the hallway.
11 Daniel travelled to the office.
12 Where is Daniel? office 11
13 John went back to the garden.
14 John moved to the bedroom.
15 Where is Sandra? bathroom 8
```

In the first case (line 3), the sentence holding the answer to the question is sentence 1. A sequence like this is called a *story* in bAbI nomenclature. Storing all intervening context between a question and the sentence holding its answer clearly places a burden on the memory capacity of models. We will investigate the performance of our models under two conditions:

- Using only a question and the supporting fact
- Using all facts in a story as well as irrelevant facts to answer a particular question

The first condition can be used to assess question-answer matching in a restricted manner, and the second condition addresses picking out an answer from a large heap of unrelated data, which demands much more memory storage. How well do our models stack up to these conditions? Let's first develop procedures for getting the bAbI data ready for our models, turning stories, questions, and answers into vector representations.

We will convert stories into ordered lists of vectors and train a network to learn the relationship between a question and a word in one of the facts. This means we are modeling a (possibly long-distance) dependency. The actual deep learning part of this procedure is outlined in the following sections, where we discuss different models. Here, we will concern ourselves with the vectorization part, following the standard Keras bAbI example at, for example, http://mng.bz/QvRw. See figure 5.3.

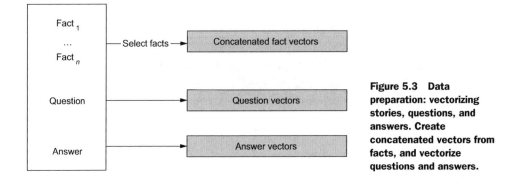

Figure 5.3 Data preparation: vectorizing stories, questions, and answers. Create concatenated vectors from facts, and vectorize questions and answers.

We need to create three lists of vectors, the reasons for which will become apparent soon:

1 A list holding all facts as vectors
2 A list of vectorized questions
3 A list of labels: word indices referring to the word that is the answer to a question

We will lump together all facts into one long vector. These vectors will be linked to questions (also vectors) and labels (pointers to words: our answers consist of just one word). We will incorporate a switch that allows us to remove irrelevant ("noisy") facts from a facts-question pair or keep them. If we keep them, we will stress our model with a lot more (irrelevant) data, but it will be interesting to see how much trouble this causes.

For starters, we need a procedure to convert the bAbI stories to vectors. The first step in this process is to create a *tokenizer,* a concept that should be familiar to you by now (see chapter 2): a lookup facility that converts words into numerical indices. This tokenizer is fitted on a vocabulary, and here, we use all words in both the training and test data.

Listing 5.1   Tokenizing stories

```
def create_tokenizer(trainingdata, testdata):
    f=open(trainingdata, "r")
    text=[]

    for line in f:
        m=re.match("^\d+\s([^\.]+)[\.].*",line.rstrip())
        if m:
            text.append(m.group(1))
        else:
            m=re.match("^\d+\s([^\?]+)[\?]\s\t([^\t]+)",
                line.rstrip())
            if m:
                text.append(m.group(1)+' '+m.group(2))
    f.close()

    f=open(testdata, "r")
    for line in f:
        m=re.match("^\d+\s([^\.]+)[\.].*",line.rstrip())
        if m:
            text.append(m.group(1))
        else:
            m=re.match("^\d+\s([^\?]+)[\?].*",line.rstrip())
            if m:
                text.append(m.group(1))
    f.close()

    vocabulary=set([word for word in text])
    max_words = len(vocabulary)
    tokenizer = Tokenizer(
        num_words=max_words, char_level=False, split=' ')
    tokenizer.fit_on_texts(text)
    return tokenizer, max_words
```

> After open the training data file, read a fact: a line starting with a number and closed with a period. Pick up the text from the fact.

> Similarly, read a question and pick up the text.

> Read a fact from the test data file and store the text.

> Read a question from the test data file and store the text.

> Create a vocabulary from the collected texts: a set of words.

> Declare a tokenizer. Keras offers a Tokenizer class in keras.preprocessing.text.

> Fit the tokenizer on the vocabulary. The fitted tokenizer converts words into unique numbers.

With the generated tokenizer at hand, we can process our bAbI stories. We represent every list of facts (including intervening, irrelevant facts or just the fact(s) holding the answer to the question) as one big vector. So, we basically concatenate the entire list of facts into one big string and tokenize that string (convert it to a numerical vector). This is a rather crude data representation, but it works out well on average, as we will see shortly. Figure 5.4 explains what's going on here in a bit more detail.

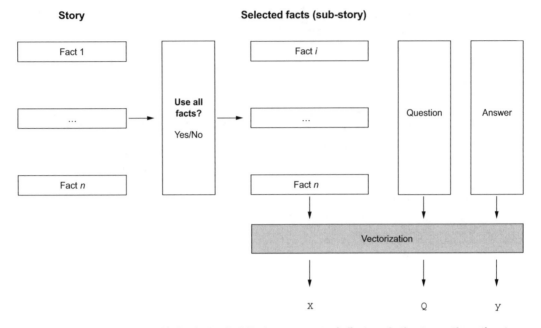

Figure 5.4   Story vectorization in detail. A Boolean parameter indicates whether to use the entire story ("Use all facts?") or just the one fact holding the answer to the question. The diagram generalizes this to a situation where multiple facts may be holding the answer to the question, but in our case, it's always just one fact. After the relevant facts to answer the question have been determined, we vectorize the facts, the question, and the answer and append the results to designated output variables for the entire training and test data sets (X for facts, Q for questions, and y for answers).

Listing 5.2   Processing stories.

```
def process_stories(filename,tokenizer,max_story_len,max_query_len,
     vocab_size,use_context=False):
     f=open(filename,"r")
     X=[]
     Q=[]
     y=[]
     n_questions=0

     for line in f:
         m=re.match("^(\d+)\s(.+)\.",line.rstrip())
         if m:
             if int(m.group(1))==1:
                 story={}
             story[int(m.group(1))]=m.group(2)
         else:
             m=re.match("^\d+\s(.+)\?\s\t([^\t]+)\t(.+)",
             line.rstrip())
             if m:
                 question=m.group(1)
                 answer=m.group(2)
                 answer_ids=[int(x) for x in m.group(3).split(" ")]
```

The flag use_context is a Boolean flag (True or False) that indicates whether to use all facts (the entire story) for answering the question (True) or just the facts (in our case, a single fact) holding the answer to the question.

Read a fact.

If the fact number is 1, start a new story (implemented as a dictionary).

Store the text of the fact at an index that matches the fact number.

Read a question. Notice that a question ends a story. Questions list their answer, and the numbers referring to the fact(s) holding the answer.

The fact(s) holding the answer to the question are collected in one array.

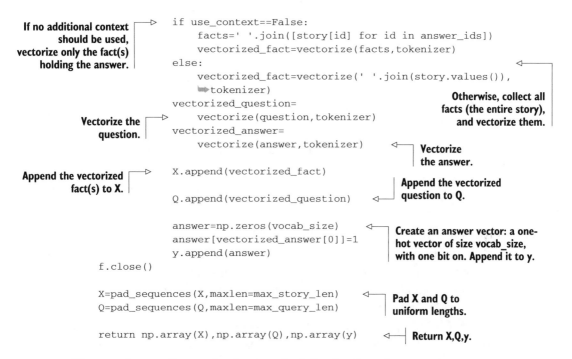

If no additional context should be used, vectorize only the fact(s) holding the answer.

Otherwise, collect all facts (the entire story), and vectorize them.

Vectorize the question.

Vectorize the answer.

Append the vectorized fact(s) to X.

Append the vectorized question to Q.

Create an answer vector: a one-hot vector of size vocab_size, with one bit on. Append it to y.

Pad X and Q to uniform lengths.

Return X,Q,y.

```
if use_context==False:
    facts=' '.join([story[id] for id in answer_ids])
    vectorized_fact=vectorize(facts,tokenizer)
else:
    vectorized_fact=vectorize(' '.join(story.values()),
        tokenizer)
vectorized_question=
    vectorize(question,tokenizer)
vectorized_answer=
    vectorize(answer,tokenizer)

X.append(vectorized_fact)

Q.append(vectorized_question)

answer=np.zeros(vocab_size)
answer[vectorized_answer[0]]=1
y.append(answer)
f.close()

X=pad_sequences(X,maxlen=max_story_len)
Q=pad_sequences(Q,maxlen=max_query_len)

return np.array(X),np.array(Q),np.array(y)
```

To vectorize a string, we implement the following function.

Listing 5.3 Vectorization

```
def vectorize(s, tokenizer):
    vector=tokenizer.texts_to_sequences([s])
    return vector[0]
```

This function produces an array of numbers for a string by assigning each word a unique integer:

```
Mary moved to the bathroom => [8, 19, 1, 2, 10]
```

The `process_stories()` function produces a triple consisting of an array of vectorized facts, an array of vectorized questions, and an array of one-hot vectors representing the answer word. So, for the following story

```
Mary moved to the bathroom
John went to the hallway
Where is Mary? bathroom
```

this function produces

```
[8, 19, 1, 2, 10, 6, 5, 1, 2, 12] (Mary moved to the bathroom
John went to the hallway)

[3, 4, 8] (Where is Mary)
```

```
[0. 0. 0. 0. 0. 0. 0. 0. 0. 0. 1. 0. 0. 0. 0. 0. 0. 0. 0. 0. 0. 0. 0.
 0. 0. 0. 0. 0. 0. 0. 0. 0. 0. 0. 0. 0. 0. 0. 0. 0. 0. 0. 0. 0. 0. 0.
 0. 0. 0. 0. 0. 0. 0. 0. 0. 0. 0. 0. 0. 0. 0. 0. 0. 0. 0. 0. 0. 0. 0.
 0. 0. 0. 0. 0. 0. 0. 0. 0. 0. 0. 0. 0. 0. 0. 0. 0. 0. 0. 0. 0. 0. 0.
 0. 0. 0. 0. 0. 0. 0. 0. 0. 0. 0. 0. 0. 0. 0. 0. 0. 0. 0. 0. 0. 0. 0.
 0. 0. 0. 0. 0. 0. 0. 0. 0. 0. 0. 0. 0. 0. 0. 0. 0. 0. 0. 0. 0. 0. 0.
 0. 0. 0. 0.] (bathroom)
```

Notice how these three arrays are in a one-to-one correspondence: X[i], Q[i], and y[i] represent the facts for a specific question at index *i* with its corresponding answer label.

We are finished turning our bAbI stories into something we can feed to a sequential model. Let's proceed with that.

5.3   *Question Answering with sequential models*

Deep learning provides a number of sequential mechanisms for handling sequences. We have seen a couple of those in previous chapters: LSTMs and RNNs were discussed in chapters 2 and 3. How can we deploy these models to handle Question Answering? We will start with an approach using RNNs, basing our model on the ideas from the implementation in the Keras demo repository (formerly available from https://github.com/keras-team/keras/blob/master/examples/babi_rnn.py; as of 2022, this code appears to have been removed) for processing bAbI with RNNs (see figure 5.5).

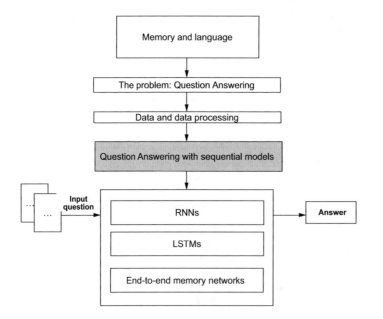

Figure 5.5   Sequential models for Question Answering

5.3.1 RNNs for Question Answering

We will implement a branching model with two RNNs. These two RNNs handle the facts (stories) and the question. Their output is merged by concatenation and sent through a `Dense` layer that produces a scalar of the size of our answer vocabulary, consisting of probabilities. The model is seeded with answer vectors with one bit on (one-hot), so the highest probability in the output layer reflects the most probable bit, indicating a unique answer word in our lexicon. The model is depicted in figure 5.6.

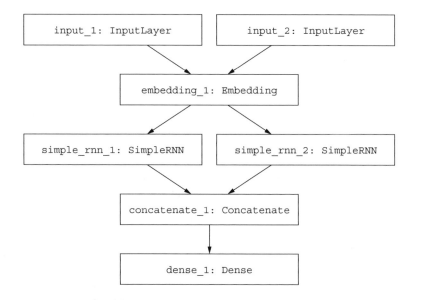

Figure 5.6   RNNs for Question Answering. Two RNNs are combined: one for analyzing facts and one for analyzing questions.

The idea behind the branching model is that we combine two temporal processes: one for analyzing a story and one for analyzing a question. The questions are uniformly short sequences in the bAbI task (they consist of just three words). The stories can be quite long: up to 58 words in this task. We will use a single embedding to embed both stories and questions; you can also experiment with separate embeddings. (Doing this increases the number of parameters in the model, and we found no significant gains in doing so.)

Exercise
Several other options are open here; we could also concatenate stories and questions to one vector and use a single RNN. Experiment with a single RNN, and compare its results with the branching RNN results.

Listing 5.4   Creating a model and preparing the data

Fit a tokenizer on the training and test data.

Process the stories in the training data. The parameter use_context specifies the amount of irrelevant facts we factor in.

```
def create_model(trainingData, testData, context=False):
    tokenizer,vocab_size, max_story_len, max_query_len=create_tokenizer(
        ➡trainingData,testData)

    X_tr,Q_tr,y_tr=process_stories(trainingData,tokenizer,max_story_len,
        max_query_len,vocab_size,use_context=context)

    X_te,Q_te,y_te=process_stories(testData,tokenizer,max_story_len,
        max_query_len,vocab_size,use_context=context)

    embedding=layers.Embedding(vocab_size,100)

    story = layers.Input(shape=(max_story_len,),
        dtype='int32')
    encoded_story = embedding(story)
    encoded_story = SimpleRNN(30)(encoded_story)

    question = layers.Input(shape=(max_query_len,),
        dtype='int32')
    encoded_question = embedding(question)
    encoded_question = SimpleRNN(30)(encoded_question)

    merged = layers.concatenate([encoded_story,
        encoded_question])
    preds = layers.Dense(vocab_size, activation=
        'softmax')(merged)

    model = Model([story, question], preds)
    model.compile(optimizer='adam',
                        loss='categorical_crossentropy',
                        metrics=['accuracy'])

    return X_tr,Q_tr,y_tr,X_te,Q_te,y_te,model
```

Similarly, process the test data stories.

Define an input layer for the stories.

Embed the input story.

An input layer for questions is defined.

Define an embedding that produces 100-dimensional vectors for the word indices coming out of the tokenizer. We will use the same embedding for encoding stories and questions.

The embedded story is passed on to a SimpleRNN layer, the output of which has a dimensionality of 30.

Embed the question, using the embedding defined earlier.

The encoded question is passed on to a SimpleRNN layer with output dimensionality 30.

The output of both SimpleRNN layers is combined through concatenation.

Compile the model, and return the model plus the processed data.

Define a Dense output layer. This layer has an output dimensionality of vocab_size: it produces a tensor of probabilities (through its softmax activation); the most probable component in that vector reflects the bit that is "on" for the output (answer) word.

We summarize the model with the Keras procedure `model.summary()`:

Layer (type)	Output Shape	Param #	Connected to
input_1 (InputLayer)	(None, 58)	0	
input_2 (InputLayer)	(None, 3)	0	
embedding_1 (Embedding)	multiple	14800	input_1[0][0] input_2[0][0]

simple_rnn_1 (SimpleRNN)	(None, 30)	3930	embedding_1[0][0]
simple_rnn_2 (SimpleRNN)	(None, 30)	3930	embedding_1[1][0]
concatenate_1 (Concatenate)	(None, 60)	0	simple_rnn_1[0][0] simple_rnn_2[0][0]
dense_1 (Dense)	(None, 148)	9028	concatenate_1[0][0]

```
=============================================================================
Total params: 31,688
Trainable params: 31,688
Non-trainable params: 0
```

The following listing trains the model and evaluates it on test data.

Listing 5.5 Training and evaluating the model

```
def run_evaluate(trainingData, testData, context=False):

    X_tr,Q_tr,y_tr,X_te,Q_te,y_te,model=create_model(
    ➥trainingData,testData,context)

    print('Training')
    model.fit([X_tr, Q_tr], y_tr,
              batch_size=32,
              epochs=10,
              verbose=1,
              validation_split=0.1)

    print('Evaluation')
    loss, acc = model.evaluate([X_te,Q_te], y_te,
                               batch_size=32)
    print('Test loss / test accuracy = {:.4f} / {:.4f}'.format(loss, acc))
```

We will run the model on the following data in the unzipped bAbI folder (you will find the zipped data in the data folder for this chapter). This data consists of 10,000 training items and 1,000 test items:

- Training data: /tasks_1-20_v1-2/en-10k/qa1_single-supporting-fact_train.txt
- Test data: /tasks_1-20_v1-2/en-10k/qa1_single-supporting-fact_test.txt

Recall that we have a binary switch for either using or discarding irrelevant context sentences. Also, recall that *irrelevant sentences* are sentences that do not contribute to the answer; there is only one such sentence for every story in our task. This switch will allow us to (crudely) estimate the memory performance of our model: can it handle a certain amount of irrelevant data? Let's first investigate this before turning to a more fine-grained analysis where we plot the model's performance as a function of the amount of stored irrelevant data.

We start with training the model without intervening irrelevant context. This works out perfectly. The RNN, simple as it is, learns the association of the single-fact vector, the question vector, and the single-word answer index without an error. Notice that the model does not know linguistic structure. It learns to associate two numerical vectors (holding word indices) with a one-hot vector representing the answer word. Here is the system log of training and evaluation:

```
Train on 9000 samples, validate on 1000 samples
Epoch 1/10
9000/9000 [==============================] - 0s - loss: 0.9990
➡- acc: 0.8367 - val_loss: 0.0493 - val_acc: 1.0000
Epoch 2/10
9000/9000 [==============================] - 0s - loss: 0.0236
➡- acc: 1.0000 - val_loss: 0.0118 - val_acc: 1.0000
Epoch 3/10
9000/9000 [==============================] - 0s - loss: 0.0082
➡- acc: 1.0000 - val_loss: 0.0057 - val_acc: 1.0000
Epoch 4/10
9000/9000 [==============================] - 0s - loss: 0.0044
➡- acc: 1.0000 - val_loss: 0.0034 - val_acc: 1.0000
Epoch 5/10
9000/9000 [==============================] - 0s - loss: 0.0028
➡- acc: 1.0000 - val_loss: 0.0023 - val_acc: 1.0000
Epoch 6/10
9000/9000 [==============================] - 0s - loss: 0.0020
➡- acc: 1.0000 - val_loss: 0.0017 - val_acc: 1.0000
Epoch 7/10
9000/9000 [==============================] - 0s - loss: 0.0014
➡- acc: 1.0000 - val_loss: 0.0012 - val_acc: 1.0000
Epoch 8/10
9000/9000 [==============================] - 0s - loss: 0.0011
➡- acc: 1.0000 - val_loss: 9.5678e-04 - val_acc: 1.0000
Epoch 9/10
9000/9000 [==============================] - 0s - loss: 8.5059e-04
➡- acc: 1.0000 - val_loss: 7.5578e-04 - val_acc: 1.0000
Epoch 10/10
9000/9000 [==============================] - 0s - loss: 6.7765e-04
➡- acc: 1.0000 - val_loss: 6.0739e-04 - val_acc: 1.0000
Evaluation
   32/1000 [..............................]
   ➡- ETA: 0sTest loss / test accuracy = 0.0006 / 1.0000
```

As you see, in the second iteration, we obtain perfect training accuracy and held-out validation data score. The final accuracy score on the test data is 100%.

Let's see what happens if we also take the intervening facts into account. Now the model is stressed much harder. For instance, the training data contains patterns like these:

```
1 Mary moved to the bathroom.
2 John went to the hallway.
3 Where is Mary? bathroom 1
4 Daniel went back to the hallway.
5 Sandra moved to the garden.
6 Where is Daniel? hallway 4
7 John moved to the office.
8 Sandra journeyed to the bathroom.
```

```
9 Where is Daniel? hallway 4
10 Mary moved to the hallway.
11 Daniel travelled to the office.
12 Where is Daniel? office 11
13 John went back to the garden.
14 John moved to the bedroom.
15 Where is Sandra? bathroom 8
```

In line 15, we observe that the answer to the question "Where is Sandra?" can be found seven facts earlier. This is a lot of context to take into account. Here is what we get:

```
Test loss / test accuracy = 1.2145 / 0.5100
```

This 51% accuracy is a very significant drop in performance. Our RNN clearly is not equipped to store this amount of data.

Let's implement a procedure to incrementally add context to our model rather than the *no context* or *all context* of our binary switch.

Listing 5.6   Incremental context

```
def process_stories_n_context(
    filename,tokenizer,vocab_size,use_context=0):       ◁─── Pass a use_context flag (see the
    f=open(filename,"r")                                     last annotation on this page)
    X=[]                                                     that specifies the amount of
    Q=[]                                                     irrelevant facts we tolerate.
    y=[]
    max_story_len=0
    max_query_len=0

    for line in f:
        m=re.match("^(\d+)\s(.+)\.",line.rstrip())       ◁─── We encounter a fact. If the fact identifier
        if m:                                                 equals 1, we open a new story (encoded as a
            if int(m.group(1))==1:                            Python dictionary). The dictionary maps fact
                story={}                                      identifiers to the accompanying text.
            story[int(m.group(1))]=m.group(2)
        else:
            m=re.match("^\d+\s(.+)\?\s\t([^\t]+)\t(.+)",    We encounter a question.
                line.rstrip())                      ◁───   Questions indicate the
            if m:                                            end of a story in our task.
                question=m.group(1)                          We vectorize the story we
                answer=m.group(2)                            gathered up to this point.
                answer_ids=[int(x) for x in m.group(3).split(" ")]
                facts=' '.join([story[id] for id in answer_ids])
                all_facts=' '.join([story[id] for id in story])
                facts_v=vectorize(facts,tokenizer)
                all_facts_v=vectorize(all_facts,tokenizer)

                if use_context==0:                  ◁───   Use the following switches: 0 for using
                    vectorized_fact=facts_v                 no context, −1 for using all context,
                elif use_context==-1:                       and an integer for using a specified
                    vectorized_fact=all_facts_v             number of (irrelevant) facts. These
                else:                                       facts are appended to the fact holding
                    x=min(use_context, len(story))          the answer, effectively pushing that
                                                            fact leftward in the context window.
```

```
            facts=' '.join([story[id] for id in answer_ids])+' '
            n=0
            for id in story:
                if n<x and id not in answer_ids:
                    facts+=story[id]+' '
                    n+=1
            vectorized_fact=vectorize(facts,tokenizer)
        l=len(vectorized_fact)
        if l>max_story_len:
            max_story_len=l
        vectorized_question=vectorize(question,
            tokenizer)
        l=len(vectorized_question)
        if l>max_query_len:
            max_query_len=l

        vectorized_answer=vectorize(answer,
            tokenizer)

        X.append(vectorized_fact)
        Q.append(vectorized_question)
        answer=np.zeros(vocab_size)
        answer[vectorized_answer[0]]=1
        y.append(answer)
    f.close()

    return np.array(X),np.array(Q),np.array(y), max_story_len, max_query_len
```

Vectorize the question. →

Vectorize the answer (this produces an array with one number, a word index). ←

Accumulate the vectorized story, question, and answer, and proceed. ←

The correspondence between the number of irrelevant facts we test and the number of words these facts cover is as follows:

- Context size = 1 fact: story length = max. 12 words
- Context size = 2 facts: story length = max. 18 words
- Context size = 4 facts: story length = max. 30 words
- Context size = 6 facts: story length = max. 41 words
- Context size = 8 facts: story length = max. 52 words
- All facts: story length = max. 58 words

The use_context parameter has turned from a Boolean (True or False) into a number. Our results with this procedure are more accurate than with the previous Boolean-valued procedure. The new procedure puts the answer facts first in the list and then adds extra irrelevant facts. This ensures that, for every increment of use_context, we increase the distance between the answer and the question. The previous procedure concatenates, for use_context=True, all facts in the story to one string. But the answer can be closer to the question in one case and further away in another case, given how the bAbI data is organized. This means the obtained 51% accuracy score is optimistic.

Our procedure for creating a model changes now into the following listing (the difference being the processing of the stories, so we only list that part).

Listing 5.7 Creating an RNN model: new story processing

```
def create_model(trainingData, testData, context):

    tokenizer,vocab_size=create_tokenizer(trainingData,testData)

    X_tr,Q_tr,y_tr,max_story_len_tr, max_query_len_tr=
        process_stories_n_context(trainingData,tokenizer,vocab_size,
        use_context=context)
    X_te,Q_te,y_te, max_story_len_te, max_query_len_te=
        process_stories_n_context(testData,tokenizer,vocab_size,
        use_context=context)

    max_story_len=max(max_story_len_tr, max_story_len_te)
    max_query_len=max(max_query_len_tr, max_query_len_te)

    X_tr, Q_tr=pad_data(X_tr,Q_tr,max_story_len, max_query_len)
    X_te, Q_te=pad_data(X_te,Q_te,max_story_len, max_query_len)

    (...)
```

We obtain the following results when we train our model for 100 iterations and test it on our test data:

- Context size = 0, test accuracy = 100%
- Context size = 2 facts (story length = max. 18 words): test accuracy = 100%
- Context size = 4 facts (story length = max. 30 words): test accuracy = 100%
- Context size = 6 facts (story length = max. 41 words): test accuracy = 100%
- Context size = 8 facts (story length = max. 52 words): test accuracy = 80.4%
- All facts (story length = max. 58 words): test accuracy = 51%

From these results, we can conclude that RNNs have limited capacity for storing large pieces of information. Performance drops significantly after 41 words. Recall from chapter 2 that RNNs blindly pass on all historical information, imposing a heavy memory burden on themselves.

What about LSTMs? Would a more careful gating of historical (temporal) information boost performance? Let's find out.

5.3.2 *LSTMs for Question Answering*

LSTMs come in *stateless* and *stateful* modes. In both modes, an LSTM processes a batch of labeled training vectors. An LSTM works one step (*feature*) at a time through an input vector, updating its cell state at each step. In stateless mode, after a sequence has been processed, the weights of the surrounding network layers are updated through backpropagation, and the cell state of the LSTM is reset. This means the LSTM will have to learn from a new sequence (vector) its gating weights (the various weights controlling which information is passed along and which is forgotten) all over again; its notion of time is limited to one sequence.

TIP   Keras presupposes no specific order in a batch. If your batch consists of labeled vectors, Keras will—in the default setting for any model—blindly shuffle your batches of training data (validation data is never shuffled), so any temporal order you put in your batch is destroyed. You can override this default setting by setting `shuffle=False` in the `model.fit()` function.

Let's quickly recap some issues pertaining to getting data into an LSTM layer. An LSTM expects triples of data, (number of samples, time steps, features per timestep), as follows:

- *Number of samples*—The number of samples in our data.
- *Time steps*—The length of the sequences fed to an LSTM. If we are feeding sentences to an LSTM, this addresses the words in every (length-padded) sentence.
- *Features*—The dimensionality of the objects at every position of a sequence: for example, vectors of a certain dimension if we're embedding words.

Luckily, LSTMs can figure out these parameters from a preceding input layer. Let's go into some detail.

Assume that we have input data consisting of 10 features:

```
f~1~,f~2~,f~3~,f~4~,f~5~,f~6~,f~7~,f~8~,f~9~,f~10~
```

Suppose we apply a sliding window of two features over this sequence (treating it as a time sequence, with two features for each time tick). We obtain $10 - 2 + 1 = 9$ subsequences:

```
[f~1~,f~2~]
[f~2~,f~3~]
[f~3~,f~4~]
[f~4~,f~5~]
[f~5~,f~6~]
[f~6~,f~7~]
[f~7~,f~8~]
[f~8~,f~9~]
[f~9~,f~10~]
```

A simple model where an LSTM is the first layer, like this

```
model=Sequential()
model.add(LSTM())
```

needs a specification of the data in terms of time ticks and features. The batch size (set by the `model.fit()` function) is deduced automatically:

```
model=Sequential()
model.add(LSTM(input_shape=(9,2)))
```

Assuming our data is initially represented as a nested array like this

```
X=array([[1,2],[2,3],[3,4],[4,5],[5,6],[6,7],[7,8],[8,9],[9,10]])
```

with shape

```
X.shape: (9,2)
```

an explicit `reshape()` action is needed to recast the data into the required (`number of samples, time steps, features`) format

```
X=X.reshape\((1,9,2))
```

resulting in

```
X.shape: (1,9,2)
```

But suppose we have another input layer preceding our LSTM layer:

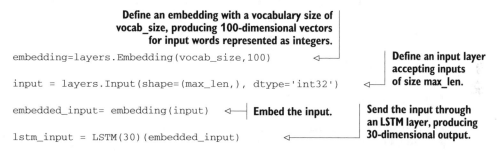

The LSTM layer, yielding an output vector of dimension 30, deduces that it will receive batches of some unspecified size consisting of a matrix of (`max_len, 100`) vectors: the embedding embeds a total of `vocab_size` vectors in a 100-dimensional vector space, and the input layer accepts input of size `max_len`. So, our LSTM layer cleverly assumes that we have arranged our data in slices of `max_len` windows, with each cell of the windows containing a vector of dimension 100, and no further input shape specification is necessary at this point.

Returning to batches, in stateful mode, vectors across batches are synchronized so that when the LSTM processes a new batch, every vector proceeds with the cell state for a corresponding vector in the previous batch. What does *corresponding* mean here? It means that in stateful mode, batches contain *temporally linked* vectors: a vector v_i in batch B_j is continued by a vector v_{i+1} in batch B_{j+1}, in such a way that vector v_{i+1} picks up the cell state left behind by vector v_i. So, we might say that v_{i+1} is a continuation of the observation formed by vector v_i. This allows use to analyze temporal patterns, like repeated measurements, each of which contributes to a global decision. Let's make this clear with an example.

Scenario: Stateful models

Imagine that you are inspecting a Twitter feed of a set of persons, consisting of consecutive tweets ordered on a timeline. A batch in stateful mode connects a tweet of a separate user to the next tweet on the timeline in the next batch. Suppose you are assigning a sentiment polarity score (positive or negative) to such Twitter feeds per user, maybe around a certain topic. Then knowledge of previous tweets on the timeline for that user will contribute to the overall sentiment score of the entire Twitter feed.

Stateful batches do not play a role in our current approach to Question Answering. We predict a word index referring to an answer based on a long, unstructured vector. Under this approach, it does not make sense to go through the facts one by one and collect different predictions over time; since we do not predict an outcome per fact and since only one fact contains the answer to the question, all other facts do not bear any useful information.

Exercise

Can you come up with a scenario where stateful batches would be relevant for Question Answering?

Our LSTM model is similar to the RNN model. It has two LSTM layers processing stories and questions, and the results (the output layers) are merged by concatenation. Figure 5.7 depicts its structure.

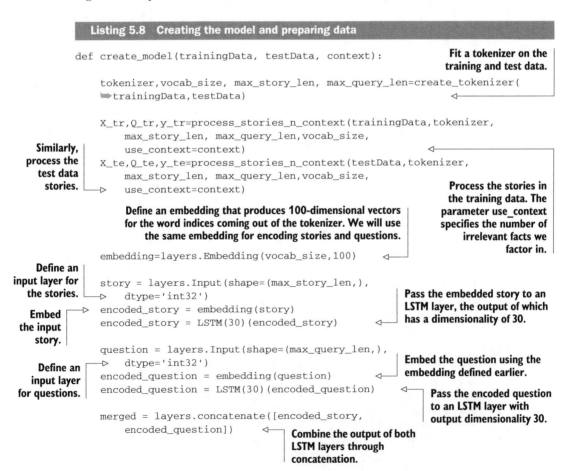

Listing 5.8 Creating the model and preparing data

```
def create_model(trainingData, testData, context):

    tokenizer,vocab_size, max_story_len, max_query_len=create_tokenizer(
    ➥trainingData,testData)

    X_tr,Q_tr,y_tr=process_stories_n_context(trainingData,tokenizer,
        max_story_len, max_query_len,vocab_size,
        use_context=context)
    X_te,Q_te,y_te=process_stories_n_context(testData,tokenizer,
        max_story_len, max_query_len,vocab_size,
        use_context=context)

    embedding=layers.Embedding(vocab_size,100)

    story = layers.Input(shape=(max_story_len,),
        dtype='int32')
    encoded_story = embedding(story)
    encoded_story = LSTM(30)(encoded_story)

    question = layers.Input(shape=(max_query_len,),
        dtype='int32')
    encoded_question = embedding(question)
    encoded_question = LSTM(30)(encoded_question)

    merged = layers.concatenate([encoded_story,
        encoded_question])
```

Fit a tokenizer on the training and test data.

Similarly, process the test data stories.

Process the stories in the training data. The parameter use_context specifies the number of irrelevant facts we factor in.

Define an embedding that produces 100-dimensional vectors for the word indices coming out of the tokenizer. We will use the same embedding for encoding stories and questions.

Define an input layer for the stories.

Embed the input story.

Pass the embedded story to an LSTM layer, the output of which has a dimensionality of 30.

Define an input layer for questions.

Embed the question using the embedding defined earlier.

Pass the encoded question to an LSTM layer with output dimensionality 30.

Combine the output of both LSTM layers through concatenation.

Define a Dense output layer. This layer has an output dimensionality of vocab_size. It produces a tensor of probabilities (through its softmax activation); the most probable component in that vector reflects the bit that is on for the output (answer) word.

```
preds = layers.Dense(vocab_size, activation='softmax')
    (merged)

model = Model([story, question], preds)
model.compile(optimizer='adam',
                loss='categorical_crossentropy',
                metrics=['accuracy'])
model.summary()

return X_tr,Q_tr,y_tr,X_te,Q_te,y_te,model
```

Compile the model, and return the model plus the processed data.

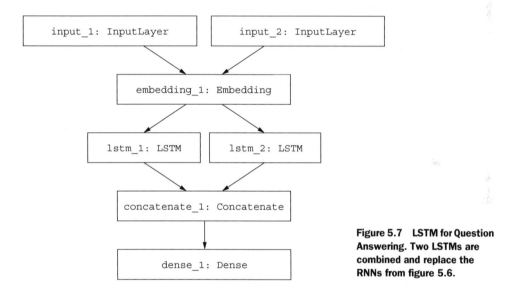

Figure 5.7   LSTM for Question Answering. Two LSTMs are combined and replace the RNNs from figure 5.6.

Using Keras's `model.summary()` procedure, the model is summarized as follows:

Layer (type)	Output Shape	Param #	Connected to
input_1 (InputLayer)	(None, 58)	0	
input_2 (InputLayer)	(None, 3)	0	
embedding_1 (Embedding)	multiple	14800	input_1[0][0] input_2[0][0]
lstm_1 (LSTM)	(None, 30)	15720	embedding_1[0][0]
lstm_2 (LSTM)	(None, 30)	15720	embedding_1[1][0]

```
concatenate_1 (Concatenate)    (None, 60)        0        lstm_1[0][0]
                                                           lstm_2[0][0]
_____
dense_1 (Dense)          (None, 148)            9028       concatenate_1[0][0]
========================================================================
Total params: 55,268
Trainable params: 55,268
Non-trainable params: 0
```

We apply LSTMs to our data in a stateless mode with the same single-vector approach used for RNNs. Training the model for 100 iterations for context sizes (number of irrelevant sentences separating the answer from the one relevant fact) 0, 2, 4, 6, and 8 yields uniform 100% accuracy on the test data. But running the model on all contexts (leading to a maximum of 58 intervening words) produces a poor score, 48.5% accuracy:

- Context size = 0, test accuracy = 100%
- Context size = 2 facts (story length = max. 18 words): test accuracy = 100%
- Context size = 4 facts (story length = max. 30 words): test accuracy = 100%
- Context size = 6 facts (story length = max. 41 words): test accuracy = 100%
- Context size = 8 facts (story length = max. 52 words): test accuracy = 100%
- All facts (story length = max. 58 words): test accuracy = 48.5%

LSTMs push the boundary a bit further than RNNs. But, similar to RNNs, they fail on long sequences, displaying an abrupt decline in accuracy.

We conclude that neither LSTMs nor RNNs are adequate tools to handle very long sequences of facts for Question Answering. LSTMs outperform RNNs for moderately long contexts but fail on extensive sequences.

Let's now take a look at end-to-end memory networks.

5.3.3 *End-to-end memory networks for Question Answering*

End-to-end memory networks embody responsive memory mechanisms. In the context of our Question Answering task, rather than just teaching a network to predict an answer word index from a combined vector of facts and a question, these networks produce a *memory response* of a series of facts (a story) to the question posed and use that response to weigh the fact vector.

Only after this weighting has been carried out is the question recombined with the weighted fact vector and used to predict a word index. So, we might say that facts are weighted by the question before prediction.

While this looks like a modest step, it makes quite a difference. For one thing, explicit information about the match between question and facts is now used for prediction. Recall that in our previous approaches, we merely lumped together facts and questions without addressing the match between the two.

How is this matching done, and why does it make a difference? Let's take a look at figure 5.8 (based on Sukhbaatar et al. 2015).

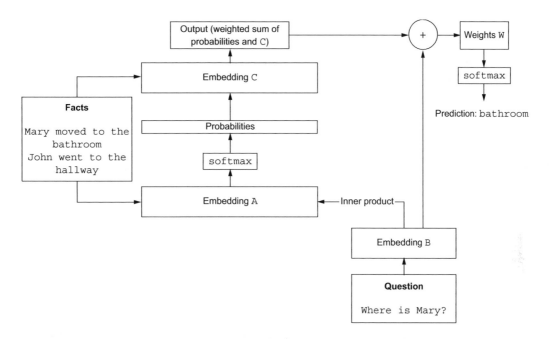

Figure 5.8   End-to-end memory networks (see Sukhbaatar et al. (2015) for the original diagram). Facts and questions are vectorized, and their match (relevant facts to answer a question) is learned in a supervised two-stage process, including the predicted answers.

Facts (here called *sentences*) are embedded with an embedding A. The question Question is embedded with an embedding B. Simultaneously, facts are embedded with a separate embedding C. The *response* of the memory bank consisting of the embedded facts is computed by first deriving an inner product of the embedded facts with the A-embedded question, after which a softmax layer produces probabilities based on the inner product. Notice that these are trainable probabilities that will be tuned during training through backpropagation. Finally, the probabilities are combined with the fact embedding produced by embedding C using a weighted sum operation. This operation adds the weights (probabilities) to the fact vector produced by C. This means the facts are now weighted based on their relevance to answering the question Question. At this point, the embedded question is combined through concatenation with the weighted sum (slightly deviating from Sukhbaatar et al. 2015, where another addition step is used). The result is sent to a final weights layer feeding into a dense output layer, the latter of which specifies the word index of the answer.

We adopt the original formalization of Sukhbaatar et al. (2015) closely in our code and, by doing so, largely follow the implementation in the (former) Keras demo repository (as mentioned, this example implementation has been removed from the Keras examples folder), with one difference: as in Sukhbaatar et al. (2015), we will use a weight matrix in the final steps of the algorithm rather than an LSTM (see the implementation in the Keras demo folder for comparison). We found that this yields better performance on our Question Answering task. One thing to keep in mind is that, unlike the original paper, this implementation treats the story (the facts) as one unstructured block. So, we may dub this approach *block-based memory networks*.

For data processing, we use exactly the same procedure as before. Listing 5.9 shows how we create our model, processing our data on the fly. Figure 5.9 shows the model.

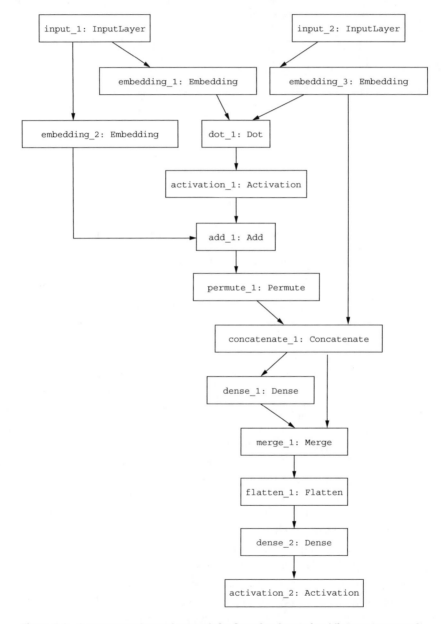

Figure 5.9   A memory end-to-end network for Question Answering (diagram generated by Keras' `plot_model()` function)

As before, we allow the specification of a context parameter that specifies the number of non-answer facts (an integer) we allow in our fact vector.

Listing 5.9   Creating a memory network model

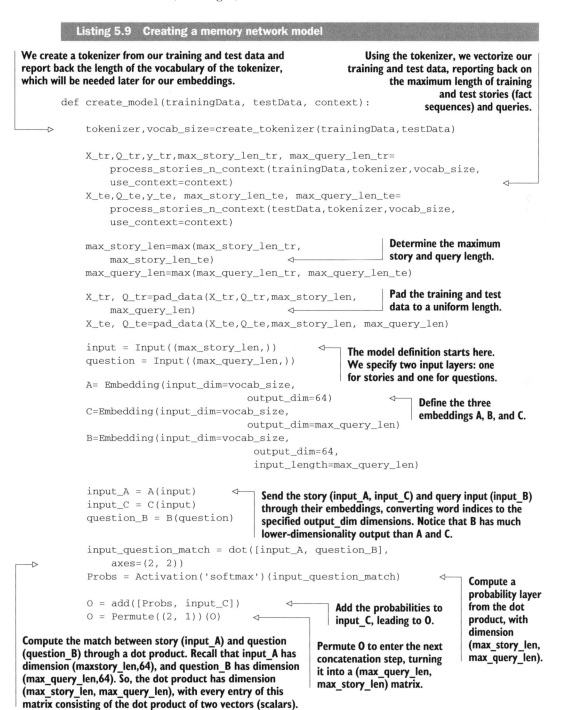

We create a tokenizer from our training and test data and report back the length of the vocabulary of the tokenizer, which will be needed later for our embeddings.

Using the tokenizer, we vectorize our training and test data, reporting back on the maximum length of training and test stories (fact sequences) and queries.

```
def create_model(trainingData, testData, context):

    tokenizer,vocab_size=create_tokenizer(trainingData,testData)

    X_tr,Q_tr,y_tr,max_story_len_tr, max_query_len_tr=
        process_stories_n_context(trainingData,tokenizer,vocab_size,
        use_context=context)
    X_te,Q_te,y_te, max_story_len_te, max_query_len_te=
        process_stories_n_context(testData,tokenizer,vocab_size,
        use_context=context)

    max_story_len=max(max_story_len_tr,
        max_story_len_te)
    max_query_len=max(max_query_len_tr, max_query_len_te)

    X_tr, Q_tr=pad_data(X_tr,Q_tr,max_story_len,
        max_query_len)
    X_te, Q_te=pad_data(X_te,Q_te,max_story_len, max_query_len)

    input = Input((max_story_len,))
    question = Input((max_query_len,))

    A= Embedding(input_dim=vocab_size,
                          output_dim=64)
    C=Embedding(input_dim=vocab_size,
                          output_dim=max_query_len)
    B=Embedding(input_dim=vocab_size,
                          output_dim=64,
                          input_length=max_query_len)

    input_A = A(input)
    input_C = C(input)
    question_B = B(question)

    input_question_match = dot([input_A, question_B],
        axes=(2, 2))
    Probs = Activation('softmax')(input_question_match)

    O = add([Probs, input_C])
    O = Permute((2, 1))(O)
```

Determine the maximum story and query length.

Pad the training and test data to a uniform length.

The model definition starts here. We specify two input layers: one for stories and one for questions.

Define the three embeddings A, B, and C.

Send the story (input_A, input_C) and query input (input_B) through their embeddings, converting word indices to the specified output_dim dimensions. Notice that B has much lower-dimensionality output than A and C.

Compute a probability layer from the dot product, with dimension (max_story_len, max_query_len).

Add the probabilities to input_C, leading to O.

Compute the match between story (input_A) and question (question_B) through a dot product. Recall that input_A has dimension (maxstory_len,64), and question_B has dimension (max_query_len,64). So, the dot product has dimension (max_story_len, max_query_len), with every entry of this matrix consisting of the dot product of two vectors (scalars).

Permute O to enter the next concatenation step, turning it into a (max_query_len, max_story_len) matrix.

Concatenate O with the embedded question, producing a final story-question pair.

Determine the size of the next weight layer based on the result of this concatenation. We need one weight for every entry in the stories-question scalar.

```
final_match = concatenate([O, question_B])

size=keras.backend.int_shape(final_match)[2]
weights = Dense(size, activation='softmax')
        (final_match)
```

The weight matrix uses softmax as activation, meaning these weights are in the range [0,1]. The final_match result is sent through this layer.

```
merged=merge([final_match, weights], mode='mul')
answer=Flatten()(merged)

answer = Dense(vocab_size)(answer)
answer = Activation('softmax')(answer)

model = Model([input_sequence, question], answer)
model.compile(optimizer='rmsprop', loss='categorical_crossentropy',
        metrics=['accuracy'])

return X_tr,Q_tr,y_tr,X_te,Q_te,y_te,model
```

Multiply the weights with the final_match values. The result is flattened to one vector.

Specify the input and output to the model, and compile the model.

A final Dense layer produces a vector of size vocab_size. This vector will be instantiated with answer vectors once we invoke the model with labeled data.

This model is summarized by Keras (`model.summary()`) as follows:

Layer (type)	Output Shape	Param #	Connected to
input_1 (InputLayer)	(None, 12)	0	
input_2 (InputLayer)	(None, 3)	0	
embedding_1 (Embedding)	(None, 12, 64)	9472	input_1[0][0]
embedding_3 (Embedding)	(None, 3, 64)	9472	input_2[0][0]
dot_1 (Dot)	(None, 12, 3)	0	embedding_1[0][0] embedding_3[0][0]
activation_1 (Activation)	(None, 12, 3)	0	dot_1[0][0]
embedding_2 (Embedding)	None, 12, 3)	444	input_1[0][0]
add_1 (Add)	(None, 12, 3)	0	activation_1[0][0] embedding_2[0][0]
permute_1 (Permute)	(None, 3, 12)	0	add_1[0][0]
concatenate_1 (Concatenate)	(None, 3, 76)	0	permute_1[0][0] embedding_3[0][0]

dense_1 (Dense)	(None, 3, 76)	5852	concatenate_1[0][0]
merge_1 (Merge)	(None, 3, 76)	0	concatenate_1[0][0] dense_1[0][0]
flatten_1 (Flatten)	(None, 228)	0	merge_1[0][0]
dense_2 (Dense)	(None, 148)	33892	flatten_1[0][0]
activation_2 (Activation)	(None, 148)	0	dense_2[0][0]

```
=================================================================
Total params: 59,132
Trainable params: 59,132
Non-trainable params: 0
```

Running our model first produces the graph shown in figure 5.10 for context sizes (number of intervening, irrelevant facts) 0, 2, 4, and 6. This graph presents the training accuracies per epoch (for a maximum of 30 epochs), as reported by Keras during training. We observe a clear effect of context size on training performance: the shorter the context, the better. But we also see that contexts 2 and 4 quickly reach 100% accuracy during training.

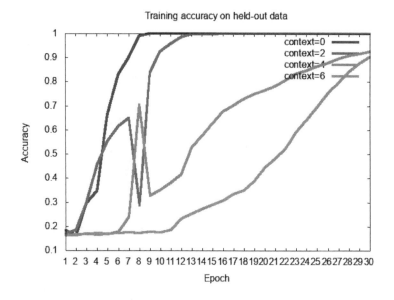

Figure 5.10 Training performance (30 epochs) on held-out data for a number of context sizes of the memory end-to-end network

The accuracies obtained per context size on the actual test data, with 100 epochs for training, are the following (as always, these numbers may fluctuate per run):

- Context size = 0, test accuracy = 100%
- Context size = 2 facts (story length = max. 18 words): test accuracy = 100%

- Context size = 4 facts (story length = max. 30 words): test accuracy = 100%
- Context size = 6 facts (story length = max. 41 words): test accuracy = 99.8%
- Context size = 8 facts (story length = max. 52 words): test accuracy = 99%
- All facts (story length = max. 58 words): test accuracy = 67.7%

These results are much better than for RNNs. For contexts up to 8, they are on a par with the LSTM results. Even though all models reach 100% accuracy on the 0 context case, memory networks show a less steep decrease in performance when the context size is increased and reach a better score in the all-facts situation. While not perfect, end-to-end memory networks perform much better on our Question Answering task.

Figure 5.11 shows a graph with the aggregated differences between RNNs, LSTMs, and memory networks on our data. It demonstrates the better performance of memory networks on long contexts. The context size listed corresponds with the number of irrelevant facts:

- 1 irrelevant fact: maximum context length = 12 words
- 2 irrelevant facts: maximum context length = 18 words
- 4 irrelevant facts: maximum context length = 30 words
- 6 irrelevant facts: maximum context length = 41 words
- 8 irrelevant facts: maximum context length = 52 words
- All facts: maximum context length = 58 words

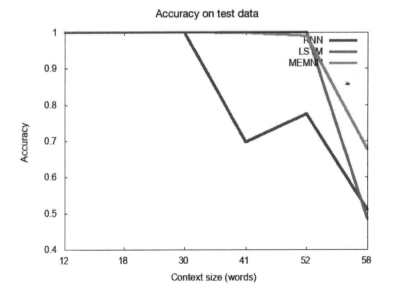

Figure 5.11   Test performance (100 training epochs) for RNNs, LSTMs, and memory end-to-end networks

Memory networks provide interesting perspectives on NLP. Recent work demonstrates that most NLP problems can be cast into a question-answer formalization. Based on our decent Question Answering results with memory networks, we will apply memory networks in the next chapter to a set of well-known other sequential NLP problems and see how that works out.

Summary

- Three approaches to Question Answering with differing memory capacity involve using RNNs, LSTMs, and end-to-end memory networks.
- For Question Answering, RNNs perform worse than LSTMs in remembering long sequences of data.
- End-to-end memory networks work by memorizing sample questions, supporting facts, and answers to the questions in memory banks.
- End-to-end memory networks outperform LSTMs for Question Answering.

Episodic memory for NLP

This chapter covers

- Applying strongly supervised end-to-end memory networks to sequential NLP problems
- Implementing a multi-hop memory network that allows for semi-supervised training
- Strongly supervised vs. semi-supervised memory networks

In this chapter, essentially, we will attempt to extend the use of episodic memory to an array of NLP problems by rephrasing them as instance of Question Answering problems. For the data we will use in this chapter, strongly supervised memory networks easily produce above-baseline results with very little effort. Semi-supervised memory networks produce better accuracy in some cases, but not consistently.

6.1 Memory networks for sequential NLP

When was the last time you stroked a cat? If it wasn't long ago, you will recall specific details of the situation. In addition, based on previous experience and knowledge, you will have a general understanding of what it means to stroke cats and what cats are in the first place. The American neuroscientist Larry Squire (1986) hypothesized that humans store experiences (concepts, facts, events) in a heterogeneous type of memory called *declarative memory*, as opposed to *procedural memory*, which stores skills or behavioral patterns (like the muscle memory you use when riding a bike). According to cognitive neuroscientist Endel Tulving (1989), procedural memory consists of a *semantic* component and an *episodic* component. Semantic memory is used to store generic, more abstract conceptual information, like prototypical information about what makes up a cat. Episodic memory stores specific memories and personal experiences (facts, events, timestamps) related to concepts, such as the memory of the last time you stroked a cat. See figure 6.1.

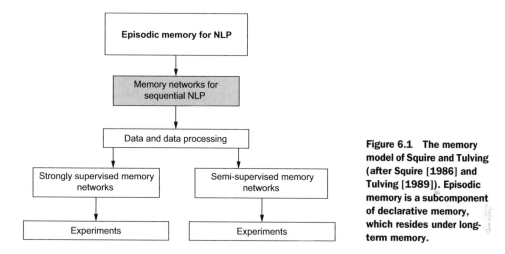

Figure 6.1 The memory model of Squire and Tulving (after Squire [1986] and Tulving [1989]). Episodic memory is a subcomponent of declarative memory, which resides under long-term memory.

While many things are unclear about the exact organization of episodic memory (for one thing, whether it is localized in a specific location in the brain or is a distributed type of memory (Chen et al. 2017), the general concept of episodic memory comes closest to the memory we implemented in the memory networks in chapter 5. We worked with descriptions of specific events (which we called *facts*), combined into *stories*. The Question Answering mechanism of memory networks implements a form of memory access or retrieval: memory networks address a memory base of stored facts to carry out an analysis by asking for the relevant facts in memory.

The end-to-end memory networks in chapter 5 apply a form of supervised attention during processing. When confronted with a story, a question, and an answer during training, they learn to hone in on an informative part of the story that holds the answer to the question posed. Those informative parts are specified in the training data, which, as you will recall, looks like this:

```
1 Mary moved to the bathroom.
2 John went to the hallway.
3 Where is Mary?        bathroom        1
```

This supervised learning mechanism can serve as a metaphor for many NLP problems—most of NLP is about picking out contextual information from a sequence of sounds or text to make a step toward interpretation.

In this chapter, we apply our own memory networks to NLP data represented as a Question Answering task (see figure 6.2). The first technique we implement, in line with the approach from chapter 5, is based on *strong supervision*: we indicate explicitly which facts contribute to answering a question in the training data of our models, plus the labels (outcomes) associated with the stories.

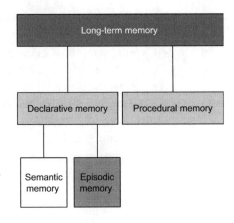

Figure 6.2   Using memory networks for sequential NLP tasks

NOTE   Alternatively—and this is the approach taken by dynamic memory networks (Kumar et al. 2016)—we can let the network determine the relevant facts for answering questions using attention mechanisms. These *semi-supervised* networks zoom in on certain information and leave other, irrelevant information unused. We will apply semi-supervised models in this chapter as well.

To give you a first flavor of this approach, suppose we encode a part-of-speech tagger as a Question Answering module. In part-of-speech tagging, the parts of speech of the words in the context of an ambiguous word, together with lexical properties, determine the part of speech of that word. For example, in the following sentence

I took a random walk through the park

the following words are ambiguous:

- Walk (noun or verb)
- Park (noun or verb)

Given the presence of *a* (which is unambiguous: it's a determiner) and the adjective *random*, the word *walk* cannot be a verb—it must be a noun. Similarly, the presence of *the* disambiguates *park* to be a noun. A Question Answering representation of this story could be as follows:

```
1 pronoun verb determiner          "I took a"_
2 verb determiner adjective        "took a random"
3 determiner adjective noun_verb   "a random walk"
4 adjective noun_verb preposition  "random walk through"
5 pos noun_verb ? noun 3 4
6 noun preposition determiner      "walk through the"
7 preposition determiner noun_verb "through the park"
8 determiner noun_verb             "the park"
9 pos noun_verb ? noun 7 8
```

Notice how we turn a sequential NLP task into a Question Answering task. We apply a moving window over a part-of-speech-tagged text. We regenerate ambiguities based on a lexicon derived from this data (in the example, we assume *walk* and *park* have been tagged as both nouns and verbs in the data). The questions we pose address the disambiguation of these ambiguities: which part of speech should a noun/verb ambiguity be assigned in this context?

Using such an approach, we need to make sure the exact order of the facts is preserved since it is crucial for strictly sequential tasks. Our vectorization procedure (see chapter 5; repeated in the following listing) does just that using the Keras built-in `Tokenizer` procedure `texts_to_sequences` (see https://keras.io/preprocessing/text/).

Listing 6.1   Vectorization

```
def vectorize(s, tokenizer):
    vector=tokenizer.texts_to_sequences([s])
    if vector[0]!='':
        return vector[0]
```

This produces an ordered vector of integers corresponding to the original word sequence of its input, such as

```
[1, 2, 3, 4, 1, 5, 6]
```

for "the (1) cat (2) jumped (3) over (4) the (1) lazy (5) dog (6)."

Now, let's see how we can transform arbitrary NLP data to the native format of memory networks: Question Answering data, yielding *linguistic Question Answering*.

6.2   Data and data processing

We will use the following data in our experiments:

- Data for PP-attachment (prepositional phrases)
- The Dutch diminutive formation data we used earlier
- Spanish part-of-speech tagging data

Let's see how we can massage this data into the required format for memory networks: data organized as Question Answering tasks consisting of facts and questions (figure 6.3).

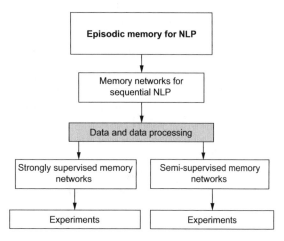

Figure 6.3   Processing the data for linguistic Question Answering

6.2.1   *PP-attachment data*

In natural language, prepositional phrases (phrases consisting of a preposition and a noun phrase) are used as *modifiers* of other words: they restrict (*specify*) the meaning of those other words (usually nouns or verbs). For instance, in

He ate a pizza with anchovies

the prepositional phrase *with anchovies* modifies the noun *pizza* rather than *ate*: it says something about the pizza, and not about the act of eating it.

Ratnaparkhi (1994) put forward a well-known benchmark dataset for PP-attachment. Here is a typical entry of this data, presented as a five-column CSV file:

```
eats,pizza,with,anchovies,N
```

The (simplified) prepositional phrase *with anchovies* modifies the noun (N) *pizza*. Notice the rigid format of this data: every entry invariably consists of a verb, a noun, a preposition, and a noun, plus an N (noun) or V (verb) label.

In this example

```
dumped,sacks,into,bin V
```

the PP *into bin* modifies the verb (V) *dumped*.

Another example is

```
gives,authority,to,administration,V
```

where *to administration* modifies the verb *gives* rather than the noun *administration*.

Let's convert this data to the Question Answering format that a memory network needs. First, we need to use only the first two "facts": not all four features are relevant for predicting the outcome. Recall that the facts are encoded as "memories": we can supply the words in the question with their parts of speech to obtain richer facts. Also recall that the first word in this data is invariably a verb, and the second word is a noun:

```
1 fetch V.
2 price N.
```

Second, our question needs to contain some information to arouse a response from those memories. One way to do this is to list the prepositional phrase in the question:

```
attach of profit ? N 1 2
```

This reads as follows: "To which part of speech should the prepositional phrase *of profit* be attached? Answer: the noun (N), on the basis of facts 1 and 2."

So, the entire story for this example is

```
1 fetch V.
2 price N.
3 attach of profit? N 1 2
```

Here is a function for performing this conversion.

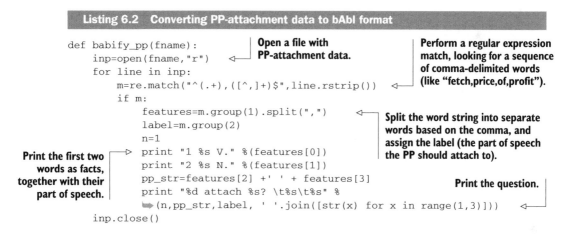

Listing 6.2 Converting PP-attachment data to bAbl format

```
def babify_pp(fname):
    inp=open(fname,"r")
    for line in inp:
        m=re.match("^(.+),([^,]+)$",line.rstrip())
        if m:
            features=m.group(1).split(",")
            label=m.group(2)
            n=1
            print "1 %s V." %(features[0])
            print "2 %s N." %(features[1])
            pp_str=features[2] +' ' + features[3]
            print "%d attach %s? \t%s\t%s" %
                (n,pp_str,label, ' '.join([str(x) for x in range(1,3)]))
    inp.close()
```

Open a file with PP-attachment data.

Perform a regular expression match, looking for a sequence of comma-delimited words (like "fetch,price,of,profit").

Split the word string into separate words based on the comma, and assign the label (the part of speech the PP should attach to).

Print the first two words as facts, together with their part of speech.

Print the question.

6.2.2 *Dutch diminutive data*

Recall the Dutch morphological diminutive formation task:

```
=,=,=,=,+,k,e,=,-,r,@,l,T      "kerel"=>"kereltje" (small man)
=,=,=,=,+,l,I,=,-,x,a,m,P      "lichaam=>lichaampje" (small body)
=,=,=,=,=,=,=,=,+,tr,A,p,J     "trap=>trapje" (small stairs)
...
```

Here we have 12 prosodic and morphological features.

NOTE As stated in the TiMBL manual (http://languagemachines.github.io/timbl), these features indicate "whether the syllable is stressed or not (values - or +), the string of consonants before the vocalic part of the syllable (i.e. its onset), its vocalic part (nucleus), and its post-vocalic part (coda). Whenever a feature value is not present (e.g. a syllable does not have an onset, or the noun has less than three syllables), the value '=' is used. The class to be predicted is either E (-etje), T (-tje), J (-je), K (-kje), or P (-pje)."

How can we turn this task into a Question Answering task? A suitable representation for this data turns out to be a single-fact representation, where we put all features in one fact.

Exercise
Experiment with a number of other schemes, like creating windowed representations. Which representation works best compared to the results listed for the experiments in this chapter?

We must take special care of special phoneme characters (such as =, +, -, @, {, and }) in the data, since our tokenizer will ignore them and will not assign an integer value to them. To keep these symbols from being erased by the tokenization process, we substitute surrogate labels for these symbols:

- + => plus
- = => eq
- - => dash
- @ => schwa (a phoneme symbol for "sounds like the *a* in *about*")
- { => lbr (left bracket)
- } => rbr (right bracket)

This leads to the following representations of the previous examples:

```
1 eq eq eq eq plus k e eq dash r schwa l.
2 suffix l?      T         1

1 eq eq eq eq plus l I eq dash x a m.
2 suffix m?      P         1

1 eq eq eq eq eq eq eq eq plus tr A p.
2 suffix p?      J         1
```

For example, the first question

```
2 suffix l? T 1
```

reads as "What is the suffix to be attached to *l*, based on fact 1? Answer: *T*." The following listing performs the conversion.

Listing 6.3 Converting Dutch diminutive data to bAbI format

```
def babify_dimin(fname):
    f=open(fname,"r")
    for line in f:
        features=line.rstrip().split(",")
        label=features.pop()
        fA=[]                               ◁── Define an array for holding
        for feature in features: )          ◁── our substitutions.
            if feature=="=":                    Fill the array with
                feature="eq"                    substitutions.
            elif feature =="-":
                feature="dash"
            elif feature=="+":
                feature="plus"
            elif feature=="@":
                feature="schwa"
            elif feature=='{':
                feature="lbr"
            elif feature=='}':
                feature="rbr"
            fA.append(feature)              Print the
        print "1 %s."%(' '.join(fA))      ◁── (one) fact.
        print "2 suffix %s? \t%s\t%s"%(fA[-1],label,"1")   ◁── Print the
    f.close()                                                   question.
```

6.2.3   *Spanish part-of-speech data*

CoNLL, the annual SIGNLL Conference on Computational Natural Language Learning (www.conll.org), publishes annual NLP benchmarks with accompanying training and test datasets. From CoNLL 2002, we use Spanish part-of-speech data from a named entity recognition task (www.clips.uantwerpen.be/conll2002/ner), which looks like this:

```
l DA O
Abogado NC B-PER
General AQ I-PER
del SP I-PER
Estado NC I-PER
, Fc O
Daryl VMI B-PER
Williams NC I-PER
, Fc O
subrayó VMI O
hoy RG O
la DA O
necesidad NC O
de SP O
tomar VMN O
medidas NC O
para SP O
proteger VMN O
al SP O
sistema NC O
judicial AQ O
australiano AQ O
...
```

Here, the second column consists of a part-of-speech label for the first column, and the last column indicates phrasal information, such as starting a named entity (B-PER, *B* for *beginning*), being part of a named entity (I-PER, *I* for *inside*), or being none of those (O). We will only use the first two columns of this data.

The rather involved procedure in listing 6.4 converts this data into bAbI format with a window of three parts of speech. It first builds a lexicon for storing ambiguities (one word receiving multiple part-of-speech tags in the data) and then windows the data. For a designated focus position (a fixed cell in the three-cell window: in our case, the middle position), it lists the eventual ambiguity and its resolution. Upon encountering an ambiguity, it composes a story consisting of the current window and its predecessor and starts a new story.

Listing 6.4   Converting Spanish part-of-speech data to bAbI format

```
def babify_conll02(fname):
    f=open(fname,"r")
    Lex={}
    for line in f:
        if re.match(".+DOCSTART.+",line):
            continue
```

Define a dictionary holding the assignment of parts of speech to words in our data.

```
m=re.match("^([^\s]+)\s+([^\s]+)\s+(.+)$",line.rstrip())
if m:
    word=m.group(1)
    pos=m.group(2)
    if word in Lex:
        if pos not in Lex[word]:
            Lex[word].append(pos)
    else:
        Lex[word]=[pos]
f.seek(0)

ngramsize=3
focus=1
story=""
for line in f:
    if re.match(".+DOCSTART.+",line):
        continue
    if re.match("^\s*$",line.rstrip()):
        ngrs=ngrams(story,ngramsize)
        n=1
        ambig=False
        for ngr in ngrs:
            fact="%d"%(n)
            i=0
            for w in ngr:
                word_plus_pos=w.split("#")
                word=word_plus_pos[0]
                pos=word_plus_pos[1]
                lex_pos='_'.join(Lex[word])
                if i==focus:
                    fact+=" %s"%(lex_pos)
                    if '_' in lex_pos:
                        ambig=True
                        unique_pos=pos
                        ambig_word=word
                        ambig_pos=lex_pos
                elif i==ngramsize-1:
                    fact+=" %s."%(lex_pos)
                    print fact
                else:
                    fact+=" %s"%(lex_pos)
                i+=1
            if ambig:
                n+=1
                ambig=False
                if n>2:
                    print "%d pos %s? \t%s\t%d %d"%(n,ambig_pos,
                    ➥unique_pos,n-2,n-1)
                else:
                    print "%d pos %s? \t%s\t%d"%(n,ambig_pos,
                    ➥unique_pos,n-1)
                n=0

        n+=1
        story=""
    else:
```

Split lines into words and parts of speech, and store the combination in the lexicon.

Keep track of ambiguities (words receiving more than one part of speech).

Rewind the input file; we're making another pass through the data.

Define the n-gram size (3).

Define a focus position: the word position addressed in the question. This only happens when the word is an ambiguity; unambiguous words do not need to be resolved.

Blank lines indicate the end of a sentence in our data. This is the trigger for converting the current sentence into a story. We start by generating n-grams of the specified size (3) for the story.

For every n-gram in our story (a triplet of parts of speech), we start a new fact.

At the focus position, check if we have an ambiguity.

Print the fact.

If we encountered an ambiguity, print the question with the answer (the disambiguated part-of-speech unique_pos).

```
m=re.match("^([^\s]+)\s+([^\s]+)\s+(.+)$",line.rstrip())
        if m:
                story+=m.group(1)+"#"+m.group(2)+" "
    f.close()
    exit(0)
```

Here is some sample output:

```
1 DA NC AQ.
2 NC AQ SP.
3 AQ SP NC.
4 SP NC Fc.
5 NC Fc VMI.
6 Fc VMI NC_AQ.
7 VMI NC_AQ Fc.
8 pos NC_AQ?     NC        6 7
```

Notice how ambiguities are indicated with underscores. In this story, `NC_AQ` is disambiguated to `NC` based on the two facts 6 and 7.

6.3   *Strongly supervised memory networks: Experiments and results*

We are now ready to run experiments on the transformed NLP data with the strongly supervised memory networks from chapter 5 (figure 6.4).

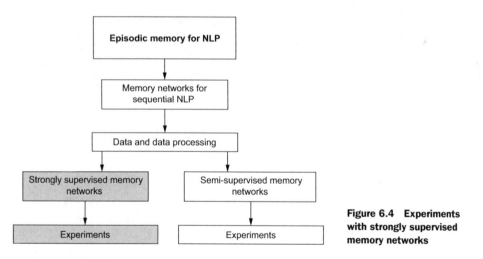

Figure 6.4 Experiments with strongly supervised memory networks

6.3.1   *PP-attachment*

First we will run the memory network from chapter 5 on the processed PP-attachment data. We train the network for 30 iterations; when it is applied to the test data, it produces

```
Test loss / test accuracy = 0.4298 / 0.8162
```

This accuracy is on par with average and above-baseline results obtained by much more complex methods for this dataset (Zavrel et al. 1997). We could probably crank up these results by resorting to external word embeddings like GloVe (chapter 3), but we will not pursue that here.

> **Exercise**
>
> Can you improve on our results by using pretrained or on-the-fly embeddings?

6.3.2 Dutch diminutives

Running our memory network on the single-fact diminutive bAbI data produces

```
Test loss / test accuracy = 0.1800 / 0.9137
```

This is not a spectacular result per se; good results should be above 95% accuracy. But on the positive side, with little or no effort, we obtain an above-baseline result (baseline results are around 86%; see the TiMBL manual at http://languagemachines .github.io/timbl). As with the PP data, it seems reasonable to assume that our results can improve with properly tailored embeddings.

> **Exercise**
>
> Can you improve on our results by using on-the-fly embeddings based on the training data? Specifically, create a Word2Vec embedding based on the training data by turning the comma-delimited sequences into quasi-sentences and combining all of these into a corpus. Apply the Word2Vec code from chapter 2, and derive an embedding. Use that embedding in the memory network.

6.3.3 Spanish part-of-speech tagging

With the Spanish data, after 30 iterations of training, we obtain this score:

```
Test loss / test accuracy = 0.3104 / 0.9006
```

Our part-of-speech tagger is quite simplistic, only focusing on triples of parts of speech and ignoring lexical aspects. The reported score of over 90% seems adequate from this perspective and is open to improvement by incorporating linguistically richer facts.

Notice how, in general, the facts listed per story arise from the automated data generation routines. This is a design choice, since no manual intervention (explicit labeling of facts) is part of the process, and it may hamper performance in some cases.

> **Exercise**
>
> Push the model's performance a bit higher by also incorporating lexical (word) information in the n-grams. Another option is a model with two input layers: one for part-of-speech n-grams and one for word n-grams.

To conclude, in general, the memory network we implemented in chapter 5 yields average performance on our three NLP tasks with virtually no processing cost.

6.4   *Semi-supervised memory networks*

Up to now, our memory networks have used a single retrieval pass over the stored facts in the episodic memory bank and have been explicitly provided with the relevant facts to answer a question in a supervised manner. Can we switch to a semi-supervised scenario (figure 6.5) where the network figures out by itself which facts are important for predicting an outcome and demands facts, questions, and answers but not selections of facts relevant to answering the question? This would definitively alleviate the burden of manually annotating our training data.

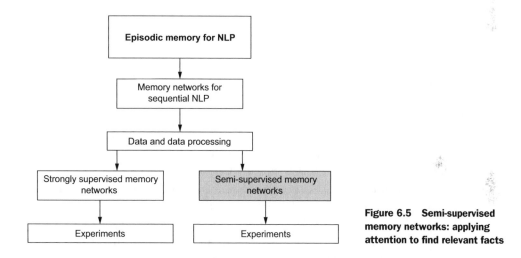

Figure 6.5   Semi-supervised memory networks: applying attention to find relevant facts

Scenario

You like the approach of memory networks for NLP, but you are weary of specifying relevant facts for a story in addition to the necessary labels. Can you resort to methods that only demand labels and no fact annotation? This will save you a lot of work: you will be able to compose NLP stories without specifying the crucial facts for answering the questions.

Recall that memory networks estimate a layer of probabilities that express the importance of a certain fact for answering a question. In our current applications of these networks (see chapter 5 and figure 6.6), we use a non-iterative approach to estimate these probabilities.

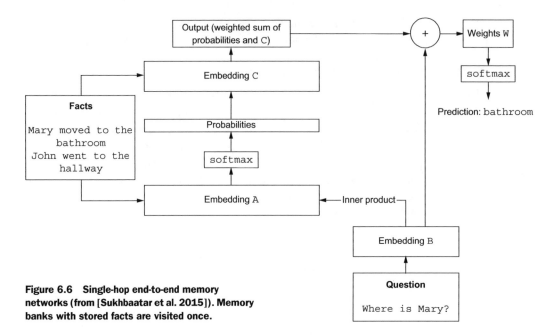

Figure 6.6   Single-hop end-to-end memory networks (from [Sukhbaatar et al. 2015]). Memory banks with stored facts are visited once.

Even though the probability layer `Probabilities` is trained during the entire training process for the network, it would make sense to add an extra facility where the probabilities can be better estimated locally by multiple exposures of facts to questions. These exposures are called *hops*: we hop one or more times over the facts when collecting their responses to an input question. Multiple hops may lead to better estimates of probabilities and, in the end, better outcomes. This idea was proposed in a 2015 paper by Sukhbaatar et al. (see figure 6.7): based on this paper, we can extend the single-hop approach we've used up to now to a multi-hop (three-hop) approach.

In figure 6.7, starting from `Question` and moving upward, we see how a question is embedded by embedding B. After that, the result is processed exactly like in the single-hop network (figure 6.6)—but three times in a row instead of just once:

1. The question is matched with the facts vector (through embedding A).
2. The result is turned into a probability vector `Output`, which is added to the result of every embedding C, also embedding the answer vector (see chapter 5 for the details). These probabilities are re-estimated during every hop, and every hop implements the same matching steps as the single-hop version.
3. The u variables (reflecting the match of the encoded question and the input) are incremented (through the + symbol, which indicates addition) with the `Output` variables, which combine encoded input with probabilities (not shown in figure 6.7; see the single-hop diagram in figure 6.6 for how they are computed).
4. The p probabilities are re-estimated during every hop, and every hop implements the same matching steps as the single-hop version.

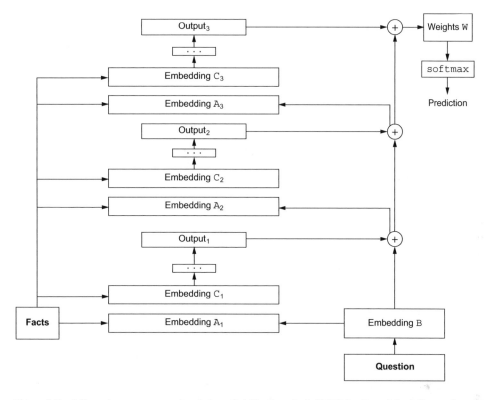

Figure 6.7 **A three-hop memory network (see Sukhbaatar et al. 2015) for the original diagram). Memory banks are visited multiple times (in *hops*), leading to better estimates of match probabilities between facts and questions.**

While embeddings A and C have different subscripts in the diagram and may be different embeddings, Sukhbaatar et al. (2015) mention that it is defensible to reuse the same A and C across these steps. So, recapitulating: we expose a question multiple times to a match with embedded answers (facts).

We implement this seemingly complex operation by inserting a loop into our network construction procedure (create_model) that iteratively refines the probability layers. Refer to chapter 5 for the model creation code for memory networks; the following listing highlights only the newly added loop.

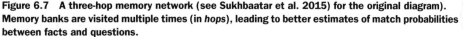

Listing 6.5 **Implementing multi-hop memory networks**

```
def create_model(trainingData, testData, context):
    tokenizer,vocab_size=create_tokenizer(trainingData,testData)

    X_tr,Q_tr,y_tr,max_story_len_tr, max_query_len_tr=process_stories_n_context(
    ➥trainingData,tokenizer,vocab_size,use_context=context)
    X_te,Q_te,y_te, max_story_len_te, max_query_len_te=process_stories_n_context(
    ➥testData,tokenizer,vocab_size,use_context=context)
```

```
max_story_len=max(max_story_len_tr, max_story_len_te)
max_query_len=max(max_query_len_tr, max_query_len_te)

X_tr, Q_tr=pad_data(X_tr,Q_tr,max_story_len, max_query_len)
X_te, Q_te=pad_data(X_te,Q_te,max_story_len, max_query_len)

input_facts = Input((max_story_len,))
question = Input((max_query_len,))

# A
A= Embedding(input_dim=vocab_size,
                          output_dim=64)
# C
C=Embedding(input_dim=vocab_size,
                          output_dim=max_query_len)
# B
B=Embedding(input_dim=vocab_size,
                          output_dim=64,
                          input_length=max_query_len)

input_A = A(input_facts)
input_C = C(input_facts)
question_B = B(question)

input_question_match = dot([input_A, question_B], axes=(2, 2))
Probs = Activation('softmax')(input_question_match)


size=keras.backend.int_shape(input_C)[2]

# Start of loop
max_hops=2
```

We define the number of hops our model should make.

```
if max_hops==0:
    O = add([Probs, input_C])
```

If we opt for zero hops, we need to generate the O result once (see chapter 5).

Apply a linear map to the input encoded by embedding C (see Sukhbaatar et al. 2015 for details).

Otherwise, we loop over the max_hops variable.

```
for i in range(max_hops):
    input_C=Dense(size)(input_C)
    O = add([Probs, input_C])
```

Add the current probability layer to the encoded, linearly transformed input of the previous step.

Match the question with the input, as in chapter 5.

```
    input_question_match = dot([input_A,
    ⮕question_B], axes=(2, 2))

    input_question_match = add([input_question_match,O])
    Probs = Activation('softmax')(input_question_match)
# End of loop
```

Add the O result to the match.

Compute new probabilities and iterate over the previous steps until termination.

```
O = Permute((2, 1))(O)
final_match = concatenate([O, question_B])
size=keras.backend.int_shape(final_match)[2]
weights = Dense(size, activation='softmax')(final_match)
merged=merge([final_match, weights], mode='mul')
answer=Flatten()(merged)
answer=Dropout(0.3)(answer) # ADDED 25.03
answer = Dense(vocab_size)(answer)   # (samples, vocab_size)
answer = Activation('softmax')(answer)
model = Model([input_facts, question], answer)
model.compile(optimizer='rmsprop', loss='categorical_crossentropy',
```

```
                 metrics=['accuracy'])

    model.summary()

    return X_tr,Q_tr,y_tr,X_te,Q_te,y_te,model
```

The create_model procedure must now receive a value of -1 for context to blindly use all facts (see chapter 5).

Let's inspect the ramifications of this loop for the model structure. Figure 6.8 shows a standard single-hop model; refer to chapter 5 (listing 5.9) for the model's source code.

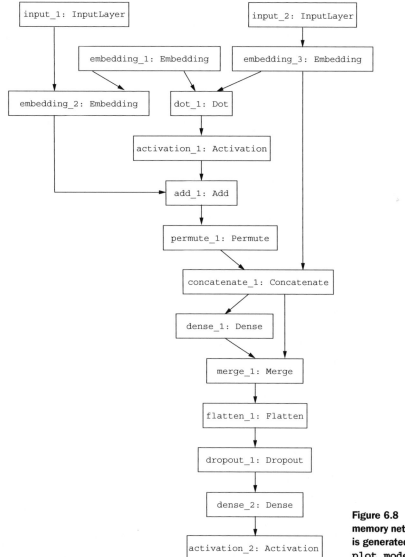

Figure 6.8   A single-hop memory network. The graph is generated by Keras' plot_model() routine.

As a point of reference, the add_1 node is where the probabilities p are combined with the result of embedding C. The concatenation node concatenates the embedded question with the weighted sum from figure 6.6.

Compare this to the three-hop version of our model, shown in figure 6.9. We clearly see the additional complexity. For instance, the second model displays iterated

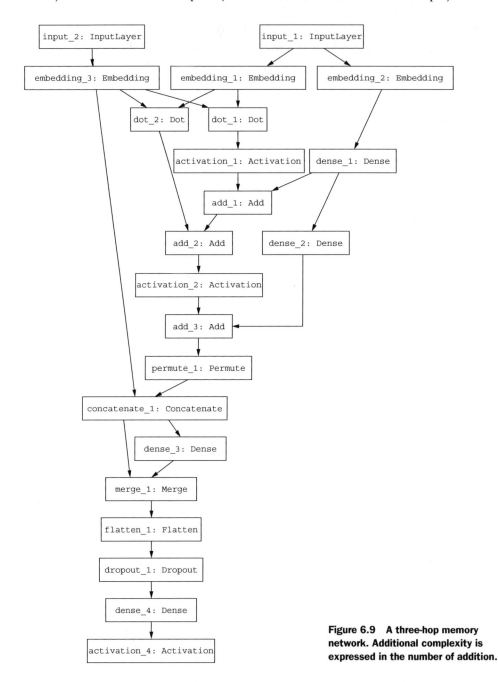

Figure 6.9   A three-hop memory network. Additional complexity is expressed in the number of addition.

additions (three rather than one in the single-hop model). The added complexity resides in the area above the `Concatenate` node and directly under the three `Embedding` nodes.

Exercise

Reason back from the three-hop graph in figure 6.9 to the diagram in figure 6.7 and the code in listing 6.5. Can you relate the diagram in figure 6.7 to figure 6.9 and listing 6.5?

6.4.1   *Semi-supervised memory networks: Experiments and results*

Let's look at experimental results with semi-supervised networks (figure 6.10). First, let's apply the semi-supervised multi-hop model to bAbI data. We choose the "indefinite knowledge" task, a reasoning task from the bAbI dataset (Weston et al. 2015). This task describes inferences based on "indefinite" facts, which consist of disjunctions (involving *or*) with answers including *maybe* for cases where a definite answer is not possible:

```
1 Fred is either in the school or the park.
2 Mary went back to the office.
3 Is Mary in the office?        yes      2
4 Bill is either in the kitchen or the park.
5 Fred moved to the cinema.
6 Is Fred in the park? no        5
7 Fred is in the office.
8 Bill moved to the cinema.
9 Is Bill in the cinema?         yes      8
10 Bill is in the park.
11 Bill is either in the office or the kitchen.
12 Is Bill in the office?        maybe    11
13 Bill is either in the cinema or the park.
14 Mary moved to the park.
15 Is Bill in the park?          maybe    13
```

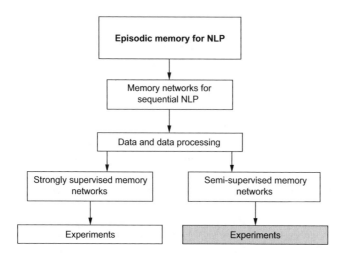

Figure 6.10   Experiments with semi-supervised memory networks

When we train and run a three-hop network on this data (300 training iterations), we obtain an accuracy of 77.10% for one hop

```
Test loss / test accuracy = 0.5571 / 0.7710
```

and a significantly improved accuracy of 88.3% for three hops:

```
Test loss / test accuracy = 0.3221 / 0.8830
```

This shows that there may be benefits in multiple hops over a memory. Sukhbaatar et al. (2015) report similar accuracy gains for a number of bAbI tasks.

Next, we turn to the bAbI task "two-argument relations" (Weston et al, 2015). This task models geographic relations between two arguments (entities), such as kitchen and office in the first story:

```
1 The office is north of the kitchen.
2 The garden is south of the kitchen.
3 What is north of the kitchen? office   1
1 The kitchen is west of the garden.
2 The hallway is west of the kitchen.
3 What is the garden east of?    kitchen 1
1 The garden is north of the office.
2 The bedroom is north of the garden.
3 What is north of the garden? bedroom 2
```

For two hops, the network (trained for 100 iterations) produces

```
Test loss / test accuracy = 0.3993 / 0.7510
```

And for three hops, we obtain

```
Test loss / test accuracy = 0.3739 / 0.7950
```

Applying the multi-hop network to our PP and diminutive data does not produce any improvement, though, and sometimes even leads to degradation of accuracy. For the Spanish part-of-speech data, after 30 training iterations, we see very slight improvement for three hops over the single-hop network we tested earlier:

```
Test loss / test accuracy = 0.2942 / 0.9023
```

As Sukhbaatar et al. (2015) note, in many cases, the semi-supervised approach performs (much) worse than the strongly supervised approach. And in quite a few cases, adding multiple hops does not increase accuracy and sometimes even leads to deteriorated performance.

> **NOTE** The multi-hop network, while offering the benefit of not relying on strong supervision, does not produce consistent quality improvements per hop, although in a number of cases, performance is boosted compared to the single-hop network. In virtually all cases, the performance of semi-supervised memory networks is not on par with that of strongly supervised networks.

Semi-supervised memory networks are less accurate than (strongly) supervised memory networks, but they offer low-complexity, reasonably accurate solutions in many cases. Similarly, data for strongly supervised memory networks is relatively easy to generate from already-available NLP data. You have seen how to generate this data for a number of tasks. The fact representation per story boils down to a design choice, with possible drawbacks for performance. The performance of these networks may not always be state of the art but can nonetheless be acceptable in many practical application scenarios where interpretability and maintenance of NLP training data are important.

Factoring probabilities into a neural network implements a form of *attention* that weights (emphasizes) aspects of our data. Neural attention is a widely researched topic. It is time we turn to these techniques to see whether we can benefit from them in terms of reducing supervision efforts. This is the topic of the next chapter.

Summary

- Memory networks can be applied to NLP tasks beyond Question Answering by implementing the metaphor of Question Answering.
- Baseline results can be produced with little effort using memory networks.
- Multi-hop memory networks generally improve results compared to single-hop networks.
- Strongly supervised memory networks outperform semi-supervised memory networks in general but not consistently.

Part 3

Advanced topics

Part 3 starts by introducing neural attention (chapter 7). This chapter shows how simple forms of attention may improve models and our understanding of what these models do with data. Chapter 8 introduces the concept of multitask learning, where several tasks are learned at the same time, a technique that may assist with learning the separate tasks involved. Chapter 9 introduces Transformers, including BERT and its competitor, XLNet. In chapter 10, we get hands-on with BERT and inspect the embeddings it produces.

Attention 7

This chapter covers

- Implementing attention in MLPs and LSTMs
- Using attention to improve the performance of a deep learning model
- Explaining model outcomes by highlighting attention patterns connected to input data

7.1 Neural attention

In the field of neurocognition, *attention* is defined as a form of cognitive focus arising from the limited availability of computational resources. The brain, while powerful, is vulnerable to distraction during cognitive processing and tends to block out certain irrelevant information. For example, if you're engaged in an intense phone call at work, you block out irrelevant stimuli from your coworkers in your context. On the other hand, if you are focusing on a hard cognitive task and someone starts a phone call next to you, your attention may wane, and it may be difficult to maintain focus. In humans, these attention facilities are developed during infancy, and problems during this development process can lead to attention-related pathologies in later life (such as autism or attention deficit disorder; see Posner et al. 2016). Interestingly, the human brain appears to deploy different attention mechanisms: for instance, a mechanism for assigning voluntary attention to parts of a stimulus (like words in a text you read) and a mechanism for attending to neglected parts of a stimulus (such as the words you initially skipped). The first mechanism might be described as *goal-driven* and the second as *stimulus-driven* (see Vossel et al. 2014).

What would an attention mechanism bring to our artificial neural networks? Attention can be used to weigh information. If we can implement such a mechanism in an NLP task, we may be able to catch a glimpse of important aspects of texts, such as the words drawing most of the neural network's attention during topic classification. In addition, we can imagine that such attentive information will benefit our models: weeding out irrelevant information should be beneficial for performance. In this chapter, we address these ideas by implementing attention mechanisms for multilayer networks and long short-term memory networks (LSTMs). The latter will take the temporal dimension into account by allowing attention values to travel through a time series.

Let us discuss two scenarios for which all this is relevant.

Scenario: Attention for explanations

You are supporting analysts by processing large amounts of textual data. Specifically, these analysts would like to have topic and sentiment classifiers that assign topics and sentiment labels to raw texts. The analysts would like to understand why their classifier assigns a certain topic or sentiment label to a text: which words were largely responsible for the assigned label? Knowing these words will enable them to understand the outcomes of the topic classifier and explain classifier results to users.

Scenario: Attention for handling messy data

You are building a document classifier, but your data is messy. Many documents in your dataset contain irrelevant words that do not seem to correlate with the intended document topics and sentiment labels. This may hamper the performance of your classifier. Can attention mechanisms diminish the need for elaborate data cleanup or term-selection procedures by demoting (paying less attention to) noisy words and promoting (paying more attention to) the really important words? In other words, can attention save you some data cleanup work?

How should attention be encoded in a neural network setting? Interpreting attention as a means to weigh information, it makes sense to encode attention as numerical values, preferably in a fixed, normalized interval. This suggests that we should encode attention as a weight layer, with weights in the interval [0,1]. A weight close to 1 indicates a high amount of attention, unlike weights close to 0. To be able to interpret these weights, we want them to be connected to the input layer of a network rather than to some intermediate layer higher in the network. This means we need a *softmax* layer: a layer with an activation function that produces outputs in the range [0,1]. This layer should directly follow the input layer. It should be trainable end to end, meaning it can be tuned like any other weight layer during the optimization phase of the model. To weigh the input data with these probabilities—putting the attention probabilities to use—we combine them with the input layer in a multiplicative way. The mechanism of weighing information can be inserted at arbitrary points in a deep learning network, either close to the input layer or higher in the network.

Attention is one of the most intensively researched topics in deep learning. This has led to a wide variety of attention types. Recall from chapter 5 that we deployed exactly such probability layers in our memory networks for Question Answering. We repeat the setup of these networks in figure 7.1. The layer of probabilities is essentially an attention layer, allowing the network to focus on relevant facts for answering questions.

Xu et al. (2015) proposed a distinction between *soft* and *hard* attention. Soft attention can be interpreted as a *global* form of attention, whereas attention is devoted in varying degrees to all features (words, image patches, pixels, or hidden states) in the input data. Local or *hard* attention only attends to a specific part of the input features at a time. A similar distinction was proposed in Luong et al. (2015) for neural machine translation.

In this chapter, we implement simple forms of soft or global attention in such a way that we can interpret the attention in terms of input data (figure 7.2). As mentioned, we look at two scenarios: an

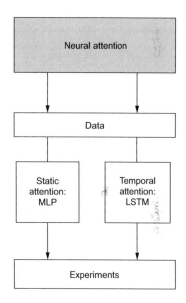

Figure 7.1   End-to-end memory networks (from [Sukhbaatar et al. 2015])

explanation scenario, where we would like attention to explain why a document has received a certain label by a classifier; and a scenario that addresses the use of attention for handling noisy data: can attention ignore messy parts (words) and focus on the really important information? We will implement attention for both multilayer perceptrons (MLPs) and LSTMs. Attention layers in an MLP are essentially *static*: unlike an LSTM, an MLP has no temporal memory and is not fit for handling time series. Therefore, incorporating attention into an LSTM calls for a different approach, such as gating (and preserving) attention through time.

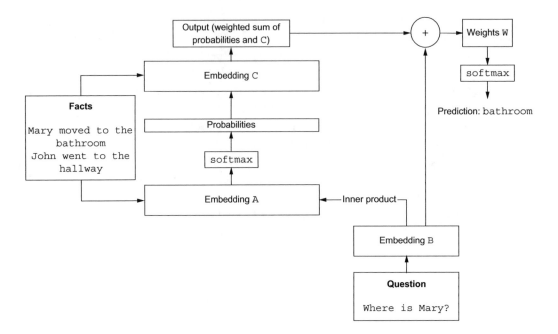

Figure 7.2   Modeling artificial attention relies (to some extent) on insights from natural neural attention.

To interpret the attention produced by our models, the word cloud visualization is a good candidate. A *word cloud* is a visual representation of a text where frequent words are denoted with larger font sizes than less frequent words. Figure 7.3 shows an example of a word cloud based on this text (an IMDB movie review):

```
Probably my all-time favorite movie, a story of selflessness, sacrifice and
dedication to a noble cause, but it's not preachy or boring. It just never
gets old, despite my having seen it some 15 or more times in the last 25
years. Paul Lukas' performance brings tears to my eyes, and Bette Davis, in
one of her very few truly sympathetic roles, is a delight. The kids are, as
grandma says, more like "dressed-up midgets" than children, but that only
makes them more fun to watch. And the mother's slow awakening to what's
happening in the world and under her own roof is believable and startling.
If I had a dozen thumbs, they'd all be "up" for this movie.
```

The word *more* outnumbers the word *movie* (it appears three times in the text versus two); stopwords (like *the*) are filtered out. The visualization is attractive and provides an immediate overview of important words. But in this document, with its limited repetitions, most non-stopwords appear only once.

To use this type of visualization for attention—with a large font expressing words that draw a lot of attention—we need to turn attention probabilities into proportional quantities. We will get to that later in the chapter, after we sort out how to incorporate attention layers into the main standard architectures for deep learning: the MLP and the LSTM. But first, let's turn to our data.

Figure 7.3 A word cloud for an IMDB document. Words with bigger fonts are more prominent than others (because they occur more frequently).

7.2 Data

We will use both news data and movie review data for this chapter (figure 7.4). The tasks will be to assign topics from the news domain to articles and polarity labels to movie reviews. As noted in previous chapters, Keras provides a set of built-in datasets, one of which consists of Reuters news data. It can be imported using

```
from keras.datasets import reuters
```

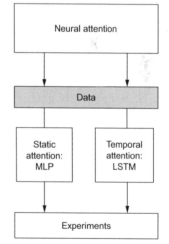

Figure 7.4 Processing data for attention modeling

Subsequently, the following code loads the preprocessed data into training and test partitions:

```
(x_train, y_train), (x_test, y_test) = reuters.load_data(num_words=None,
➥test_split=0.2)
```

Here, we specify that we put no cap on the number of words (num_words=None) and split the overall data into 80% training data and 20% test data. What does this data look like?

The dataset consists of 11,228 Reuters newswires with 46 topics. Texts are encoded as integer-based vectors, with every integer representing a unique word. Keras also assigns some extra meaning to the integers: they reflect the ordinal position of the word in the frequency listing for the entire data, so 10 means the 10th most frequent word in the entire dataset. The highest numbers reflect stopwords such as articles (or maybe a word like *movie*). The frequency information allows us to easily filter out high-frequency and (often) non-discriminatory words, if desired.

We can retrieve the vocabulary with

```
word_index = reuters.get_word_index(path="reuters_word_index.json")
```

This word index is a dictionary, mapping words to positions (integers). To map these word positions back to words, the index needs to be reversed.

Listing 7.1 Reversing a word index

```
RevWordIndex = {}

for key, value in word_index.items():
    RevWordIndex[value]=key
```

With this reverse word index, it is easy to inspect the first training document from the one-hot vector, which encodes a bag of words:

```
word_id=0
s=""

for i in x_test[0]:
    if i==1.0:
       s+=RevWordIndex[word_id]+" "
    word_id+=1
```

The document appears to be

```
of said and a mln 3 for vs dlrs it reuter 1 pct on is that its cts by year
be with will was u net as 4 but this are bank were 8 oil inc also tonnes
after rate 15 group exchange dollar we week note expected all rise meeting
18 only sale since wheat federal high term figures surplus annual likely
sell gold canadian opec dealers low news cents according way 49 signed
november financing 64 trust adding bank's weather review efforts mines
accounts commodities bureau baldrige pension managing expensive lifting
supplied argue
```

Similarly, Keras provides us with sentiment-labeled movie review data: a set of 25,000 reviews from IMDB. The documents are labeled with positive or negative sentiment (polarity) and are, like the Reuters data, represented as sequences of integers.

7.3 Static attention: MLP

Our first shot at attention involves equipping an MLP with an attention layer (figure 7.5). Recall that we insert a probability layer just after the input layer, with probabilities linked to input words. We will start with constructing a standard MLP, which we extend with an attention layer. The MLP will be applied to the Reuters news data.

We will convert the numerical vectors of the Keras dataset to one-hot format and eliminate stopwords based on a dictionary, which we derive from `nltk`:

```
from nltk.corpus import stopwords

stopwords = set(stopwords.words('english'))
```

The diagram in figure 7.6 shows the data processing procedure, and the following listing has the code.

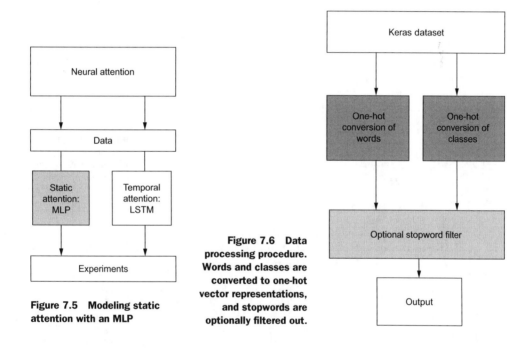

Figure 7.5   Modeling static attention with an MLP

Figure 7.6   Data processing procedure. Words and classes are converted to one-hot vector representations, and stopwords are optionally filtered out.

Listing 7.2   Data collection and processing for the MLP

```
def createData(stopwords, filterStopwords=False):

    (x_train, y_train), (x_test, y_test) = reuters.load_data(
    ➥num_words=None, test_split=0.2)          ◁─┐  Load the raw
                                                  │  data from Keras.
    num_classes=max(y_train)+1

    word_index = reuters.get_word_index(path="reuters_word_index.json")

    # Inverse index: number=>word            │  Define a reverse map, mapping
    RevWordIndex = {}                    ◁─┘  word indexes back to words.
    for key, value in word_index.items():
        RevWordIndex[value]=key
```

```
max_words = 10000

tokenizer = Tokenizer(num_words=max_words)          ◁──────────────┐
x_train = tokenizer.sequences_to_matrix(x_train, mode='binary')
x_test = tokenizer.sequences_to_matrix(x_test, mode='binary')

y_train = keras.utils.to_categorical(y_train, num_classes)
y_test = keras.utils.to_categorical(y_test, num_classes)

if filterStopwords:    ◁──┐  Optionally, apply a stopword filter to the
   j=0                       data, weeding out non-discriminatory
   for x in x_train:         words by setting positive indices (1) in the
      n=1                     one-hot encoded word vectors to zero (0).
      for w in x:
         if RevWordIndex[n] in stopwords:
            x_train[j][n-1]=0.0           Define a Tokenizer for converting the
         n+=1                             sequences of integers into sequences
      j+=1                                     of one-hot encoded vectors
                                          (effectively creating matrices) and
   j=0                                    create vectors encoding the classes.
   for x in x_test:
      n=1
      for w in x:
         if RevWordIndex[n] in stopwords:   Return the processed data (now
            x_test[j][n-1]=0.0               in one-hot format), together
         n+=1                               with the reverse word index and
      j+=1                                    the number of classes, for
                                                     further processing.
   return x_train, y_train, x_test, y_test, RevWordIndex,
➥num_classes                                            ◁──────────────┘
```

To demonstrate the effect of defining the Tokenizer, the following is the first training document in this dataset, (from the Keras dataset):

```
[1, 27595, 28842, 8, 43, 10, 447, 5, 25, 207, 270, 5, 3095, 111, 16, 369,
186, 90, 67, 7, 89, 5, 19, 102, 6, 19, 124, 15, 90, 67, 84, 22, 482,
26, 7, 48, 4, 49, 8, 864, 39, 209, 154, 6, 151, 6, 83, 11, 15, 22, 155,
11, 15, 7, 48, 9, 4579, 1005, 504, 6, 258, 6, 272, 11, 15, 22, 134, 44,
11, 15, 16, 8, 197, 1245, 90, 67, 52, 29, 209, 30, 32, 132, 6, 109, 15,
17, 12]
```

It is a sequence of integers, with each integer encoding a specific word. We turn this into a one-hot vector with the tokenizer.sequences_to_matrix() method, which produces

```
[0. 1. 0. 0. 1. 1. 1. 1. 1. 1. 1. 1. 1. 0. 0. 1. 1. 1. 0. 1. 0. 0. 1. 0.
 0. 1. 1. 0. 0. 1. 1. 0. 1. 0. 0. 0. 0. 0. 0. 1. 0. 0. 0. 1. 1. 0. 0. 0.
 1. 1. 0. 0. 1. 0. 0. 0. 0. 0. 0. 0. 0. 0. 0. 0. 0. 0. 1. 0. 0. 0. 0.
 0. 0. 0. 0. 0. 0. 0. 0. 0. 0. 1. 1. 0. 0. 0. 1. 1. 0. 0. 0. 0. 0.
 0. 0. 0. 0. 0. 0. 1. 0. 0. 0. 0. 0. 1. 0. 1. 0. 0. 0. 0. 0. 0. 0.
 0. 0. 0. 0. 1. 0. 0. 0. 0. 0. 0. 1. 0. 1. 0. 0. 0. 0. 0. 0. 0. 0.
 0. 0. 0. 0. 0. 0. 0. 1. 0. 0. 1. 1. 0. 0. 0. 0. 0. 0. 0. 0. 0. 0.
 0. 0. 0. 0. 0. 0. 0. 0. 0. 0. 0. 0. 0. 0. 0. 0. 1. 0. 0. 0. 0. 0.
 ...

]
```

Every integer that refers to a word is mapped onto a specific position in the vector, with a 1 indicating its presence. The vector is zero-based, meaning it starts at offset 0. For instance, word 1 in this Keras data vector leads to a 1 in the second position (position 1 in the zero-offset vector). Since there is no word 0 in the Keras vector, the first position (0) in the binary vector has a zero value.

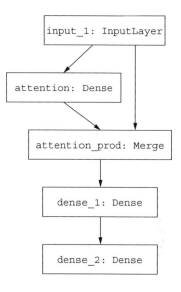

This binary representation is capped at 1,000 (`max_words`) words, meaning the second word, with index 27595, is not present in this vector—just like every word with an index higher than 1,000. The entire training and test datasets are represented as huge matrices of binary values.

We are now ready to implement an attention layer for an MLP (see https://github.com/philip peremy/keras-attention-mechanism for the code and discussion that inspired the MLP approach implemented here). Figure 7.7 shows the model, and the following list has the code.

Figure 7.7   MLP model with attention. Attention values are merged with the binary input through multiplication.

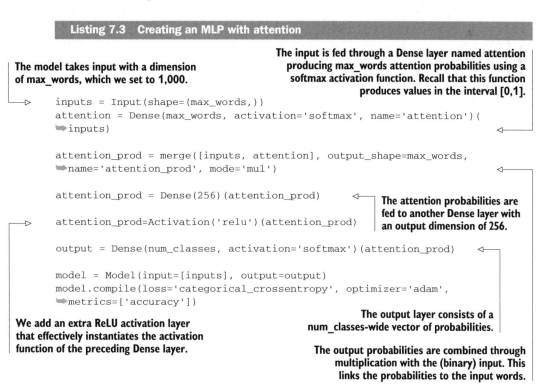

Listing 7.3   Creating an MLP with attention

The model takes input with a dimension of max_words, which we set to 1,000.

The input is fed through a Dense layer named attention producing max_words attention probabilities using a softmax activation function. Recall that this function produces values in the interval [0,1].

```
inputs = Input(shape=(max_words,))
attention = Dense(max_words, activation='softmax', name='attention')(
    inputs)

attention_prod = merge([inputs, attention], output_shape=max_words,
    name='attention_prod', mode='mul')

attention_prod = Dense(256)(attention_prod)

attention_prod=Activation('relu')(attention_prod)

output = Dense(num_classes, activation='softmax')(attention_prod)

model = Model(input=[inputs], output=output)
model.compile(loss='categorical_crossentropy', optimizer='adam',
    metrics=['accuracy'])
```

The attention probabilities are fed to another Dense layer with an output dimension of 256.

We add an extra ReLU activation layer that effectively instantiates the activation function of the preceding Dense layer.

The output layer consists of a num_classes-wide vector of probabilities.

The output probabilities are combined through multiplication with the (binary) input. This links the probabilities to the input words.

Visualizing the attention probabilities involves extracting the attention probabilities for a given input document from the model and converting them to proportional integer values. Here is how to do that.

First, to extract the activation values from a certain layer in a Keras model, we need to refer to that layer by its name, which we assigned in listing 7.3 for our model definition.

Let's start with a naive implementation that reveals how we can inspect Keras models. The following procedure extracts from a trained model the layer activation from the named layer for a specific input.

Listing 7.4 Extracting activations from a layer

The Keras backend is a library for performing low-level operations on models, layers, and the like. We need a particular low-level function.

We specify how we use the model: for training (MODE=1) or testing (MODE=0). In our case, we will always use the model in test mode: after it has been trained, we apply it to input data.

```
import keras.backend as K

def getLayerActivation(model, inputData, layerName):
    activation = []
    MODE=0
    inp = model.layers[0].input

    for layer in model.layers:

        if layer.name==layerName:

            func = K.function([inp, K.learning_phase()], [layer.output])
            activation = [func([inputData,MODE])[0]]
            break

    return activation
```

Keras models can be polled for the layers they contain. We work through the model layer by layer.

We have hit the layer with the specified name and can start extracting the activation values of that layer.

Run the function, producing an output array called activation.

Using the Keras backend K specifies a function func that, from the specified input data and all layers preceding the current layer, generates the output values (the activation values) of that layer.

Return the activation values.

It turns out this code can be simplified further, as follows:

```
def getLayerActivation(model, inputData, layerName):
    m = Model(inputs=model.input,
              outputs=model.get_layer(layerName).output)
    activation=m.predict(inputData)
    return activation
```

This omits the backend function and retrieves the named layer directly by its name.

Next, we turn the attention probabilities extracted from a model for a given input into proportional integer values to be used in a word cloud. Figure 7.8 illustrates what we have in mind.

For this to happen, we need to detect the minimal multiplier that will turn a set of probabilities with a variable number of decimal places into integers, keeping the decimal digits intact. For instance, for these values

- 0.123
- 0.0456

the minimal multiplier is 10,000:

- $0.123 \times 10{,}000 = 1230$
- $0.0456 \times 10{,}000 = 456$

The helper function in listing 7.5 takes a string-based approach to this problem. Notice that Python encodes small probabilities (below 0.0001) internally with negative exponentials:

```
>>> str(0.0001)
'0.0001'
>>> str(0.00001)
'1e-05'
```

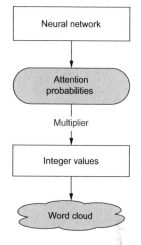

Figure 7.8 From attention probabilities to a word cloud: converting attention values to discrete integer values for visualization

---

Listing 7.5 Discretizing attention probabilities

```
def discretize_attention(normalized_attention):
    multiplier=1
    for p in normalized_attention:
        p_str=str(p)
        if 'e-0' in p_str:
            p_decomposed=p_str.split(".")
            if len(p_decomposed)>1:
                decimals=p_decomposed[1].split("e-0")
                x=10**(len(decimals[0])+int(decimals[1]))
        else:
            x=10**(1+np.floor(np.log10(np.abs(x))))*-1
        if x>multiplier:
            multiplier=x
    discrete_attention=[]
    for p in normalized_attention:
        discrete_attention.append(int(p*multiplier))
    return discrete_attention
```

The function produces output like this:

```
>>> discretize_attention([0.1,0.000123,0.0000345,0.7])

[1000000, 1230, 345, 7000000]
```

These values are adequate for word cloud visualization: they preserve differences of magnitude between probabilities (0.7 is 7 times higher than 0.1, and this is preserved in 1,000,000 versus 7,000,000) and encode these with properly scaled integers.

The next listing shows how to generate a word cloud from the discretized probabilities and an array holding lists of integer-encoded documents from the Keras datasets (we work with the first document, at index 0).

Listing 7.6   Generating a word cloud

```
from wordcloud import WordCloud        ◄─┐   Load an open source word cloud package (see
import matplotlib.pyplot as plt          │   https://github.com/amueller/word_cloud).

# Process attention
P={}
n=0                                          Our input is an array       ... and an array of integer-
                                             of discretized              encoded documents. We
for attval in discrete_attention:    ◄──┘    attention values ...        use the first document
    word_id=DOCUMENTS[0][n]                                         ◄─┘  only, at index 0.
    if RevWordIndex[word_id] in P:                        ◄─┐
            P[RevWordIndex[word_id]]+=attval                 │  Collect the discretized
        else:                                                   attention probabilities for the
            P[RevWordIndex[word_id]]=attval                     words in the documents.
    n+=1

# Use ordinal positions                              Sort these values in increasing
n=1                                                  order and assign integers to the
Q={}                                                 values based on their order,
for w in sorted(P, key=P.get, reverse=False):  ◄─┘   stored in a dictionary.
    Q[w]=n
    n+=1
                                                     Hand over the dictionary
                                                     to the WordCloud class in
wc = WordCloud(background_color="white",             the wordcloud package.
 ➥max_words=1000).generate_from_frequencies(Q)  ◄─┘

plt.imshow(wc, interpolation='bilinear')   ◄─┐  Visualize the word
plt.axis("off")                                 cloud with Matplotlib.
plt.show()
```

7.4   *Temporal attention: LSTM*

We intend to equip the standard LSTM with an extra gate for attention (figure 7.9). We will implement a mechanism for transporting attention probabilities through time by overwriting the standard Keras source code for the LSTM layer with attention extensions. Our `AttentionLSTM` differs from a standard LSTM only in having an extra gate that lets through attention probabilities. The Keras code base for the LSTM layer is too long to be listed in this book. Therefore, we will highlight the relevant portions and refer you to the code directory accompanying this chapter for the full source code. First, we quickly recap the LSTM architecture and discuss our extension. After that, we look at the process for defining new layers in Keras.

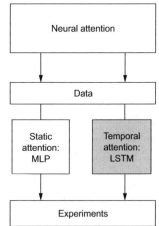

Figure 7.9   Temporal attention with an LSTM: adding an extra gate for attention

Recall that LSTMs consist of linked cells that contain a number of gates. For every time step, information passes through all these units, with time steps corresponding to discrete linguistic units, like words. The cell looks globally like figure 7.10 (see chapter 2 for details).

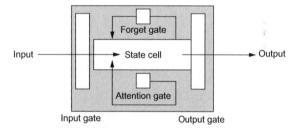

Figure 7.10 The LSTM cell

In its cell states, the LSTM gates information through three gates: an input gate (i_t), an output gate (o_t), and a forget gate (f_t). The gates receive the current input (x_t) and the hidden state at the previous time step (h_{t-1}). We add another gate to this architecture: an attention gate a_t through which attention probabilities are passed. This leads to the diagram in figure 7.11.

Figure 7.11 Attention-equipped LSTM cell state. The cell state gets an extra gate for attention values from history.

From the Keras documentation on writing proprietary layers (https://keras.io/layers/writing-your-own-keras-layers), we learn that we need to implement at least these two methods:

- `build(input_shape)`—This is where you will define your weights. This method must set `self.built = True` at the end, which can be done by calling `super([Layer], self).build()`.
- `call(x)`—This is where the layer's logic lives. Unless you want your layer to support masking, you only have to care about the first argument passed to call: the input tensor.

The Keras documentation includes the following example.

Listing 7.7 Sample proprietary layer in Keras

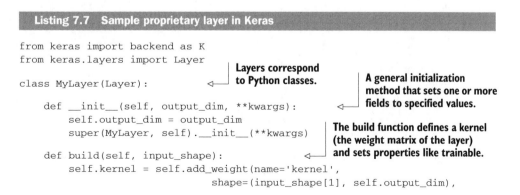

```
from keras import backend as K
from keras.layers import Layer

class MyLayer(Layer):                        ◁── Layers correspond
                                                 to Python classes.
    def __init__(self, output_dim, **kwargs):        ◁── A general initialization
        self.output_dim = output_dim                     method that sets one or more
        super(MyLayer, self).__init__(**kwargs)          fields to specified values.

    def build(self, input_shape):            ◁── The build function defines a kernel
        self.kernel = self.add_weight(name='kernel',   (the weight matrix of the layer)
                          shape=(input_shape[1], self.output_dim),   and sets properties like trainable.
```

```
                         initializer='uniform',
                         trainable=True)
        super(MyLayer, self).build(input_shape)

    def call(self, x):
        return K.dot(x, self.kernel)

    def compute_output_shape(self, input_shape):
        return (input_shape[0], self.output_dim)
```

The call function specifies the computation of the layer: in this case, a dot product of the input and the weights.

The optional compute_output_shape specifies eventual shape transformations performed by the layer computations.

For our purposes, we will implement two proprietary layers: `AttentionLSTMCell`, which is used by an `AttentionLSTM`. Both are extended versions of standard Keras classes (`LSTMCell` and `LSTM`): they keep everything in place but add special ingredients for dealing with attention. Figure 7.12 compares the standard `LSTM` class and `AttentionLSTM`, and figure 7.13 compares `LSTMCell` and `AttentionLSTMCell`.

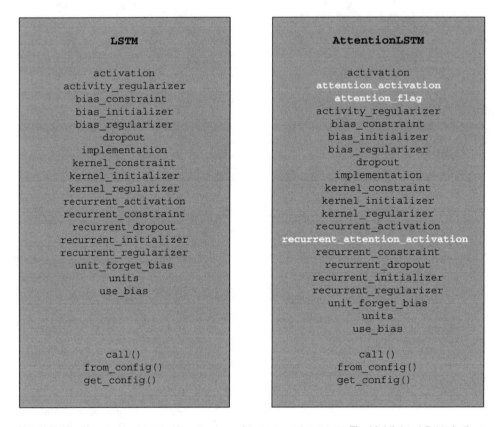

Figure 7.12   The standard `LSTM` class compared to `AttentionLSTM`. The highlighted fields indicate the points of difference (implemented class methods) between the two implementations.

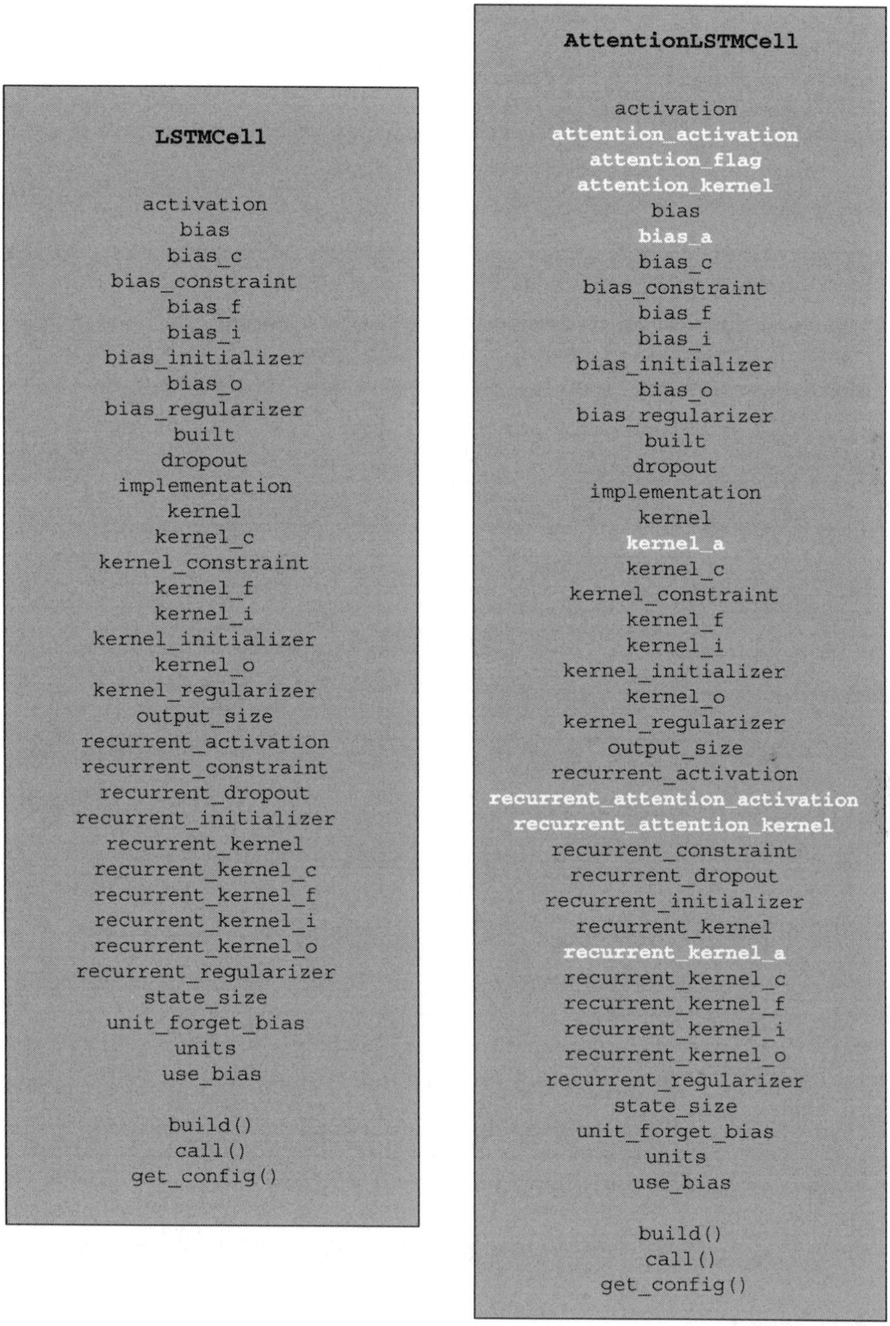

LSTMCell

activation
bias
bias_c
bias_constraint
bias_f
bias_i
bias_initializer
bias_o
bias_regularizer
built
dropout
implementation
kernel
kernel_c
kernel_constraint
kernel_f
kernel_i
kernel_initializer
kernel_o
kernel_regularizer
output_size
recurrent_activation
recurrent_constraint
recurrent_dropout
recurrent_initializer
recurrent_kernel
recurrent_kernel_c
recurrent_kernel_f
recurrent_kernel_i
recurrent_kernel_o
recurrent_regularizer
state_size
unit_forget_bias
units
use_bias

build()
call()
get_config()

AttentionLSTMCell

activation
attention_activation
attention_flag
attention_kernel
bias
bias_a
bias_c
bias_constraint
bias_f
bias_i
bias_initializer
bias_o
bias_regularizer
built
dropout
implementation
kernel
kernel_a
kernel_c
kernel_constraint
kernel_f
kernel_i
kernel_initializer
kernel_o
kernel_regularizer
output_size
recurrent_activation
recurrent_attention_activation
recurrent_attention_kernel
recurrent_constraint
recurrent_dropout
recurrent_initializer
recurrent_kernel
recurrent_kernel_a
recurrent_kernel_c
recurrent_kernel_f
recurrent_kernel_i
recurrent_kernel_o
recurrent_regularizer
state_size
unit_forget_bias
units
use_bias

build()
call()
get_config()

Figure 7.13 The standard `LSTMCell` class compared to `AttentionLSTMCell`. The highlighted fields indicate the points of difference (implemented class methods) between the two implementations.

If you inspect these figures carefully, you will notice exact attention counterparts of the Keras standard LSTM ingredients, such as these:

- `activation => attention_activation`
- `recurrent_activation => recurrent_attention_activation`
- `kernel_a` in addition to `kernel_c`, `kernel_f`, `kernel_i`, and `kernel_o`

Every layer in Keras has a couple of standard elements, one of which is the *kernel*: the weight matrix the layer creates. Other elements include the layer activation function and, optionally, a bias vector (a set of weights that are input independent, reflecting the bias of the layer when it is fed no (that is, `zero`) input).

We define a specific *attention kernel* (a weight matrix) in `AttentionLSTMCell` as follows.

Listing 7.8   The `build` method of `AttentionLSTMCell`

```
def build(self, input_shape):

...

    self.attention_kernel = self.add_weight(name='attention',
                              shape=(input_dim,input_dim),
                              initializer='uniform',
                              trainable=True)
...
```

Since we want our attention weights to weigh our input, the shape of this weight matrix should be square in the input dimension. We specified in listing 7.8 that the activation function of the attention layer we're building is `softmax`, producing values in the interval [0,1] that sum up to 1 (normalized probabilities). This kernel is used to compute the attention weight matrix, similar to its use for the other standard input gate:

```
self.kernel_i = self.kernel[:, :self.units]
...

self.kernel_a = self.attention_kernel[:, :input_dim]
```

It picks out a weight matrix proportional to the input dimensions from the attention kernel matrix.

In addition, a specific recurrent version of this kernel is needed to deal with temporal weights (similar to the standard kernel for `LSTMCell`).

Listing 7.9   Recurrent attention kernel of `AttentionLSTMCell` in `build`

```
...

    self.recurrent_attention_kernel = self.add_weight(
            shape=(input_dim, input_dim),
            name='recurrent_attention_kernel',
            initializer=self.recurrent_initializer,
```

```
                regularizer=self.recurrent_regularizer,
                constraint=self.recurrent_constraint)
...
```

The crucial code for attention is listed next. It is part of the `call` function of the `AttentionLSTMCell` layer.

```
def call(self, inputs, states, training=None):
        ...
        x_i = K.dot(inputs_i, self.kernel_i)        ⟵┐  Here, the various
        x_a = K.dot(inputs_a, self.kernel_a)         │  gates are applied
        x_f = K.dot(inputs_f, self.kernel_f)         │  to the input.
        x_c = K.dot(inputs_c, self.kernel_c)
        x_o = K.dot(inputs_o, self.kernel_o)
        ...

        i = self.recurrent_activation(x_i + K.dot(h_tm1_i,
            self.recurrent_kernel_i))
        f = self.recurrent_activation(x_f + K.dot(h_tm1_f,
            self.recurrent_kernel_f))
        # Attention
        a = self.recurrent_attention_activation(x_a + K.dot(
            h_tm1_a,self.recurrent_kernel_a))

        attP=a*self.attention_activation(x_a+K.dot(
            h_tm1_a,self.recurrent_kernel_a))

        c = f * c_tm1 +i * self.activation(x_c + K.dot(
            h_tm1_c, self.recurrent_kernel_c))+attP

        o = self.recurrent_activation(x_o + K.dot(h_tm1_o,
            self.recurrent_kernel_o))
        ...

    if self.attention_flag:                    ⟵┐  We have added a specific
        return a, [a, c]                         │  attention_flag field (an
    else:                                        │  attribute) to our class.
        return h,[h,c]
```

The recurrent, temporal attention probabilities are computed.

The attention probabilities are passed through the activation function specific for attention.

The `attention_flag` allows us to return different outputs from the `AttentionLSTMCell` layer: regular output (`attention_flag=False`) or the attention probabilities (`attentionFlag=True`); see listing 7.13. We will explain now how we exploit this in practice.

Exercise

Take a close look at the standard Keras source code for the `LSTM` layer, and compare it to the `AttentionLSTM` source code (see the code repository for this chapter). Compare both types of layers, and figure out their differences.

We start by outlining the data processing for our LSTM. The procedure is similar to the procedure for our MLP, but here we are using an embedding rather than a one-hot encoding for the words of our texts. Figure 7.14 shows the initial stage: turning documents into padded sequences of integers.

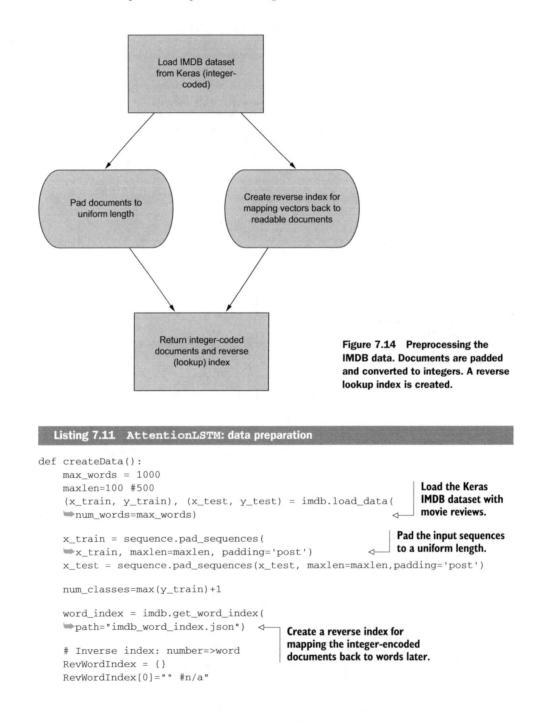

Figure 7.14   Preprocessing the IMDB data. Documents are padded and converted to integers. A reverse lookup index is created.

Listing 7.11   `AttentionLSTM`: data preparation

```
def createData():
    max_words = 1000
    maxlen=100 #500
    (x_train, y_train), (x_test, y_test) = imdb.load_data(
    ➥num_words=max_words)

    x_train = sequence.pad_sequences(
    ➥x_train, maxlen=maxlen, padding='post')
    x_test = sequence.pad_sequences(x_test, maxlen=maxlen,padding='post')

    num_classes=max(y_train)+1

    word_index = imdb.get_word_index(
    ➥path="imdb_word_index.json")

    # Inverse index: number=>word
    RevWordIndex = {}
    RevWordIndex[0]="" #n/a"
```

Load the Keras IMDB dataset with movie reviews.

Pad the input sequences to a uniform length.

Create a reverse index for mapping the integer-encoded documents back to words later.

```
for key, value in word_index.items():
    RevWordIndex[value]=key

return x_train, y_train, x_test, y_test, RevWordIndex,
➥num_classes
```

> **Return the data, the index, and the number of classes found in the data.**

Listing 7.12 `AttentionLSTM`: model creation

```
def createModel(attention_flag=False, return_sequences=False, timesteps=1,
➥input_dim=1, maxlen=64, num_classes=1):
    maxwords= 1000
    maxlen=100
    vlen=maxlen

    model = Sequential()
    model.add(Embedding(maxwords, vlen, input_length=maxlen))
    model.add(AttentionLSTM(maxlen,
                            return_sequences=return_sequences,
                            attention_flag=attention_flag,
                            input_shape=(maxlen,vlen),
                            dropout=0.2,name='attention_lstm',
                            recurrent_dropout=0.2))
    model.add(Dense(1, activation='sigmoid'))
    model.compile(loss='binary_crossentropy',
                  optimizer='adam',
                  metrics=['accuracy'])
    return model
```

> **Start with an Embedding for the integer-valued documents.**

> **A Dense layer encodes the class probability: close to zero for negative sentiment, and close to 1 for positive sentiment.**

> **Compile the model.**

> **Add an AttentionLSTM layer. Notice the use of attention_flag, which allows us to switch from regular output to attention probabilities for this layer. Recall that dropout takes care of overfitting by turning off neurons in a random (probabilistic) fashion. The dropout probabilities here are arbitrarily set at 0.2.**

> **The model is returned.**

Figure 7.15 shows a diagram of our model. The model is summarized as follows:

Layer (type)	Output Shape	Param #
embedding_1 (Embedding)	(None, 100, 100)	100000
attention_lstm (AttentionLSTM	(None, 100, 100)	100400
dense_1 (Dense)	(None, 100, 1)	101

Notice that we feed the LSTM three-dimensional data (as required for LSTMs): (batch size, 100,100) means 100 words with embedding size 100.

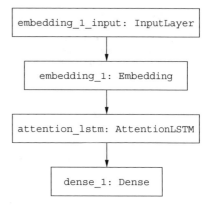

Figure 7.15 The `AttentionLSTM` model. Embeddings feed into an `AttentionLSTM` layer, ending in a `Dense` layer.

Listing 7.13 `AttentionLSTM`: model deployment

> **After data preparation, we create two models: one for training and one for testing. This is the first model.**

```
x_train,y_train,x_test,y_test, RevWordIndex,num_classes, TEST = createData()

maxlen=max([max([len(x) for x in x_train]),max([len(x) for x in x_test])])
input_dim=100 # words
timesteps=10
batch_size = 32

model1=createModel(attention_flag=False,return_sequences=False,
➥timesteps=timesteps,input_dim=input_dim,maxlen=maxlen,
➥num_classes=num_classes)

model1.fit(x_train,y_train,
          batch_size=batch_size,
          epochs=5
          )
model1.save_weights("m1.weights.h5")
score = model1.evaluate(x_test, y_test, batch_size=batch_size, verbose=1)
print('Test loss:', score[0])
print('Test accuracy:', score[1])

model2=createModel(attention_flag=True, return_sequences=True,
➥timesteps=timesteps, input_dim=input_dim,maxlen=maxlen,
➥num_classes=num_classes)

model2.load_weights("m1.weights.h5")

TEST_DATA=... # a test document from x_test
attention=getLayerActivation(
➥model2, TEST_DATA,layerName='attention_lstm')[0]
discrete_attention=[]
for window in attention:
        normalized_window=window/sum(window)
        discrete_window=discretize_attention(normalized_window)
        discrete_attention.append(discrete_window)
...
```

> **Fit the model to the training data.**

> **After training, we save the weights. They will be used by the second model.**

> **Evaluate the first model on test data.**

> **Model 1 weights are loaded into model 2.**

The attention probabilities are retrieved from model 2 for a given test document. These probabilities are returned per timestep and become normalized before being discretized. Finally, they are fed to the word cloud visualization procedure.

Create the second model. It uses the weights from the first model and outputs attention probabilities. Notice that we set return_sequences to True. This means we obtain the hidden state output for every timestep, which, in our case, consists of attention probabilities. With an embedding as input, we do not have explicit timesteps, but the data is three-dimensional, as required: (batch size, number of words, dimension of embedding).

Figure 7.16 illustrates the two-model process.

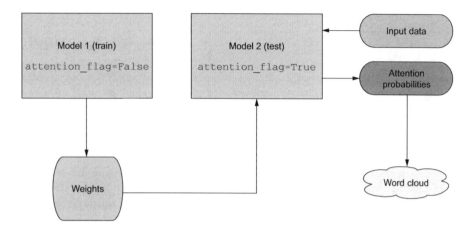

Figure 7.16 **Two-model process for LSTM attention. Model 1 (training) creates weights used by model 2 (testing).**

7.5 *Experiments*

Let's compare our two systems for the scenarios we defined (repeated here and in figure 7.17).

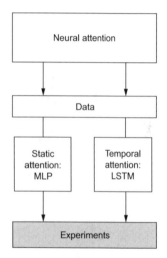

Figure 7.17 **Comparing systems for neural attention**

Scenario: Attention for explanations

You are supporting analysts by processing large amounts of textual data. Specifically, these analysts would like to have topic and sentiment classifiers that assign topics and sentiment labels to raw texts. The analysts would like to understand why their classifier assigns a certain topic or sentiment label to a text: which words were largely responsible for the assigned label? Knowing these words will enable them to understand the outcomes of the topic classifier and explain classifier results to users.

Scenario: Attention for handling messy data

You are building a document classifier, but your data is messy. Many documents in your dataset contain irrelevant words that do not seem to correlate with the intended document topics and sentiment labels. This may hamper the performance of your classifier. Can attention mechanisms diminish the need for elaborate data cleanup or term-selection procedures by demoting (paying less attention to) noisy words and promoting (paying more attention to) the really important words? In other words, can attention save you some data cleanup work?

7.5.1 *MLP*

We repeat here the test document we reconstructed earlier from the Reuters dataset:

```
of said and a mln 3 for vs dlrs it reuter 1 pct on is that its cts by year
be with will was u net as 4 but this are bank were 8 oil inc also tonnes
after rate 15 group exchange dollar we week note expected all rise meeting
18 only sale since wheat federal high term figures surplus annual likely
sell gold canadian opec dealers low news cents according way 49 signed
november financing 64 trust adding bank's weather review efforts mines
accounts commodities bureau baldrige pension managing expensive lifting
supplied argue
```

Let's apply the MLP for the purposes of our first scenario: interpretable document labeling. Our MLP model produces the attention cloud in figure 7.18 for this document when we filter out stopwords.

**Figure 7.18   A word cloud with stopwords removed. Words like *dlrs* (dollars),
bank, and *pct* (percent) appear to draw a lot of attention by the network.
Curiously, the word *also* draws attention as well.**

The direct interpretability of these visualizations provides an answer to the question raised in the first scenario: "Which words were largely responsible for the assigned label?"

Now, let's look at our second scenario, which is all about handling messy words in the data. What happens when we do not filter out stopwords? What if stopwords contribute to accuracy by enhancing the discrimination between documents with different labels?

Here are accuracy reports for the last four iterations of two runs of our MLP model
(20 iterations). This report has stopwords removed:

```
...
Epoch 17/20
8083/8083 [==============================] - 2s
➡- loss: 0.4729 - acc: 0.8653 - val_loss: 1.4041 - val_acc: 0.7241
Epoch 18/20
8083/8083 [==============================] - 2s
➡- loss: 0.4504 - acc: 0.8703 - val_loss: 1.4249 - val_acc: 0.7152
Epoch 19/20
8083/8083 [==============================] - 2s
➡- loss: 0.4248 - acc: 0.8750 - val_loss: 1.4427
➡- val_acc: 0.7253
Epoch 20/20
8083/8083 [==============================] - 2s
➡- loss: 0.4063 - acc: 0.8802 - val_loss: 1.4829 - val_acc: 0.7186
2080/2246 [=========================>...]
➡- ETA: 0s('Test loss:', 1.3930903858938921)
('Test accuracy:', 0.7248441674087266)
```

And this report is with stopwords kept in place:

```
...
Epoch 17/20
8083/8083 [==============================] - 2s
➡- loss: 0.4734 - acc: 0.8655 - val_loss: 1.3654 - val_acc: 0.7308
Epoch 18/20
8083/8083 [==============================] - 2s
➡- loss: 0.4488 - acc: 0.8741 - val_loss: 1.4007 - val_acc: 0.7353
Epoch 19/20
8083/8083 [==============================] - 2s
➡- loss: 0.4255 - acc: 0.8768 - val_loss: 1.4053 - val_acc: 0.7341
Epoch 20/20
8083/8083 [==============================] - 2s
➡- loss: 0.4023 - acc: 0.8816 - val_loss: 1.4546 - val_acc: 0.7286
1952/2246 [=========================>....]
➡- ETA: 0s('Test loss:', 1.4121399647618444)
('Test accuracy:', 0.7333036509349955)
```

These results indicate that eliminating stopwords from the bag-of-words representations of the Reuters documents downgrades accuracy a bit. Although we would need
more systematic results, this means the current attention mechanism can handle noisy
input by itself, which answers the question in the second scenario: "Can attention
mechanisms diminish the need for elaborate data cleanup or term-selection procedures by demoting noisy words and promoting the really important words?"

The word cloud produced when removing the stopwords is shown in figure 7.19,
and the word cloud produced when keeping the stopwords (20 iterations) is shown in
figure 7.20. If stopwords prove to enhance model accuracy, it makes perfect sense to
eliminate them only from the attention visualizations and use them under the hood
when we train and test our models.

Figure 7.19 Attention word cloud: no stopwords. The results look quite interpretable.

Figure 7.20 Attention word cloud: stopwords kept. We recognize the important words like *dlrs*, *inc*, *pct*, and *bank*, but they are surpassed by stopwords like *it*, *be*, and *as*.

Exercise

Investigate the effect on accuracy of removing or keeping stopwords and frequency-based filtering the Keras data (using the information implicit in the integer encoding, as discussed).

7.5.2   *LSTM*

Next, let's go through the two scenarios with the attention-equipped LSTM. For the following test document

```
the production is colossal lush breathtaking to view but the rest the
ridiculous romance Julie looking befuddled Hudson already dead the mistimed
comedy and the astoundingly boring songs deaden this spectacular film into
being irritating LILI is like a twee 1940s mega musical with some vulgar
bits to spice it up
```

our LSTM model derives the attention cloud shown in figure 7.21 when stopwords are deleted. Keeping stopwords in the document produces figure 7.22.

Figure 7.21   Attention word cloud produced by LSTM with attention gates: stopwords removed

Figure 7.22   Attention word cloud produced by LSTM with attention gates: stopwords kept. As with MLP, we see the relative importance of the previously emphasized words, but other words were also found to be important.

Now that we have implemented a temporal form of attention, the road is open to further analysis. For instance, long documents can be chopped up into consecutive paragraphs, and our `AttentionLSTM` may be able to capture, at a later stage, long-range attention dependencies by memorizing attention early in the document. In such circumstances, a stateful `AttentionLSTM` can be applied to this data, processing batch by batch and continuing the processing of the nth member of batch b_t with the nth member of batch b_{t+1}. The only thing we need to specify is that our `AttentionLSTM` should be stateful: we do so by setting the Keras `LSTM` flag `stateful=True`. See Remy 2016 for a very clear discussion of preparing the data for such a setup.

The bottom line is that we have implemented simple forms of attention in two basic architectures of deep learning: a static MLP and a temporal LSTM. Depending on the application at hand and whether temporal information plays a role, you can choose which approach to use.

Exercise

Create a stateful version of `AttentionLSTM`, and apply it to temporal data consisting of segmented documents. Is the model capable of retaining attention for certain words at the beginning of the document?

NOTE Attention to input data is an initial step in interpreting the importance of certain parts of the data. Applying attention to higher levels of abstraction on the model may reflect more meaningful attention. But the question of how linguistic abstraction occurs in deep NLP models is still unresolved.

Summary

- You can easily add a simple static soft or global attention mechanism to an MLP model. Attention close to the input layer assigns weights to input elements like words.
- You can implement temporal soft or global attention for an LSTM by implementing proprietary Keras layers.
- You can visualize attention to words with techniques like word clouds.
- Eliminating stopwords may be a bad idea from a performance point of view. Noisy stopwords appear to be able to draw valuable attention from the network.

Multitask learning 8

This chapter covers
- Understanding deep multitask learning for NLP
- Implementing hard, soft, and mixed parameter sharing for multitask learning

In this chapter, we apply different multitask learning approaches to practical NLP problems. In particular, we apply multitask learning to three datasets:

- Two sentiment datasets consisting of consumer product reviews and restaurant reviews
- The Reuters topic dataset
- A part-of-speech and named-entity tagging dataset

8.1 Introduction to multitask learning

Multitask learning is concerned with learning several things at the same time (figure 8.1). An example is learning both part-of-speech tagging and sentiment analysis simultaneously or learning two topic taggers in one go. Why would that be a good idea? For quite some time, ample research has demonstrated that multitask learning improves performance on certain separate tasks. This gives rise to the following application scenario.

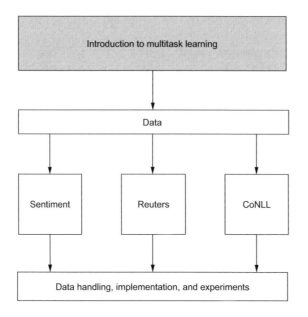

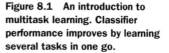

Figure 8.1 An introduction to multitask learning. Classifier performance improves by learning several tasks in one go.

Scenario: Multitask learning

You are training classifiers on a number of NLP tasks, but the performance is disappointing. It turns out your tasks can be decomposed into separate subtasks. Can multitask learning be applied here, and, if so, does performance improve on the separate tasks when they are learned together?

The main motivation for multitask learning is improving classifier performance. The reason multitask learning can boost performance is rooted in statistics. Every machine learning algorithm suffers from *inductive bias*: a set of implicit assumptions underlying its computations. An example of such an inductive bias is the maximization of distances between class boundaries carried out by support vector machines. Another example is the bias in nearest neighbor–based machine learning, where the assumption is that the neighbors (in the feature space) of a specific test data point are in the same class as the test data point. An inductive bias is not necessarily a bad thing; it incorporates a form of optimized specialization.

In multitask learning, learning two tasks simultaneously—with their own separate inductive biases—produces an overall model that aims for one inductive bias that optimizes for the two tasks at the same time. This approach may lead to better generalization properties of the separate tasks, meaning the resulting classifier can handle unseen data better. Often that classifier turns out to be a stronger classifier for both separate tasks.

A good question to ask is which tasks can be combined so that performance on the separate tasks benefits from learning them at the same time. Should these tasks be conceptually related? How should we define *task relatedness*? This is a topic beyond the scope of this book. We will focus our experiments on combining tasks that fit together reasonably well. For instance, named-entity recognition may benefit from part-of-speech tagging. Or learning to predict restaurant review sentiments may be beneficial for predicting consumer product sentiments. First, we discuss preprocessing and handling our data. After that, we go into the implementation of the three types of multitask learning.

8.2   Multitask learning

As mentioned, we will use the following datasets for multitask learning (figure 8.2):

- Two different datasets for consumer review–based sentiments (restaurant and electronic product reviews)
- The Reuters news dataset, which has 46 topics from the news domain (https://keras.io/api/datasets/reuters)
- Joint learning of Spanish part-of-speech tagging and named-entity tagging

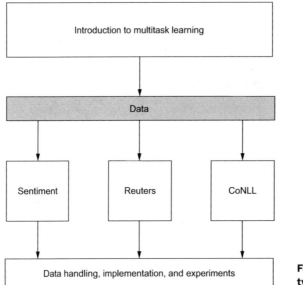

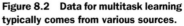

Figure 8.2   Data for multitask learning typically comes from various sources.

For the sentiment datasets, we will verify whether learning sentiments from two domains in parallel (restaurant and product reviews) improves the sentiments assignment to the separate domains. This is a topic called *domain transfer*: how to transfer knowledge from one domain to another during learning to supplement small datasets with additional data.

The Reuters news dataset entails a similar type of multitask learning. Given a number of topics assigned to documents, can we create sensible combinations of pairs of two topics (topics A+B, learned together with topics C+D) that, when learned together, benefit the modeling of the separate topics? And how can we turn such a pairwise discrimination scheme into a multiclass classifier?

Finally, the last task addresses multitask learning applied to shared data with different labelings. In this task, we create two classifiers: one focusing on part-of-speech tagging and the other on named-entity recognition. Do these tasks benefit from each other? Let's look at each of our datasets in turn.

8.3 *Multitask learning for consumer reviews: Yelp and Amazon*

We will use two sentiment datasets: sets of Yelp restaurant reviews and Amazon consumer reviews, labeled for positive or negative sentiment (figure 8.3). These datasets can be obtained from Kaggle (www.kaggle.com/rahulin05/sentiment-labelled-sentences-data-set).

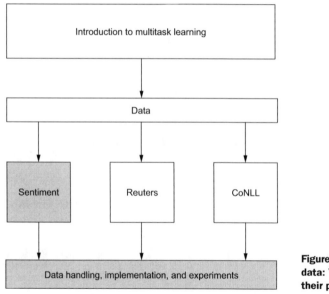

Figure 8.3 Our sentiment analysis data: Yelp and Amazon reviews and their processing

The Yelp dataset contains restaurant reviews with data like this:

```
The potatoes were like rubber and you could tell they had been made up
ahead of time being kept under a warmer.,0

The fries were great too.,1

Not tasty and the texture was just nasty.,0

Stopped by during the late May bank holiday off Rick Steve recommendation
and loved it.,1
```

The Amazon dataset contains reviews of consumer products:

```
o there is no way for me to plug it in here in the US unless I go by
a converter.,0

Good case, Excellent value.,1

Great for the jawbone.,1

Tied to charger for conversations lasting more than 45 minutes.MAJOR
PROBLEMS!!,0

The mic is great.,1

I have to jiggle the plug to get it to line up right to get decent volume.,0
```

8.3.1   *Data handling*

First, let's discuss how to load the sentiment data into our model. The overall schema
is shown in figure 8.4.

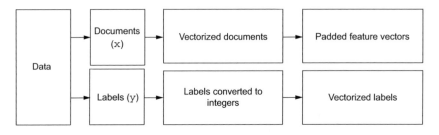

**Figure 8.4   Sentiment data processing schema. Labeled data (sentiment-labeled
documents) is turned into padded, vectorized documents and labels.**

The following procedure converts our data into vectors labeled with one-hot encoded
class labels.

Listing 8.1   Loading sentiment data

```
def loadData(train, test):

    global Lexicon

    with io.open(train,encoding = "ISO-8859-1") as f:        Read the training data
        trainD = f.readlines()                               into an array of lines.
    f.close()

    with io.open(test,encoding = "ISO-8859-1") as f:
        testD = f.readlines()                        Similar for the
    f.close()                                        test data

    all_text=[]
    for line in trainD:
```

```
        m=re.match("^(.+),[^\s]+$",line)
        if m:
            all_text.extend(m.group(1).split(" "))

    for line in testD:
        m=re.match("^(.+),[^\s]+$",line)
        if m:
            all_text.extend(m.group(1).split(" "))

    Lexicon=set(all_text)

    x_train=[]
    y_train=[]
    x_test=[]
    y_test=[]

    for line in trainD:
        m=re.match("^(.+),([^\s]+)$",line)
        if m:
            x_train.append(vectorizeString(m.group(1),Lexicon))
            y_train.append(processLabel(m.group(2)))

    for line in testD:
        m=re.match("^(.+),([^\s]+)$",line)
        if m:
            x_test.append(vectorizeString(m.group(1),Lexicon))
            y_test.append(processLabel(m.group(2)))

    return (np.array(x_train),np.array(y_train)),(np.array(x_test),
    ➥np.array(y_test))
```

Annotations (right margin):
- **Extend the all_text array with training data. We need this for a lexicon for vectorization of our data.**
- **Similar for the test data**
- **Build a lexicon.**
- **Vectorize the training data (see listing 8.2 for vectorizeString) using the lexicon.**
- **Similar for the test data**
- **Return the vectorized training and test data.**

The vectorizeString function converts a string into a vector of word indices using a lexicon. It is based on the familiar Keras one_hot function we have encountered before.

Listing 8.2 Vectorizing strings

```
def vectorizeString(s,lexicon):
    vocabSize = len(lexicon)
    result = one_hot(s,round(vocabSize*1.5))
    return result
```

The processLabel function creates a global dictionary for the class labels in the dataset.

Listing 8.3 Creating a class label dictionary

```
def processLabel(x):
    if x in ClassLexicon:
        return ClassLexicon[x]
    else:
        ClassLexicon[x]=len(ClassLexicon)
        return ClassLexicon[x]
```

The final processing of the data takes place after this: padding the feature vectors to a uniform length and converting the integer-based class labels to binary vectors with the Keras built-in `to_categorical` function:

```
x_train = pad_sequences(x_train, maxlen=max_length, padding='post')
x_test = pad_sequences(x_test, maxlen=max_length, padding='post')

y_train = keras.utils.to_categorical(y_train, num_classes)
y_test = keras.utils.to_categorical(y_test, num_classes)
```

Now that we have our data in place, let's establish a baseline result: what does a standard, single-task classifier produce for these datasets? Here is our single-task setup.

Listing 8.4 Single-task sentiment classifier

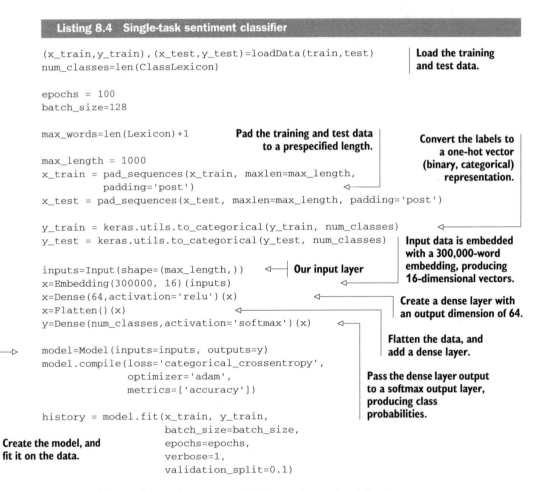

```
(x_train,y_train),(x_test,y_test)=loadData(train,test)     Load the training
num_classes=len(ClassLexicon)                              and test data.

epochs = 100
batch_size=128

max_words=len(Lexicon)+1        Pad the training and test data        Convert the labels to
                                    to a prespecified length.         a one-hot vector
max_length = 1000                                                     (binary, categorical)
x_train = pad_sequences(x_train, maxlen=max_length,                    representation.
        padding='post')
x_test = pad_sequences(x_test, maxlen=max_length, padding='post')

y_train = keras.utils.to_categorical(y_train, num_classes)
y_test = keras.utils.to_categorical(y_test, num_classes)     Input data is embedded
                                                             with a 300,000-word
inputs=Input(shape=(max_length,))      Our input layer       embedding, producing
x=Embedding(300000, 16)(inputs)                              16-dimensional vectors.
x=Dense(64,activation='relu')(x)
x=Flatten()(x)                                               Create a dense layer with
y=Dense(num_classes,activation='softmax')(x)                an output dimension of 64.

model=Model(inputs=inputs, outputs=y)                       Flatten the data, and
model.compile(loss='categorical_crossentropy',              add a dense layer.
            optimizer='adam',
            metrics=['accuracy'])                           Pass the dense layer output
                                                            to a softmax output layer,
                                                            producing class
history = model.fit(x_train, y_train,                       probabilities.
                    batch_size=batch_size,
Create the model, and       epochs=epochs,
fit it on the data.         verbose=1,
                            validation_split=0.1)
```

Running this model on Amazon and Yelp produces the following accuracy scores:

- Amazon: 76.5
- Yelp: 69.9

These single-task scores are our baseline. Does multitask learning improve on these scores? We will implement the three variants of multitask learning and find out.

8.3.2   Hard parameter sharing

In hard parameter sharing, we enforce task-specific subnetworks to explicitly share information, like a shared layer combining some of their hidden layer information (figure 8.5). Which layers are best to combine is an architectural decision that should be made based on experimentation: this effectively is a *hyperparameter optimization* problem. Separate tasks keep their task-specific input and output layers and meet in the middle by sharing intermediate layers or feeding into one shared layer together.

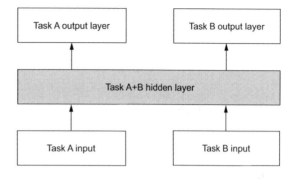

Figure 8.5   Hard parameter sharing. Two task subnetworks share information like a specific layer.

The following listing shows our implementation of hard parameter sharing. For a fair comparison with the single-task result presented earlier, we use exactly the same structure for the two subclassifiers.

Listing 8.5   Hard parameter sharing for sentiment data

```
ClassLexicon={}                                              ◁─┤ Process the data for task 1.
(x1_train,y1_train),(x1_test,y1_test)=loadData(train1,test1)
num_classes1=len(ClassLexicon)
x1_train = pad_sequences(x1_train, maxlen=max_length, padding='post')
y1_train = keras.utils.to_categorical(y1_train, num_classes1)
x1_test = pad_sequences(x1_test, maxlen=max_length, padding='post')
y1_test = keras.utils.to_categorical(y1_test, num_classes1)

ClassLexicon={}                                              ◁─┤ Process the data for task 2.
(x2_train,y2_train),(x2_test,y2_test)=loadData(train2,test2)
num_classes2=len(ClassLexicon)
x2_train = pad_sequences(x2_train, maxlen=max_length, padding='post')
y2_train = keras.utils.to_categorical(y2_train, num_classes2)
x2_test = pad_sequences(x2_test, maxlen=max_length, padding='post')
y2_test = keras.utils.to_categorical(y2_test, num_classes2)

epochs = 100
batch_size=128
max_words=len(Lexicon)+1
max_length = 1000                                 │ Define the
                                                  ◁─┤ first network.
inputsA=Input(shape=(max_length,))
x1=Embedding(300000, 16)(inputsA)
x1=Dense(64,activation='relu')(x1)
```

```
x1=Dense(32,activation='relu')(x1)
x1=Flatten()(x1)
                                            Define the
                                            second network.
inputsB=Input(shape=(max_length,))    ◄───
x2=Embedding(300000, 16)(inputsB)     Let both networks converge
x2=Dense(64,activation='relu')(x2)    on a shared layer, which is a       Define two output layers,
x2=Flatten()(x2)                      concatenation layer that            projecting the classes
                                      glues together the hidden           for both separate tasks.
merged = Concatenate()([x1, x2])  ◄── layers x1 and x2.                   This is where the two
                                                                          networks diverge again.
y1=Dense(num_classes1,activation='softmax')(merged)   ◄──┘
y2=Dense(num_classes2,activation='softmax')(merged)

model=Model(inputs=[inputsA, inputsB],outputs=[y1,y2])  ◄───  Define a model
                                                              with two input and
model.compile(loss='categorical_crossentropy',               two output arrays.
              optimizer='adam',
              metrics=['accuracy'])

history = model.fit([x1_train,x2_train], [y1_train,y2_train],
                    batch_size=batch_size,
                    epochs=epochs,
                    verbose=1,
                    validation_split=0.1)

score = model.evaluate([x1_test,x2_test], [y1_test,y2_test],
            batch_size=batch_size, verbose=1)

print(score)
```

RESULTS

First we repeat the single-task scores we obtained earlier:

- Amazon: 76.5
- Yelp: 69.9

Running the multitask classifier shows that only Yelp benefits from joint learning:

- Amazon: 64.5
- Yelp: 76.5

Sentiment	Single-task	Hard
Amazon	76.5	64.5
Yelp	69.9	76.5

Exercise

Experiment with different approaches to layer sharing. Can you combine other layers? Maybe even a few layers? What about other approaches than just concatenation, like multiplication, summing, or averaging? Keras offers different options; see https://keras.io/layers/merge.

8.3.3 Soft parameter sharing

The soft parameter approach to multitask learning consists of independent subnetworks that do not share any layers but instead are subjected to constraints that align their parameters (that is, weights) for specified layers (figure 8.6). The subnetworks adapt their weights so that the distance between the weights (as measured by some distance metric) is minimized.

We implement soft parameter sharing through a custom loss function. Remember that a loss function is a function that drives model training: during training, a model

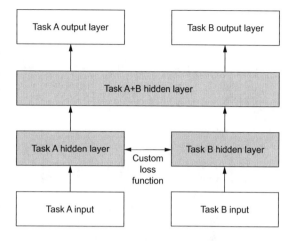

Figure 8.6 Soft parameter sharing. Two task subnetworks are jointly regulated through constraints that align their parameters (weights) for specified layers.

measures its error with such a function (for example, by comparing its predicted labels with the ground truth labels in the training data). Standard loss functions include accuracy or mean squared error, and they work on label predictions. Custom loss functions allow us to condition the loss during training on arbitrary information and not just on the mismatch between predicted and ground truth labels. This opens up possibilities for regularizing distances between weights across layers in the separate networks. The Keras pattern for writing a custom loss function is the following:

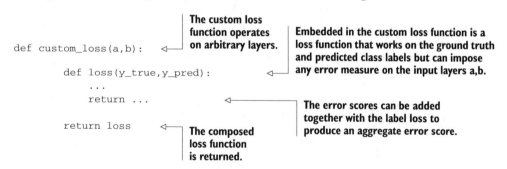

We instantiate this pattern for all implementations in this chapter as follows.

Listing 8.6 Custom loss function

```
def custom_loss(a,b):
        def loss(y_true,y_pred):
                e1=keras.losses.categorical_crossentropy(y_true,y_pred)
                e2=keras.losses.mean_squared_error(a,b)
                e3=keras.losses.cosine_proximity(a,b)
```

```
        e4=K.mean(K.square(a-b), axis=-1)
        return e1+e2+e3+e4
    return loss
```

In this custom loss function, we combine a bunch of (somewhat arbitrary) error measures. Their specific composition is open to experimentation, since no underlying theory is readily available.

> **Exercise**
>
> Experiment with other losses in your custom loss function. Can you find combinations that work better? Or can you maybe come up with a specific loss function (like a distance metric) yourself?

So, defining a custom loss function involves two major choices:

- The pair of layers it should operate on
- The composition of losses in the subordinate loss function embedded in the custom loss function

Our model is simple. Unlike in hard parameter sharing, we do not combine any layers from both tasks and transfer the regularization between the respective layers to the loss function; see listing 8.7.

> **NOTE**   As of 2020, Keras uses TensorFlow as its only backend. TensorFlow version 2 may cause an error like `SymbolicException: Inputs to eager execution function cannot be Keras symbolic tensors`. This error is also referred to in the official GitHub for TensorFlow (https://github.com/tensorflow/probability/issues/519). A solution that has been reported to work is to add the following line to your code after importing TensorFlow (as `tf`): `tf.compat.v1.disable_eager_execution()`. See the Stack Exchange discussion at http://mng.bz/o2Yv.

Listing 8.7   Soft parameter sharing for sentiment data

```
inputsA=Input(shape=(max_length,))
x1=Embedding(300000, 16)(inputsA)
x1=Dense(64,activation='relu')(x1)
x1=Flatten()(x1)

inputsB=Input(shape=(max_length,))
x2=Embedding(300000, 16)(inputsB)
x2=Dense(64,activation='relu')(x2)
x2=Flatten()(x2)

y1=Dense(num_classes1,activation='softmax')(x1)
y2=Dense(num_classes2,activation='softmax')(x2)
```

```
model=Model(inputs=[inputsA, inputsB],outputs=[y1,y2])

model.compile(loss=custom_loss(x1,x2),
              optimizer='adam',
              metrics=['accuracy'])
```

RESULTS

Here are our results on Amazon and Yelp:

- Amazon: 77.5
- Yelp: 75

which stack up to the previous results as follows.

Sentiment	Single-task	Hard	Soft
Amazon	76.5	64.5	77.5
Yelp	69.9	76.5	75

Soft parameter sharing boosts performance on Amazon and improves it on Yelp compared to the baseline (but not compared to hard parameter sharing).

8.3.4 Mixed parameter sharing

Mixed parameter sharing is just the combination of hard and soft parameter sharing. The subnetworks share one or more layers and adapt their internal parameters to each other (figure 8.7). In our experiments, we will limit the number of subnetworks to two for all three kinds of multitask learning.

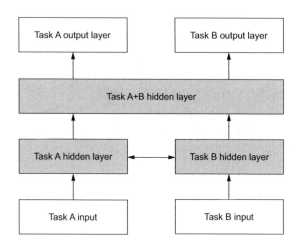

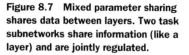

Figure 8.7 Mixed parameter sharing shares data between layers. Two task subnetworks share information (like a layer) and are jointly regulated.

For mixed parameter sharing, we simply combine hard and soft parameter sharing.

Listing 8.8   Mixed parameter sharing for sentiment data

```
(...)
merged = Concatenate()([x1, x2])

y1=Dense(num_classes1,activation='softmax')(merged)
y2=Dense(num_classes2,activation='softmax')(merged)

model=Model(inputs=[inputsA, inputsB],outputs=[y1,y2])

def custom_loss(a,b):
    def loss(y_true,y_pred):
        e1=keras.losses.categorical_crossentropy(y_true,y_pred)
        e2=keras.losses.mean_squared_error(a,b)
        e3=keras.losses.cosine_proximity(a,b)
        e4=K.mean(K.square(a-b), axis=-1)
        return e1+e2+e3+e4
    return loss

model.compile(loss=custom_loss(x1,x2),
              optimizer='adam',
              metrics=['accuracy'])
```

RESULTS

Mixed parameter sharing produces the following results:

- Amazon: 74
- Yelp: 69.5

It performs worse than soft parameter sharing and even the single-task classifiers.

Sentiment	Single-task	Hard	Soft	Mixed
Amazon	76.5	64.5	77.5	74
Yelp	69.9	76.5	75	69.5

8.4   *Multitask learning for Reuters topic classification*

The Reuters dataset is part of Keras's library of datasets (figure 8.8). Texts are encoded as integer-based vectors, with every integer representing a unique word (see chapter 7 for further details). Here is a list of all the topics in the Keras dataset (see the work of Steffen Bauer at https://github.com/keras-team/keras/issues/12072]:

```
ReutersTopics= ['cocoa','grain','veg-oil','earn','acq','wheat','copper',
    'housing','money-supply','coffee','sugar','trade','reserves','ship',
    'cotton','carcass','crude','nat-gas',   'cpi','money-fx','interest',
    'gnp','meal-feed','alum','oilseed','gold','tin','strategic-metal',
    'livestock','retail','ipi','iron-steel','rubber','heat','jobs','lei',
    'bop','zinc','orange','pet-chem','dlr','gas','silver','wpi','hog',
    'lead']
```

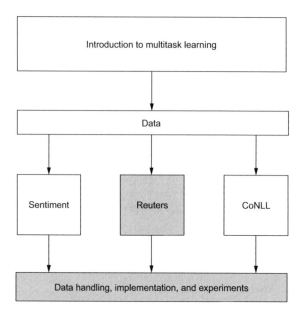

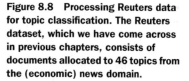

Figure 8.8 Processing Reuters data for topic classification. The Reuters dataset, which we have come across in previous chapters, consists of documents allocated to 46 topics from the (economic) news domain.

8.4.1   Data handling

The experiments we will carry out follow the same data organization. For two pairs of topics, we will investigate which other pair of two topics can be learned as a separate, additional task in such a way that both tasks benefit from each other. So, we will create pairs of topics (each pair is a task) and seek out which combination of two such pairs (covering in total four topics) benefits the separate tasks. This is an instance of *one-versus-one classification*: for N classes, train $N(N–1) / 2$ binary classifiers, learning the distinction between two classes. During testing, for each test document, compute the most-often-assigned class label, and assign that label to the document.

For instance, suppose you have a three-class problem with data labeled A, B, or C. You train three classifiers ($3 \times 2 / 2$) as follows:

- *Classifier 1*—A versus {B,C}: the data for B and C is lumped together in one composite class {B,C}.
- *Classifier 2*—B versus {A,C}: the data for A and C is lumped together in one composite class {A,C}.
- *Classifier 3*—C versus {A,B}: the data for A and B is lumped together in one composite class {A,B}.

If a given document is labeled {B,C} by classifier 1, {A,C} by classifier 2, and C by classifier 3, there are three votes for C (versus one vote each for A and B), so we assign label C to the document.

The total number of pairwise combinations of 46 topics is somewhat overwhelming: 1,035 ($46 \times 45 / 2$). For each of these pairs, we generate training and test datasets.

Some of these pairs may have training datasets that are too small, so we set a lower bound of 300 items per training.

The code in listing 8.9 generates all distinct pairs of topics based on their numerical identifier (which is used in the Keras dataset as a label) and removes datasets with fewer than 300 items. Following the topic combination, documents and labels are processed as for the sentiment data. The schema in figure 8.9 illustrates the process.

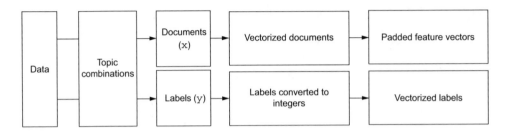

Figure 8.9   Reuters data processing schema

Listing 8.9   Generating topic combinations

```
Stored={}
for x in range(45):
    for y in range(45):
        if x==y:
            continue
        if (x,y) not in Stored and (y,x) not in Stored:
            Stored[(x,y)]=1
```

Additionally, we define a global `ClassLexicon` dictionary to convert topic labels to binary values (recall that we have only two tasks):

```
global ClassLexicon
ClassLexicon={}
```

It is used in the following listing.

Listing 8.10   Looking up class labels

```
def processLabel(x):
    if x in ClassLexicon:
        return ClassLexicon[x]
    else:
        ClassLexicon[x]=len(ClassLexicon)
        return ClassLexicon[x]
```

Next, for every combination of two pairs of topics, we build up the training and test datasets as follows.

Listing 8.11   Creating Reuters training and test datasets

```
Tried={}
for (topic1,topic2) in Stored:
    for (topic3,topic4) in Stored:
        if (topic1,topic2)==(topic3,topic4):
            continue
        if topic1 in (topic3,topic4) or topic2 in (topic3,topic4):
            continue
        if (topic1,topic2) in Tried or (topic3,topic4) in Tried:
            continue
        Tried[(topic1,topic2)]=1
        Tried[(topic3,topic4)]=1

        ClassLexicon={}
        ClassLexicon[topic1]=ClassLexicon[topic2]=0
        ClassLexicon[topic3]=ClassLexicon[topic4]=1


        indices_train1=[i for i in range(len(y_train)) if
        ➡y_train[i] in [topic1,topic2]]
        indices_test1=[i for i in range(len(y_test)) if
        ➡y_test[i] in [topic1,topic2]]
        indices_train2=[i for i in range(len(y_train)) if
        ➡y_train[i] in [topic3,topic4]]
        indices_test2=[i for i in range(len(y_test)) if
        ➡y_test[i] in [topic3,topic4]]

        x1_train=np.array([x_train[i] for i in indices_train1])
        y1_train=np.array([processLabel(y_train[i]) for i in indices_train1])

        ClassLexicon={}

        x1_test=np.array([x_test[i] for i in indices_test1])
        y1_test=np.array([processLabel(y_test[i]) for i in indices_test1])

        ClassLexicon={}

        x2_train=np.array([x_train[i] for i in indices_train2])
        y2_train=np.array([processLabel(y_train[i]) for i in indices_train2])

        ClassLexicon={}

        x2_test=np.array([x_test[i] for i in indices_test2])
        y2_test=np.array([processLabel(y_test[i]) for i in indices_test2])

        num_classes1=2
        num_classes2=2
        max_length=1000

        x1_train = pad_sequences(x1_train, maxlen=max_length,
        ➡padding='post')
        y1_train = keras.utils.to_categorical(y1_train, num_classes1)
        x1_test = pad_sequences(x1_test, maxlen=max_length, padding='post')
        y1_test = keras.utils.to_categorical(y1_test, num_classes1)
```

Define an auxiliary dictionary to keep track of topic combinations.

Check for identical topic pairs.

Similarly, exclude partially overlapping topic pairs.

Pick up the indices in the training data labels that conform with the selected topic pairs.

Create a dictionary for class labels. Notice that we relabel the selected topic labels as binary labels, creating two binary tasks.

Repeat the process for the second task, generating training and test data.

Pad the training and test data for both tasks, and convert labels to binary vectors.

```
x2_train = pad_sequences(x2_train, maxlen=max_length, padding='post')
y2_train = keras.utils.to_categorical(y2_train, num_classes2)
x2_test = pad_sequences(x2_test, maxlen=max_length, padding='post')
y2_test = keras.utils.to_categorical(y2_test, num_classes2)

if len(x1_train)<300 or len(x2_train)<300:      ◁─┐  Datasets smaller than
    continue                                       │  300 items are discarded.

min_train=min(len(x1_train),len(x2_train))      ◁─┐  Create even-sized
x1_train=x1_train[:min_train]                      │  datasets for both tasks.
x2_train=x2_train[:min_train]
y1_train=y1_train[:min_train]
y2_train=y2_train[:min_train]

min_test=min(len(x1_test),len(x2_test))
x1_test=x1_test[:min_test]
x2_test=x2_test[:min_test]
y1_test=y1_test[:min_test]
y2_test=y2_test[:min_test]
```

8.4.2   Hard parameter sharing

Here is how we implement hard parameter sharing for this dataset. For every pair of
two topics, we find another pair of two topics, and we learn those two two-class problems together. The model structure is exactly the same as we used for the sentiment
data.

Listing 8.12   Reuters hard parameter sharing

```
inputsA=Input(shape=(max_length,))          ◁─┐  The network for the first topic
x1=Embedding(300000, 16)(inputsA)              │  combination (two topics)
x1=Dense(64,activation='relu')(x1)
x1=Flatten()(x1)

inputsB=Input(shape=(max_length,))          ◁─┐  The network for the second
x2=Embedding(300000, 16)(inputsB)              │  topic combination (two topics)
x2=Dense(64,activation='relu')(x2)
x2=Flatten()(x2)

merged = Concatenate()([x1, x2])            ◁─┤  Combine two layers.

                                                  Train the model on the
y1=Dense(num_classes1,activation='softmax')(merged)    current data partitions
y2=Dense(num_classes2,activation='softmax')(merged)   (notice that we are still in
                                                      the loop of the previous
model=Model(inputs=[inputsA, inputsB],outputs=[y1,y2])  code fragment from
                                                            listing 8.11).
history = model.fit([x1_train,x2_train], [y1_train,y2_train],    ◁─────┘
                    batch_size=batch_size,
                    epochs=epochs,
                    verbose=0,
                    validation_split=0.1)
                                                      Evaluate
score = model.evaluate([x1_test,x2_test], [y1_test,y2_test],  ◁─┘  the model.
                    batch_size=batch_size, verbose=1)
```

RESULTS

Hard parameter sharing yields the following results:

```
grain+sugar improved with cocoa+trade: 0.160000 => 0.200000
grain+nat-gas improved with cocoa+crude: 0.089286 => 0.107143
grain+gnp improved with cocoa+interest: 0.022222 => 0.044444
wheat+trade improved with acq+reserves: 0.953488 => 0.976744
trade+nat-gas improved with sugar+crude: 0.102041 => 0.142857
trade+gnp improved with sugar+interest: 0.056604 => 0.113208
nat-gas+interest improved with crude+gnp: 0.068182 => 0.159091
money-fx+gnp improved with cpi+interest: 0.901961 => 0.921569
```

We see some significant improvements here, even for the low-scoring topics. How does soft parameter sharing fare?

8.4.3 Soft parameter sharing

The soft parameter implementation for Reuters is as follows.

Listing 8.13   Reuters soft parameter sharing

```
inputsA=Input(shape=(max_length,))
x1=Embedding(300000, 16)(inputsA)
x1=Dense(64,activation='relu')(x1)
x1=Flatten()(x1)

inputsB=Input(shape=(max_length,))
x2=Embedding(300000, 16)(inputsB)
x2=Dense(64,activation='relu')(x2)
x2=Flatten()(x2)

y1=Dense(num_classes1,activation='softmax')(x1)
y2=Dense(num_classes2,activation='softmax')(x2)

model=Model(inputs=[inputsA, inputsB],outputs=[y1,y2])

def custom_loss(a,b):
    def loss(y_true,y_pred):
        e1=keras.losses.categorical_crossentropy(y_true,y_pred)
        e2=keras.losses.mean_squared_error(a,b)
        e3=keras.losses.cosine_proximity(a,b)
        e4=K.mean(K.square(a-b), axis=-1)
        return e1+e2+e3+e4
    return loss

model.compile(loss=custom_loss(x1,x2),
              optimizer='adam',
              metrics=['accuracy'])
```

RESULTS

Soft parameter sharing for Reuters yields the following results:

```
veg-oil+earn improved with cocoa+grain: 0.964912 => 0.982456
earn+cpi improved with veg-oil+interest: 0.958333 => 0.979167
wheat+trade improved with acq+reserves: 0.953488 => 0.976744
```

```
coffee+money-fx improved with money-supply+interest: 0.948276 => 0.965517
trade+reserves improved with sugar+ship: 0.900000 => 0.925000
trade+cpi improved with sugar+money-fx: 0.910714 => 0.928571
ship+money-fx improved with reserves+interest: 0.931818 => 0.954545
nat-gas+money-fx improved with crude+interest: 0.952381 => 0.968254
nat-gas+interest improved with crude+gnp: 0.068182 => 0.090909
money-fx+gnp improved with cpi+interest: 0.901961 => 0.960784
interest+meal-feed improved with money-fx+hog: 0.902439 => 0.926829
```

Interestingly, we see an increase in high accuracy gains compared to hard parameter sharing. However, mixed parameter sharing does not demonstrate that kind of improvement.

8.4.4 *Mixed parameter sharing*

As before, we combine the two parameter-sharing modes.

Listing 8.14   Reuters mixed parameter sharing

```
inputsA=Input(shape=(max_length,))
x1=Embedding(300000, 16)(inputsA)
x1=Dense(64,activation='relu')(x1)
x1=Flatten()(x1) #DA for LSTM

inputsB=Input(shape=(max_length,))
x2=Embedding(300000, 16)(inputsB)
x2=Dense(64,activation='relu')(x2)
x2=Flatten()(x2)

merged = Concatenate()([x1, x2])

y1=Dense(num_classes1,activation='softmax')(merged)
y2=Dense(num_classes2,activation='softmax')(merged)

model=Model(inputs=[inputsA, inputsB],outputs=[y1,y2])

def custom_loss(a,b):
    def loss(y_true,y_pred):
        e1=keras.losses.categorical_crossentropy(y_true,y_pred)
        e2=keras.losses.mean_squared_error(a,b)
        e3=keras.losses.cosine_proximity(a,b)
        e4=K.mean(K.square(a-b), axis=-1)
        return e1+e2+e3+e4
    return loss

model.compile(loss=custom_loss(x1,x2),
          optimizer='adam',
          metrics=['accuracy'])
```

RESULTS

This approach yields the following results:

```
grain+nat-gas improved with cocoa+crude: 0.089286 => 0.107143
wheat+trade improved with acq+reserves: 0.953488 => 0.976744
trade+reserves improved with sugar+ship: 0.900000 => 0.925000
```

```
trade+cpi improved with sugar+money-fx: 0.910714 => 0.928571
trade+gnp improved with sugar+interest: 0.056604 => 0.075472
ship+money-fx improved with reserves+interest: 0.931818 => 0.954545
nat-gas+interest improved with crude+gnp: 0.068182 => 0.136364
money-fx+gnp improved with cpi+interest: 0.901961 => 0.941176
```

In conclusion, the three approaches produce overlapping but distinct results. A sensible direction for reaping the benefits of these different approaches would be to create an ensemble classifier consisting of the three types of *one-versus-all* parameter sharing.

> **Exercise**
> Create an ensemble classifier from this multitask classifier along the lines just sketched. How does it compare to a standard multiclass classifier for this data?

8.5   Multitask learning for part-of-speech tagging and named-entity recognition

The Computational Natural Language Learning (CoNLL) conference publishes a shared task every year (figure 8.10). In 2002, a task was presented addressing joint part-of-speech (POS) tagging and named-entity recognition (NER) tagging for Dutch and Spanish (http://mng.bz/nNO4). The named-entity tagging task consists of recognizing named entities ranging from isolated words to phrases. For instance, *Melbourne* is a one-word named entity, but *The United States of America* is a phrasal named entity. The CoNLL task uses a so-called *I-O-B* schema for this task. This schema tags words as being a named entity (*B*), being part of (inside) a named entity (*I*), or being outside of (not part of) a named entity (*O*).

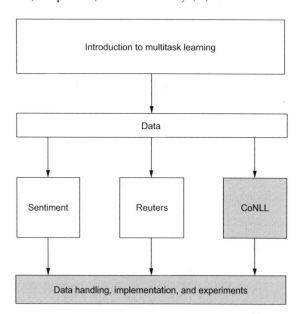

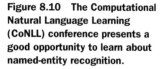

Figure 8.10   The Computational Natural Language Learning (CoNLL) conference presents a good opportunity to learn about named-entity recognition.

Here is a typical fragment of the Spanish CoNLL data:

```
El DA O
Abogado NC B-PER
General AQ I-PER
del SP I-PER
Estado NC I-PER
, Fc O
Daryl VMI B-PER
Williams NC I-PER
, Fc O
subrayó VMI O
hoy RG O
```

For each word in the string "El Abogado General del Estado, Daryl Williams, subrayó hoy (…)" ("State Attorney General Daryl Williams stressed today (…)"), we see a part of speech and an assigned I-O-B tag. The tags have been subclassed for people or job titles (PER), organizations (ORG), and locations (LOC):

```
Tribunal NC B-ORG
Supremo AQ I-ORG
del SP O
estado NC O
de SP O
Victoria NC B-LOC
```

This example uses the string "Tribunal Supremo del estado de Victoria" ("The supreme court of the state of Virginia").

8.5.1 *Data handling*

We handle the CoNLL data according to the schema shown in figure 8.11. First we define two auxiliary lexicon lookup procedures: one for the features (words) and one for the class labels (parts of speech and I-O-B tags) that will be used in our data processing code.

Listing 8.15 Lexicon lookup

```
global ClassLex
ClassLex={}

def lookup(feat):
    if feat not in Lex:
        Lex[feat]=len(Lex)
    return Lex[feat]

def class_lookup(feat):
    if feat not in ClassLex:
        ClassLex[feat]=len(ClassLex)
    return ClassLex[feat]
```

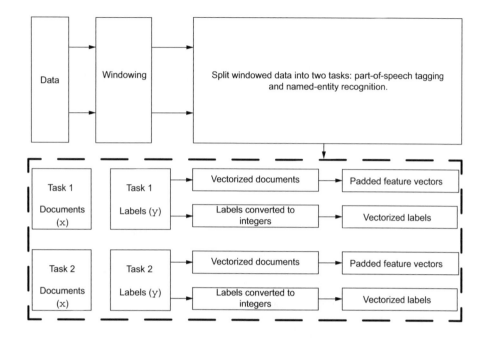

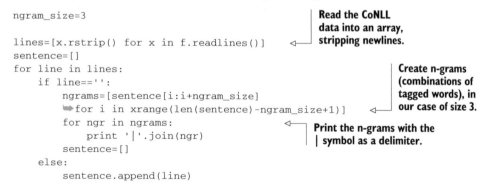

Figure 8.11   CoNLL data processing schema. Data is windowed and split for two tasks: part-of-speech tagging and named-entity recognition.

We preprocess the original format of the CoNLL data (one word per line, plus tags) into a windowed representation. We use windows of three words—the idea is to predict the tags for the third word based on the preceding two words:

```
ngram_size=3
                                                    Read the CoNLL
                                                    data into an array,
lines=[x.rstrip() for x in f.readlines()]    ⟵     stripping newlines.
sentence=[]
for line in lines:                                      Create n-grams
    if line=='':                                        (combinations of
        ngrams=[sentence[i:i+ngram_size]                tagged words), in
        ➡for i in xrange(len(sentence)-ngram_size+1)]  ⟵  our case of size 3.
        for ngr in ngrams:                         ⟵
            print '|'.join(ngr)             Print the n-grams with the
        sentence=[]                         | symbol as a delimiter.
    else:
        sentence.append(line)
```

This produces output like the following:

```
la DA O|necesidad NC O|de SP O
necesidad NC O|de SP O|tomar VMN O
de SP O|tomar VMN O|medidas NC O
tomar VMN O|medidas NC O|para SP O
medidas NC O|para SP O|proteger VMN O
para SP O|proteger VMN O|al SP O
```

The `load_conll` function reads from a training and test data file in this format and converts the data to vector format using the two lookup procedures from listing 8.14.

Listing 8.16 Generating CoNLL training and test data

```python
def load_conll(train, test):
    x1_train=[]
    y1_train=[]
    x1_test=[]
    y1_test=[]
    x2_train=[]
    y2_train=[]
    x2_test=[]
    y2_test=[]

    tr=open(train,"r")
    for line in tr:
        if line.rstrip()=='':
            continue
        features=line.rstrip().split("|")
        target=features.pop().split(" ")
        target_word=target[0]
        target_y1=target[1]
        target_y2=target[2]

        y1_train.append(class_lookup(target_y1))
        y2_train.append(class_lookup(target_y2))

        l=lookup(target_word)
        x1=[l]
        x2=[l]
        for feature in features:
            if feature=='':
                continue
            feature_split=feature.split(" ")
            x1.append(lookup(feature_split[0]))
            x1.append(lookup(feature_split[1]))
            x2.append(lookup(feature_split[0]))
            x2.append(lookup(feature_split[2]))
        x1_train.append(x1)
        x2_train.append(x2)
    tr.close()

    te=open(test,"r")
    for line in te:
        if line.rstrip()=='':
            continue
        features=line.rstrip().split("|")
        target=features.pop().split(" ")
        target_word=target[0]
        target_y1=target[1]
        target_y2=target[2]

        y1_test.append(class_lookup(target_y1))
        y2_test.append(class_lookup(target_y2))

        l=lookup(target_word)
        x1=[l]
```

Read the windowed CoNLL training data, and determine the targets (these are the two tags associated with the final word in the n-gram).

Here, we allocate words and parts of speech to the first task, and words and named-entity tags to the second task.

Similarly, process the test data.

```
    x2=[1]

    for feature in features:
        if feature=='':
            continue
        feature_split=feature.split(" ")
        x1.append(lookup(feature_split[0]))
        x1.append(lookup(feature_split[1]))
        x2.append(lookup(feature_split[0]))
        x2.append(lookup(feature_split[2]))
    x1_test.append(x1)
    x2_test.append(x2)
te.close()
```

Return all the data.

```
return (np.array(x1_train), np.array(y1_train)),(np.array(x2_train),
➥np.array(y2_train)),(np.array(x1_test),np.array(y1_test)),
➥(np.array(x2_test),np.array(y2_test))
```
⟵

The next listing shows how the `load_conll` function is used prior to generating class vector representations.

Listing 8.17 Generating class vectors

```
(x1_train, y1_train), (x2_train, y2_train), (x1_test,y1_test),
➥(x2_test, y2_test)= load_conll(train, test)

num_classes1=np.max(np.concatenate((y1_train,y1_test),axis=None))+1
num_classes2=np.max(np.concatenate((y2_train,y2_test),axis=None))+1

y1_train = keras.utils.to_categorical(y1_train, num_classes1)
y1_test = keras.utils.to_categorical(y1_test, num_classes1)
y2_train = keras.utils.to_categorical(y2_train, num_classes2)
y2_test = keras.utils.to_categorical(y2_test, num_classes2)
```

Next we implement two single-task models for this data. We start by defining a number of constants.

Listing 8.18 Defining constants

```
num_words=len(Lex)
embedding_vector_length = 32
max_length=5
batch_size=128
epochs=50
```

The single-task implementation for POS tagging is as follows.

Listing 8.19 Single-task CoNLL data analysis

```
inputs=Input(shape=(max_length,))
```
⟵ **Define an input layer.**

```
x=Embedding(num_words, embedding_vector_length)(inputs)
```
⟵

The input is embedded into an embedding layer with output dimension 32.

```
x=Conv1D(filters=32, kernel_size=3, padding='same', activation='relu')(x)
```
To safeguard the linear ordered structure of the data, we apply a convolution layer.

```
x=MaxPooling1D(pool_size=2)(x)
```
Apply MaxPooling to the convolutional layer output.

```
x=LSTM(100)(x)
```

```
y=Dense(num_classes1, activation='softmax')(x)
```
The output is fed into an LSTM layer with output dimension 100.

```
model=Model(inputs=inputsA,outputs=y)
model.compile(loss='categorical_crossentropy',
              optimizer='adam',
              metrics=['categorical_accuracy'])
history = model.fit(x_train, y_train,
                    batch_size=batch_size,
                    epochs=epochs,
                    verbose=1,
                    validation_split=0.1)

score = model.evaluate(x_test, y_test,
                       batch_size=batch_size, verbose=1)
```
A dense output layer produces class probabilities with softmax.

The model is evaluated on test data.

For NER, we have the exact same setup. Using this model, our baseline result for single-task learning is as follows:

- POS: 0.917472
- NER: 0.932256

8.5.2 *Hard parameter sharing*

Here is how we implement hard parameter sharing for CoNLL. We basically use the same subnetworks and, like before, let them converge on a shared layer.

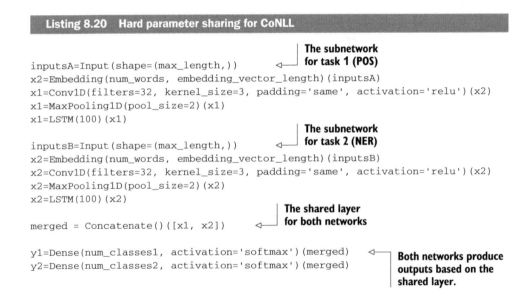

Listing 8.20 Hard parameter sharing for CoNLL

```
inputsA=Input(shape=(max_length,))
x2=Embedding(num_words, embedding_vector_length)(inputsA)
x1=Conv1D(filters=32, kernel_size=3, padding='same', activation='relu')(x2)
x1=MaxPooling1D(pool_size=2)(x1)
x1=LSTM(100)(x1)

inputsB=Input(shape=(max_length,))
x2=Embedding(num_words, embedding_vector_length)(inputsB)
x2=Conv1D(filters=32, kernel_size=3, padding='same', activation='relu')(x2)
x2=MaxPooling1D(pool_size=2)(x2)
x2=LSTM(100)(x2)

merged = Concatenate()([x1, x2])

y1=Dense(num_classes1, activation='softmax')(merged)
y2=Dense(num_classes2, activation='softmax')(merged)
```
The subnetwork for task 1 (POS)

The subnetwork for task 2 (NER)

The shared layer for both networks

Both networks produce outputs based on the shared layer.

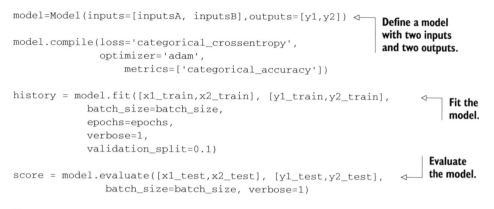

```
model=Model(inputs=[inputsA, inputsB],outputs=[y1,y2])
```
⟵ **Define a model with two inputs and two outputs.**

```
model.compile(loss='categorical_crossentropy',
              optimizer='adam',
                metrics=['categorical_accuracy'])
```

```
history = model.fit([x1_train,x2_train], [y1_train,y2_train],
            batch_size=batch_size,
            epochs=epochs,
            verbose=1,
            validation_split=0.1)
```
⟵ **Fit the model.**

```
score = model.evaluate([x1_test,x2_test], [y1_test,y2_test],
            batch_size=batch_size, verbose=1)
```
⟵ **Evaluate the model.**

RESULTS

Again, our baseline result for single-task learning is as follows:

- POS: 0.917472
- NER: 0.932256

Learning both tasks together yields

- POS: 0.918869
- NER: 0.942686

NER improves slightly, but both tasks seem to benefit from joint learning:

CoNLL	Single-task	Hard
POS	0.917472	0.918869
NER	0.932256	0.942686

8.5.3 Soft parameter sharing

For soft parameter sharing, we opt for sharing the two embedding layers.

Listing 8.21 Soft parameter sharing for CoNLL

⟵ **Define the network for POS.**
```
inputsA=Input(shape=(max_length,))
x_a=Embedding(num_words, embedding_vector_length)(inputsA)
x1=Conv1D(filters=32, kernel_size=3, padding='same', activation='relu')(x_a)
x1=MaxPooling1D(pool_size=2)(x1)
x1=LSTM(100)(x1)
```

⟵ **Define the network for NER.**
```
inputsB=Input(shape=(max_length,))
x_b=Embedding(num_words, embedding_vector_length)(inputsB)
x2=Conv1D(filters=32, kernel_size=3, padding='same', activation='relu')(x_b)
x2=MaxPooling1D(pool_size=2)(x2)
x2=LSTM(100)(x2)
```

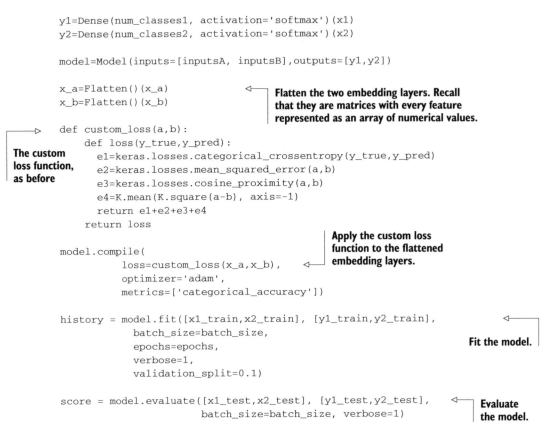

```
y1=Dense(num_classes1, activation='softmax')(x1)
y2=Dense(num_classes2, activation='softmax')(x2)

model=Model(inputs=[inputsA, inputsB],outputs=[y1,y2])

x_a=Flatten()(x_a)          ◄─┐  Flatten the two embedding layers. Recall
x_b=Flatten()(x_b)            │  that they are matrices with every feature
                              │  represented as an array of numerical values.

def custom_loss(a,b):
    def loss(y_true,y_pred):
        e1=keras.losses.categorical_crossentropy(y_true,y_pred)
        e2=keras.losses.mean_squared_error(a,b)
        e3=keras.losses.cosine_proximity(a,b)
        e4=K.mean(K.square(a-b), axis=-1)
        return e1+e2+e3+e4
    return loss
                                           Apply the custom loss
                                           function to the flattened
model.compile(                             embedding layers.
        loss=custom_loss(x_a,x_b),    ◄─┘
        optimizer='adam',
        metrics=['categorical_accuracy'])

history = model.fit([x1_train,x2_train], [y1_train,y2_train],      ◄─┐
        batch_size=batch_size,
        epochs=epochs,                               Fit the model.
        verbose=1,
        validation_split=0.1)

score = model.evaluate([x1_test,x2_test], [y1_test,y2_test],   ◄─┐ Evaluate
                batch_size=batch_size, verbose=1)                 the model.
```

The custom loss function, as before

RESULTS

Soft parameter sharing for CoNLL produces the following accuracy scores:

- POS: 0.916965
- NER: 0.948174

Compared to the baseline single-task scores (POS: 0.917472, NER: 0.932256), we see that soft parameter sharing outperforms hard parameter sharing for NER (0.942686) and produces a similar result for POS (0.918869).

CoNLL	Single-task	Soft	Hard
POS	0.917472	0.916965	0.918869
NER	0.932256	0.948174	0.942686

8.5.4 *Mixed parameter sharing*

For mixed parameter sharing, as before, we share intermediate layers as in hard parameter sharing and also deploy the custom loss used for soft parameter sharing.

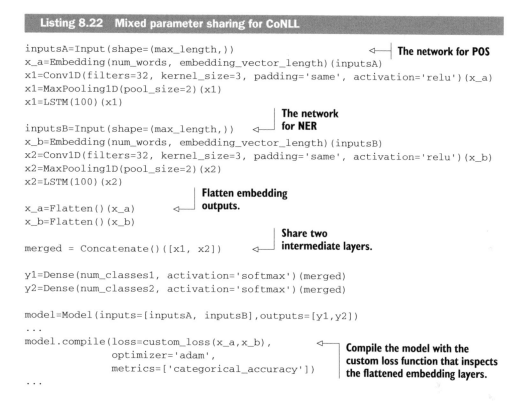

Listing 8.22   Mixed parameter sharing for CoNLL

```
inputsA=Input(shape=(max_length,))                          ◁─┤ The network for POS
x_a=Embedding(num_words, embedding_vector_length)(inputsA)
x1=Conv1D(filters=32, kernel_size=3, padding='same', activation='relu')(x_a)
x1=MaxPooling1D(pool_size=2)(x1)
x1=LSTM(100)(x1)
                                                   ┌ The network
inputsB=Input(shape=(max_length,))      ◁─┘ for NER
x_b=Embedding(num_words, embedding_vector_length)(inputsB)
x2=Conv1D(filters=32, kernel_size=3, padding='same', activation='relu')(x_b)
x2=MaxPooling1D(pool_size=2)(x2)
x2=LSTM(100)(x2)
                                     ┌ Flatten embedding
x_a=Flatten()(x_a)          ◁─┘ outputs.
x_b=Flatten()(x_b)
                                          ┌ Share two
merged = Concatenate()([x1, x2])    ◁─┘ intermediate layers.

y1=Dense(num_classes1, activation='softmax')(merged)
y2=Dense(num_classes2, activation='softmax')(merged)

model=Model(inputs=[inputsA, inputsB],outputs=[y1,y2])
...
model.compile(loss=custom_loss(x_a,x_b),           ◁─┐ Compile the model with the
              optimizer='adam',                        custom loss function that inspects
              metrics=['categorical_accuracy'])        the flattened embedding layers.
...
```

RESULTS

Mixed parameter sharing improves performance slightly for NER compared to the baseline scores (POS: 0.91747, NER: 0.932256). It does slightly better than hard parameter sharing and slightly worse than soft parameter sharing:

- POS: 0.917067
- NER: 0.946068

CoNLL	Single-task	Hard	Mixed
POS	0.917472	0.918869	0.917067
NER	0.932256	0.942686	0.946068

Summary

- You can implement and apply deep multitask learning with hard parameter sharing (sharing layers across subclassifiers), soft parameter sharing, and mixed parameter sharing (a combination of hard and soft parameter sharing).
- Multitask learning can produce significantly better results for one or all of the subtasks learned.

- Soft parameter sharing yields the best results overall, but differences compared to hard parameter sharing are usually small.
- Mixed parameter sharing does not stand out compared to the other two approaches.
- It is up to the NLP engineer to come up with optimal combinations of layers, task combinations, and custom loss functions using practical experimentation guided by trial and error.

Transformers

In late 2018, researchers from Google published a paper introducing a deep learning technique that would soon become a major breakthrough: *Bidirectional Encoder Representations from Transformers*, or *BERT* (Devlin et al. 2018). BERT aims to derive word embeddings from raw textual data just like Word2Vec, but does it in a much more clever and powerful manner: it takes into account both the left and right contexts when learning vector representations for words (figure 9.1). In contrast, Word2Vec uses a single piece of context. But this is not the only difference. BERT is grounded in *attention* and, unlike Word2Vec, deploys a *deep* network (recall that Word2Vec uses a *shallow* network with just one hidden layer.)

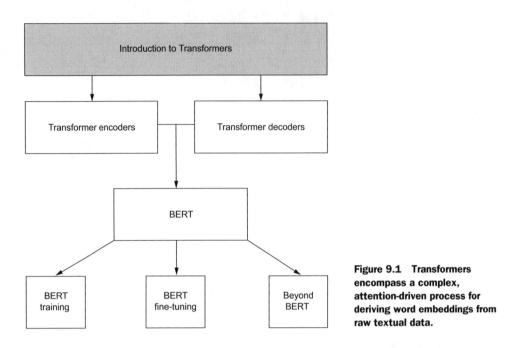

Figure 9.1   Transformers encompass a complex, attention-driven process for deriving word embeddings from raw textual data.

BERT smashed existing performance scores on all tasks it was applied to and (as we see later in this chapter) led to some not-so-trivial insights into deep neural language processing through the analysis of its attention patterns. So, how does BERT do all that? Let's trace BERT back to its roots: Transformers. We will go through the technical background of Transformers in this chapter and defer applications and detailed code to chapter 10.

9.1   *BERT up close: Transformers*

BERT descends from so-called *Transformers*, which are encoder-decoder models developed by Google (Vaswani et al. 2017). Similar to Word2Vec, BERT models are trained to produce a prediction (a word under a mask) based on an internal representation of context information. Recall from chapter 3 that in Word2Vec, we predict a word given its immediate neighbor words (the *continuous bag-of-words [CBOW]* variant) or, vice versa, a context given a certain word (*skipgram*).

Figure 9.2 repeats these approaches. The CBOW approach aims to infer a missing word w_t from its context based on a single hidden layer representing the projected context words w_{t-2}, w_{t-1}, w_{t+1}, w_{t+2}. In contrast, the skipgram approach attempts to predict contexts from the single word w_t.

Word2Vec is centered around a prediction task similar to what BERT addresses: predicting words in contexts, with the aim of representing separate words with vector memories of the contexts they occur in. Since this process can be interpreted as a form of encoding, it is similar to *autoencoders*. Such networks also compress or *encode* input data

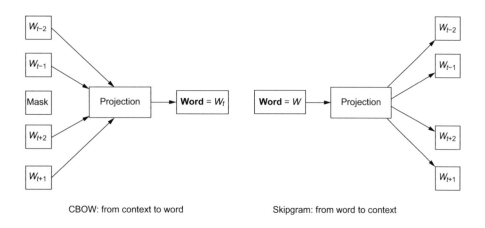

CBOW: from context to word   Skipgram: from word to context

Figure 9.2   Skipgram and CBOW prediction by Word2Vec (Mikolov et al. 2013)

into intermediate representations, and they are trained to minimize *reconstruction loss*: the error the network makes when attempting to reconstruct (*decode*) the original input from the encoded (latent) representation. This type of learning is known as *bottleneck learning*. Figure 9.3 shows the typical structure of an autoencoder; the encoded layer forms a bottleneck, which is usually a lower dimension than the original input, and the network learns to eliminate noise and focus on the important dimensions of the input data, not unlike dimensionality reduction techniques such as principal component analysis (PCA) (https://en.wikipedia.org/wiki/Principal_component_analysis).

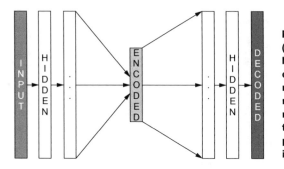

Figure 9.3   An autoencoder. Input is encoded (represented) in one (often lower-dimensional) hidden layer after passing through several other hidden layers. The original input is then reconstructed from this lower-dimensional representation: the model is trained to reproduce the original input. If done properly, the lower-dimensional input captures intrinsic properties of the input and abstracts away irrelevant noise and variation.

Transformers are complex encoder-decoder models. A transformer consists of multiple cross-linked encoder and decoder layers and an extensive self-attention mechanism: words paying attention to themselves and to others. Transformers can be used to map one sequence into another, as in machine translation (translating an English sentence into a German sentence, for instance). Figure 9.4, based on the original Transformer paper (Vaswani et al. 2017), depicts the canonical Transformer architecture.

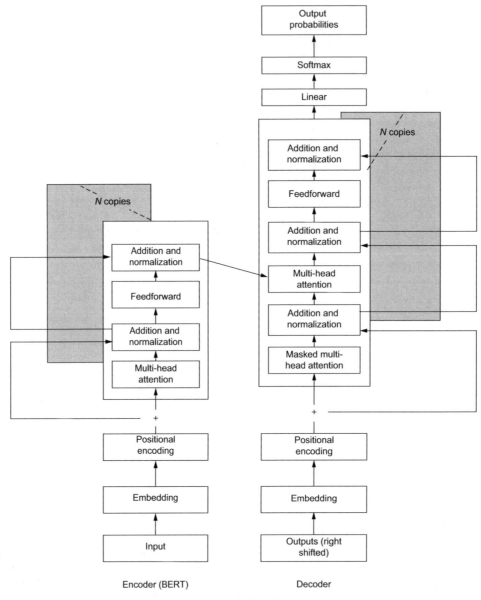

Figure 9.4   The Transformer architecture (see Vaswani et al. 2017). The left part is the encoder, and the right part is the decoder. Both encoder and decoder blocks have multiple copies, and they are connected one by one (every encoder block is connected to a corresponding decoder block).

Let's dissect the architecture in detail starting with the part on the left: the encoder layers. As it turns out, BERT, as a member of the Transformer family, only has the encoder part of this architecture.

9.2   *Transformer encoders*

An encoder layer or block in a Transformer (figure 9.5) has two internal layers: a *self-attention* layer and a fully connected feedforward network layer. The structure of the encoder is laid out in figure 9.6.

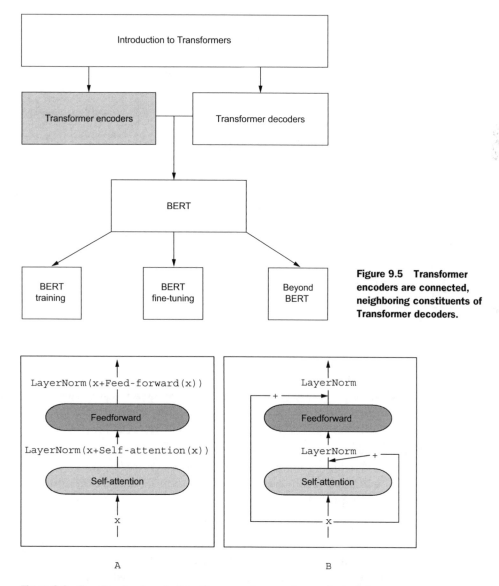

Figure 9.5   Transformer encoders are connected, neighboring constituents of Transformer decoders.

Figure 9.6   Encoder structure for Transformers, shown as two equivalent diagrams. Input x is passed through a self-attention layer, then the original input is added to the output of the self-attention layer, and finally the result is normalized. After that, a feedforward layer is applied, followed again by adding the original input to that result and normalizing it. Adding the unaltered x to subsequent layer outputs is called a *residual* or *skip* connection, made explicit in diagram B.

TIP   *Self-attention* means a relational attention mechanism that relates differ-ent parts of a sequence (like the words in a text). An alternative name for this is *intra-attention*.

Every sublayer has access to the incoming input vector x, which therefore is a form of *residual* or *skip* connection: a connection between two layers bypassing intervening lay-ers. Diagram B in the figure makes this a bit more explicit. The `LayerNorm` operation normalizes the output of the layer based on the mean and standard deviation for all the summed inputs to the neurons in that layer, which has shown measurable effects on training time (see Ba et al. 2016). A standard type of fea-ture normalization in machine learning is *z-score normaliza-tion*, where we first compute the mean and standard deviation for every feature in a dataset, subtract each fea-ture's mean from that feature, and divide the result by the standard deviation for that feature. In layer normalization, the mean (mu) and standard deviation (sigma) are defined *per layer (l)* as in figure 9.7. For example, figure 9.8 shows how a three-neuron layer is normalized by subtracting its mean from every neuron activation and then dividing by the standard deviation for the layer.

$$\mu^l = \frac{1}{H} \sum_{i=1}^{H} a_i^l$$

$$\sigma^l = \sqrt{\frac{1}{H} \sum_{i=1}^{H} \left(a_i^l - \mu^l\right)^2}$$

Figure 9.7   Layer normalization. H is the number of nodes in a (hidden) layer *l*; a_i^l is the summed input to neuron i in layer *l*.

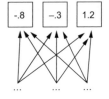

μ = 1/3 [−.8 + −.3 + 1.2]=0.033

σ = √ 1/3 [.694 + .11 + 1.36] = .845

−.985   −.393   1.38

(−.8−μ)/σ   (−.3−μ)/σ   (1.2−μ)/σ

Figure 9.8   Layer normalization example: normalizing three neuron activations based on the mean and standard deviation

TIP   In layer normalization, different inputs receive different normalizations and do not depend on the batch statistics for the entire batch they belong to. Since the batch size is a hyperparameter that can be set before training, this eliminates an important source of variability.

All encoder layers are equipped with attention: every input "pays attention" to every other input (but itself). This is done with *attention heads* that derive embeddings of every separate input element in the context of surrounding input elements. The trick here is that within the context window, all context is modeled, and the embeddings for separate input elements contain weighted attention information for every other input element in the context.

Let's dive a bit deeper into attention heads. An attention head is a triple of three matrices W_Q, W_K, W_V containing separate weights. They are initialized with random values. Given an input $x_1,...,x_n$, with an embedding for every part x_i, we compute three matrix-vector products, resulting in three vectors:

$$k_i = W_K x_i \quad q_i = W_Q x_i \quad v_i = W_V x_i$$

TIP If we multiply a matrix with r rows and c columns by a vector with c components (of size $(c,1)$), we end up with a matrix of shape $(r,1)$. Such a matrix is called a *column vector*.

These values populate three matrices K, Q, V of size (r,c), where c is the fixed length of the input sequences x, and r is an arbitrary number of rows.

   The two matrices K and Q seem to encode similar information, but they are distinct. To compute attention weights between all input elements x_i and x_j, we perform the following matrix computation involving the familiar softmax operation we used previously to compute attention

$$\text{ATTENTION}(Q,K,V) = \text{softmax}(QK^T/\sqrt{d_k})V$$

where the V matrix is used as a final weighting factor, and the quantity QK^T is normalized for the dimension of the key vectors k ($\sqrt{d_k}$). K^T is the transpose of K (rows and columns reversed).

   Any attention value a_{ij} computed with $\text{ATTENTION}(Q,K,V)$ encodes the attention token i pays to token j. Note that this is an asymmetric relation; it does not entail that token j pays the same attention to token i. That's why there are two weight matrices involved: a *query* matrix Q and a *key* matrix K.

NOTE Suppose we have input data that is represented as a batch of N examples, each of which is a 512×768 matrix: (padded) sequences of 512 words, with each word represented with a 768-dimensional embedding. Given an attention head, every such matrix (corresponding to one input example) is multiplied by three matrices: the query, key, and value matrices for the attention head. Let these be of size $(64,512)$ for Q and K and $(64,768)$ for V. We end up with a matrix sized $(64,64)$ from the product QK^T. After multiplication with V, the computation of $\text{ATTENTION}(Q,K,V)$ produces a matrix of shape $(64,768)$: $(64,64) \times (64,768) = (64,768)$.

But this is by no means the end of the story. Why not have multiple attention heads?

TIP Recall that every attention head is a triple of three matrices W_Q, W_K, W_V containing separate weights.

This is where one of the marvels of Transformers comes to light. Having multiple attention heads jointly at work leads to a situation where heads *specialize* in different kinds of attention focus. For instance, when Transformers are fed raw text to produce embeddings, certain attention heads specialize in prepositional phrase patterns, emphasizing the relation between prepositions and their noun objects (<u>on</u> the <code>table</code>). Other heads specialize in transitive verb-direct object relations (<code>Mary</code> <u>eats</u> an <u>apple</u>) or even reflexive pronoun-antecedent relations (<u>John</u> shaves <u>himself</u>). See Clark et al. (2018) for examples.

The various attention matrices per attention head are then combined into one big matrix, which finally is multiplied by the *V* matrix. This produces the output for the current encoder layer. In our example, for 8 attention heads per layer, we end up with 512,768-dimensional output. The result of this process is that the original word embeddings assigned to the input words (starting as random embeddings) are incrementally updated with this contextual self-attention information: words paying attention to themselves and each other. In that sense, word embeddings become increasingly tuned for modeling words as a function of their context, similar to Word2Vec, but using much more contextual information.

> **Exercise**
> Reflect on the convolutional filters in CNNs (chapter 2). What are the differences from and similarities to attention heads?

Figure 9.4 shows we can have multiple encoder layers stacked onto each other (the *N* copies), each with its own multiple attention heads. This creates *hierarchies of attention*. The first encoding layer is a bit different from subsequent layers: it encodes information of the embeddings corresponding to the inputs while preserving their word position through something called *positional encoding*. We clearly need this information, since Transformers do not treat texts as bags of words; word order is important to encode contextual information in the word embeddings they produce. It is also important to understand how Transformers, in this respect, differ from sequential models like recurrent neural networks and long short-term memory. Transformers explicitly do not use memory facilities like cell states to encode temporal memory. They oversee more information in their input sequences and look back and forth in those sequences. So, how do they keep track of word positions?

9.2.1   *Positional encoding*

Positional encoding is a trick to encode word positions into vectors (representing words) by using the cyclic aspects of the sine and cosine functions. Recall from high school algebra that sine and cosine are periodic functions: at fixed increments of their inputs, they produce the same minimum and maximum values. Furthermore, the <code>sin</code> and <code>cos</code> functions, while similar from a periodic point of view, are phase-shifted variants of each other. This is illustrated in figure 9.9.

Notice how the values of the cosine and sine lie in the interval [–1,1]. For every position, the positional embedding approach generates a vector consisting of sine and

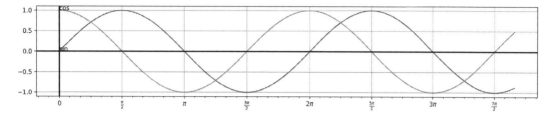

Figure 9.9 **Sine and cosine. The y-axis demonstrates the value range of these functions ([–1,1]). On the x-axis, we see that cos x = 0 when x = ±π/2, ±3π/2, ±5π/2, and so on (at uneven multiples of π/2) and sin x = 0 for x = 0, π, 2π, 3π, and so on.**

cosine values. These sine and cosine values are computed as a function of both the word position and the current dimension of the vector and uniquely tie words to word positions. These vectors are subsequently added to the original word embedding vector for a word at a given position. The computed values can be interpreted as a continuous alternative to discrete bits, as we see shortly. The computations are as follows:

$$\text{positional\_encoding}(p, d, 2i) = \sin(p/(10000^{2i/d}))$$
$$\text{positional\_encoding}(p, d, 2i+1) = \cos(p/(10000^{2i/d}))$$

So, we're using `sin` for even word positions (0,2,4,…) and `cos` for uneven word positions (1,3,5,…).

Let's walk through an example. Suppose we have four-dimensional word embeddings for a sequence of 10 words. For every word position 1 to 10, we will generate a positional vector of dimension 4; then we will add these vectors to the original four-dimensional word embeddings, fusing them with positional information.

Listing 9.1 Positional encoding

```
import sys
from math import sin, cos
import numpy as np

dimension=4
max_len=10
pos_enc=np.zeros(shape=(max_len,dimension))     ← Define a container array
for pos in range(max_len):                          consisting of zeros.
    i=0
    while (i<=dimension-2):              ←    Fill the array with the
        x = pos/(10000**(2.0*i/dimension))      positional sin and cos values.
        pos_enc[pos][i] = sin(x)
        pos_enc[pos][i+1] = cos(x)
        i+=2
print(pos_enc)          ←   Print the result.
```

This produces 10 four-dimensional vectors, one for every word:

```
[[ 0.00000000e+00   1.00000000e+00   0.00000000e+00   1.00000000e+00]
 [ 8.41470985e-01   5.40302306e-01   9.99999998e-05   9.99999995e-01]
 [ 9.09297427e-01  -4.16146837e-01   1.99999999e-04   9.99999980e-01]
 [ 1.41120008e-01  -9.89992497e-01   2.99999995e-04   9.99999955e-01]
 [-7.56802495e-01  -6.53643621e-01   3.99999989e-04   9.99999920e-01]
 [-9.58924275e-01   2.83662185e-01   4.99999979e-04   9.99999875e-01]
 [-2.79415498e-01   9.60170287e-01   5.99999964e-04   9.99999820e-01]
 [ 6.56986599e-01   7.53902254e-01   6.99999943e-04   9.99999755e-01]
 [ 9.89358247e-01  -1.45500034e-01   7.99999915e-04   9.99999680e-01]
 [ 4.12118485e-01  -9.11130262e-01   8.99999879e-04   9.99999595e-01]]
```

Exercise

Compute these values by hand and check the results with those shown here.

For example, for word 1 (with word index 0, as we're using zero-based counting), the four-dimensional vector is built up as follows:

```
[cjn(0/(10000=1))=0, vaz(0/(10000=1))=1, nja(0/(100002/4=100))=0,
aks(0/(100002/4=100))=1]
```

Notice how we shift from $i = 0$ to $i = 2$ in the code. At every position i in the result vector, we generate a value for i itself and $i+1$, and then we skip over to $i+2$ in order not to overwrite the value at $i+1$.

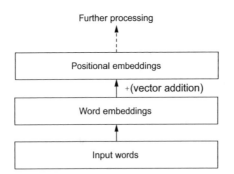

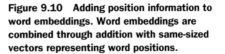

Figure 9.10   **Adding position information to word embeddings. Word embeddings are combined through addition with same-sized vectors representing word positions.**

Adding these positional vectors v to the original (in this example, four-dimensional) word embeddings w for every word in a sequence ($v + w$) leads to vectors that represent positional information, as expressed by the diagram in figure 9.10.

Interestingly, only part of the vector space allocated to this positional information is used. Look again at the situation for our toy example: 10 words, with word embeddings of size 4. We visualize the positional vectors (based on the `sin` and `cos` computations) with `matplotlib` like this (using the `pos_enc` array computed in listing 9.1), which gives us figure 9.11:

```python
import numpy as np
import matplotlib.pyplot as plt
import matplotlib.cm as cm

x=range(dimension)
y=range(max_len)
x, y = np.meshgrid(x,y)           Define a grid
                                  of size (x,y).

                                  Plot pos_enc with the position
plt.xticks(range(dimension))      encodings on the grid in grayscale.
plt.pcolormesh(x, y, pos_enc ,cmap=cm.gray)
plt.colorbar()
plt.xlabel('Embedding dimension')
plt.ylabel('Word position in sequence')
plt.show()
```

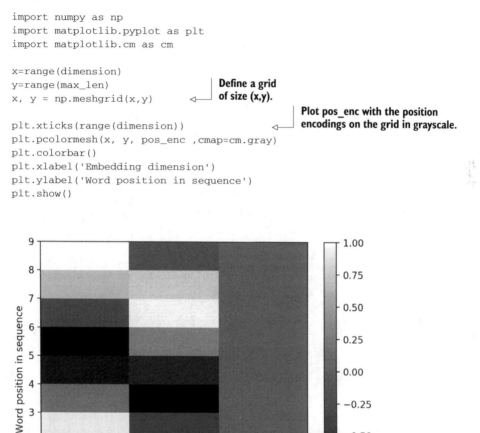

Figure 9.11 Positional embedding for sequences of maximally 10 words, embedding size = 4. Each row is a vector to be added to the word embedding vector for the word in the corresponding position (the y-axis values).

Here you see that the first two dimensions of the positional vector are discriminating between the various word positions in a nonbinary, continuous manner: the gray shades (to which the computed `cos` and `sin` values, all in the interval [–1,1], have been converted by `matplotlib`) demonstrate this. Consider trying to discriminate between these positions with binary values, on the other hand: that would demand 4 bits ($2^4 = 16$).

Compare this to a more realistic situation: sequences of at most 100 words, 300 dimensions. This produces the picture in figure 9.12. Again, notice how the first, say, 50 dimensions appear to dominate the positional encoding.

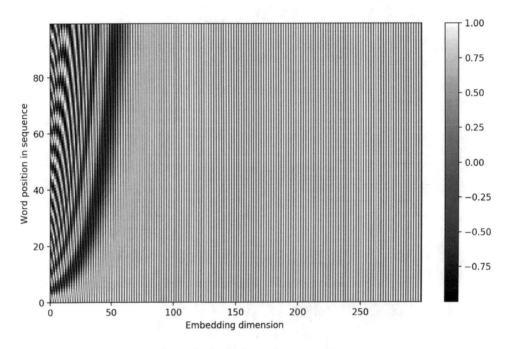

Figure 9.12　Positional embedding for sequences with a maximum of 100 words, embedding size = 300. Each row is a vector to be added to the word embedding vector for the word in the corresponding position (the y-axis values).

So, how is this raw text processed to enter the encoding layers? BERT uses a tokenizer called *WordPiece* (Schuster and Nakajima 2012) that chunks words into subwords. For example, WordPiece chops *echoscopy* into *echo*, *sco*, and *py*. This significantly reduces the chance of encountering out-of-vocabulary words: just as only 26 characters make up English words, the subword combinations create rare words. With this trick, BERT manages to keep its tokenizer vocabulary to just over 30,000 for English.

For example, figure 9.13 shows how raw text enters the first encoder layer. All layers pass on the attention weights their attention heads compute (concatenated) and feed these weights into a `Dense` layer that is the input for the subsequent layer.

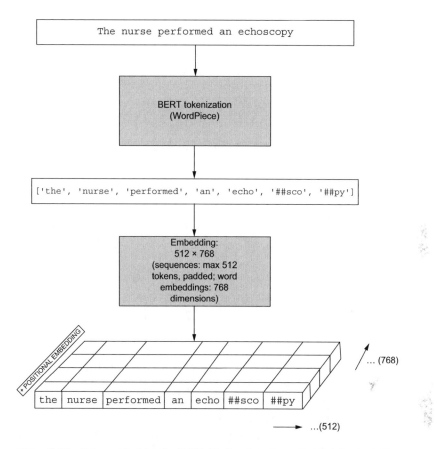

Figure 9.13 Token embedding for BERT. The input sentence first is tokenized. The ## prefixes indicate word pieces: subwords split off from a word by the BERT tokenizer. After that, the sentence is embedded in a 512 × 768 embedding (padded up to 512 token positions) to which the positional vectors are added.

9.3 *Transformer decoders*

Recall that a Transformer is meant to *transform* sequences (figure 9.14): it can be used for any sequence-to-sequence task like machine translation. The decoder essentially attempts to generate an output sequence word by word based on the encoder representation of the input data. However, feeding some extra information to the decoder helps greatly. Take a look at the Transformer decoder architecture shown in figure 9.15. The first thing to notice is that the decoder also has access to the desired output symbols, excluding the word it should currently predict. That is, it cannot peek into the future: it should generate a current word based on the previous words it has generated. Such a decoder is called *autoregressive.*

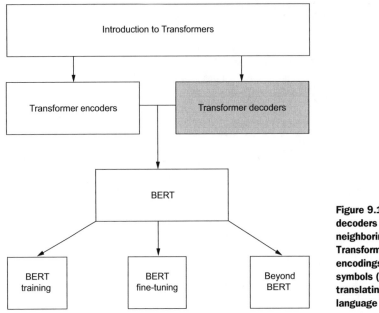

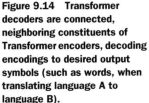

Figure 9.14 Transformer decoders are connected, neighboring constituents of Transformer encoders, decoding encodings to desired output symbols (such as words, when translating language A to language B).

Let's now turn to the right side of the Transformer architecture: the decoders. We repeat the Transformer architecture picture in figure 9.15.

During training, feeding the ground truth data to the decoder mimics this generation process: we act like the decoder has generated the ground truth. One important caveat is that the decoder starts at a *shifted* position compared to the encoder: one word to the right. This is implemented by prefixing the desired output sequence to the encoder with a designated symbol. An extra symbol is added to the desired output to denote the end of the sequence (the ground truth) for the decoder, and decoding stops when the decoder generates this symbol. If the decoder were working on a *nonshifted* version of the desired output sequence, it would be trained to copy that sequence rather than infer the next words.

As an example, suppose we are teaching a Transformer to translate "The nurse performed an echoscopy" to German:

> *The nurse performed an echoscopy => Die Krankenschwester führte eine Echoskopie durch*

During training, the decoder receives the following (assuming a windowed presentation of training data) for predicting "führte"

> *The latent encoded representation for the entire sentence 'The nurse performed an echoscopy' [START] 'Die Krankenschwester'*

and therefore never sees "führte" in its ground truth input when predicting "führte." It cannot see the word it should be predicting.

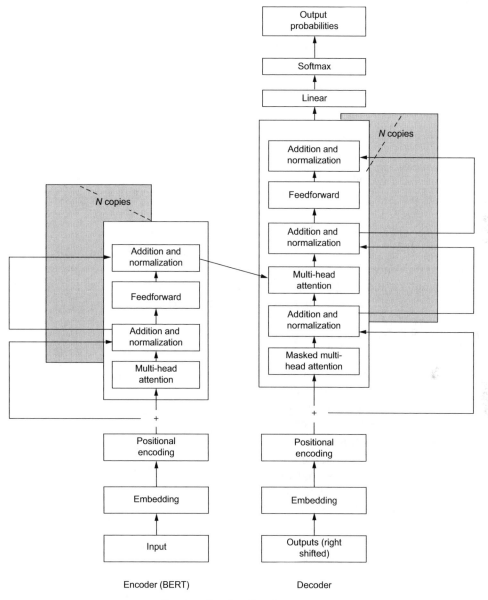

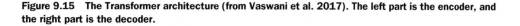

Figure 9.15   The Transformer architecture (from Vaswani et al. 2017). The left part is the encoder, and the right part is the decoder.

TIP   Giving the decoder access to the output ground truth data is called *teacher forcing*. It allows us to safeguard the decoder from derailing when making its predictions, since its loss function will take this ground truth into account. Errors made by the decoder are fed all the way back down to the encoder.

In addition to applying the decoder to shifted data, self-attention for a word at position i in the decoder is limited to the words preceding that position: words $w_1,...,w_{i-1}$. This is implemented by masking out those words with a binary filter (a *mask*).

Once trained, the decoder operates in this stepwise fashion:

1 The decoder receives an empty sequence prefixed with the designated start symbol. We refer to that symbol with [START]. Similarly, we denote the end symbol with [END].
2 The decoder generates the first word based on the encoder representation that the trained encoder uses to encode its input.
3 In an iterative manner, the decoder completes its decoded sequence word by word. In the second step, it produces the second word based on (again) the encoded representation and [START] <first word>, and so on, until it generates the [END] symbol.

This implements the autoregressive_property for Transformers: the decoder bases its next step (prediction) on its own previously produced output; as said, this is mimicked during training by pretending the input data sent to the decoder is generated by the decoder itself. Now, how does BERT relate to the Transformer architecture?

9.4   *BERT: Masked language modeling*

BERT is not a full Transformer: it only has the encoder part. Recall, for that matter, its full name: Bidirectional Encoder Representations from Transformers. This makes sense: BERT is not meant to transform sequences into other sequences; it was created to produce word representations (vector embeddings), just like Word2Vec (figure 9.16). Toward this end, BERT uses *masked language models*, which model word distribution patterns by masking out certain words, and has the models predict the words under the masks. Technically, BERT performs *denoising autoencoding*. It attempts to reconstruct a sequence of words from a corrupted, noisy signal: a sequence of

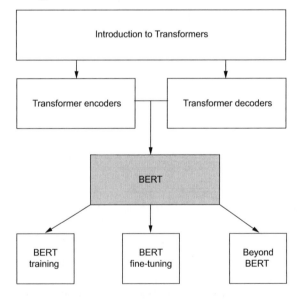

Figure 9.16   BERT represents masked language models, and its task is to pack word context information into word embeddings.

words containing masks, indicated with a specific masking symbol. Such masking symbols are not used in Word2Vec. On the fly, BERT infers an optimal encoding of words.

Masked language modeling draws inspiration from a well-established test for assessing the mastery of a native or secondary language and the readability of texts: the *Cloze* test, developed in the 1950s (Taylor 1953). In this test, participants are asked to fill in the blanks in sentences like these:

- The _ performed an echoscopy ('nurse','doctor')
- The _ recovered quickly from the procedure ('patient')

Again, recall from Word2Vec that a limited, unidirectional form of the Cloze test was at the heart of context prediction (predicting, for a given word, a neighbor word or an immediate context). BERT takes this idea further by exploiting *remote* and *non-adjacent* left and right (bidirectional) contexts for predicting a blanked-out, masked word.

9.4.1 Training BERT

As mentioned earlier, BERT consists of the encoder part of a Transformer. BERT is trained on two objectives simultaneously (figure 9.17):

- Predicting words hidden under masks as a bidirectional, masked language model.
- Predicting, for an arbitrary pair of two sentences, whether the second sentence is a natural progression of the first sentence. This task establishes additional relations between words across sentences, and it was added to BERT with question-answering applications in mind, where these relations between sentences often play a role.

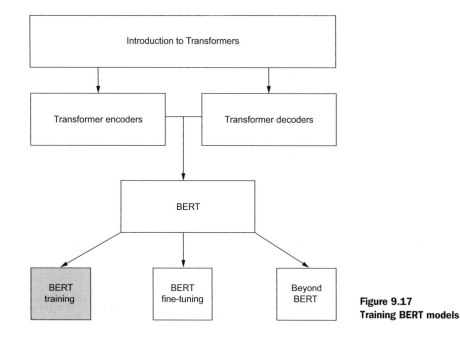

**Figure 9.17
Training BERT models**

The first objective is implemented in BERT as follows. BERT needs to work on input text in this format:

```
[CLS] The nurse performed an echoscopy [SEP] The patient recovered quickly [SEP]
```

After internal preprocessing, BERT receives a large set of such sentence pairs. The CLS tag at the beginning of each pair denotes whether the two sentences form a natural pair for the second objective (it is a binary class label). BERT input data consists of a set of sentences in the specified format, which is partially permuted: it contains real sentence pairs and artificial pairs. The SEP tag separates sentences.

> **TIP**   Refer to our implementation of Word2Vec (see chapter 3), where we did something similar when generating context samples.

After we apply the WordPiece tokenizer to the tokens in each sentence in a pair, tokens are embedded with a (1,768)-sized vector. The sentence positions are added as vectors, followed by the positional vectors. The maximum sequence length in BERT is 512, so we end up with a matrix of $(N,512,768)$ for N sentence pairs. See figure 9.18.

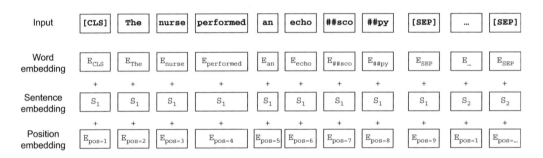

Figure 9.18   BERT input data. Position embedding and sentence flags (indicating the sentence in which a word piece occurs) are combined into word embeddings. These word embeddings are fine-tuned with attention during training BERT.

Internally, BERT generates its training data as follows:

1 From a raw, sentence-based corpus, create sentence pairs (50% natural pairs, 50% random pairs). Create [CLS] ... [SEP] ... [SEP] sequences.

2 Choose 15% random tokens from the WordPiece-processed corpus.

3 For every such token, 80% of the time, mask the token in its sequence with a designated MASK token; 12% of the tokens become masked. In 10% (1.5% of the tokens), replace the token with a random token from the BERT vocabulary (which has 30,000 tokens total). In the remaining 10% (1.5% of the tokens), leave the selected token unchanged.

The rationale behind this process is that BERT wants to limit the mismatch of corrupted data (as a result of inserting MASK symbols) with subsequent uncorrupted input data in applications or uncorrupted *downstream* data during fine-tuning (more about that later). The random tokens infuse some random noise into this process, which is a familiar machine learning technique to prevent overfitting models.

The following code implements the masking procedure. It is typically tucked away in BERT; there is no need to explicitly preprocess input data in this manner.

Listing 9.2 Masking

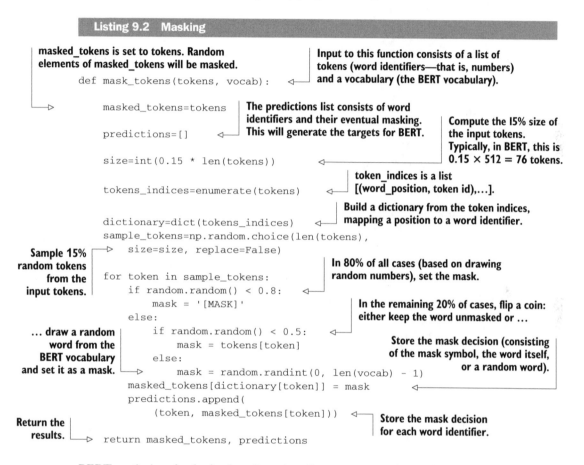

masked_tokens is set to tokens. Random elements of masked_tokens will be masked.

Input to this function consists of a list of tokens (word identifiers—that is, numbers) and a vocabulary (the BERT vocabulary).

```
def mask_tokens(tokens, vocab):
```

```
    masked_tokens=tokens
```

The predictions list consists of word identifiers and their eventual masking. This will generate the targets for BERT.

```
    predictions=[]
```

Compute the 15% size of the input tokens. Typically, in BERT, this is 0.15 × 512 = 76 tokens.

```
    size=int(0.15 * len(tokens))
```

```
    tokens_indices=enumerate(tokens)
```

token_indices is a list [(word_position, token id),...].

Build a dictionary from the token indices, mapping a position to a word identifier.

```
    dictionary=dict(tokens_indices)
    sample_tokens=np.random.choice(len(tokens),
         size=size, replace=False)
```

Sample 15% random tokens from the input tokens.

```
    for token in sample_tokens:
        if random.random() < 0.8:
```

In 80% of all cases (based on drawing random numbers), set the mask.

```
            mask = '[MASK]'
        else:
```

In the remaining 20% of cases, flip a coin: either keep the word unmasked or ...

```
            if random.random() < 0.5:
                mask = tokens[token]
            else:
```

... draw a random word from the BERT vocabulary and set it as a mask.

```
                mask = random.randint(0, len(vocab) - 1)
        masked_tokens[dictionary[token]] = mask
        predictions.append(
            (token, masked_tokens[token]))
```

Store the mask decision (consisting of the mask symbol, the word itself, or a random word).

Store the mask decision for each word identifier.

Return the results.

```
    return masked_tokens, predictions
```

BERT optimizes both the loss function for sentence pair prediction ("Do these two sentences form a natural pair?") and the loss function for unveiling the masked tokens.

BERT comes in two ready-made flavors:

- *BERT-BASE*—12 encoder layers, 768-size embeddings, 12 multi-attention heads per layer, 110 million parameters
- *BERT-LARGE*—24 encoder layers, 1,024-size embeddings, 16 multi-attention heads per layer, 340 million parameters

Empirically, it was shown in Vaswani et al. (2017) that summing the last four hidden layers of BERT to produce the final embedding for a word produced optimal results, with an additional slight improvement by not summing but concatenating those four layers (producing an unwieldy $4 \times 768 = 3{,}072$-dimensional vector).

It is important to notice here that BERT, unlike Word2Vec, produces a *contextual embedding*: we typically feed a pretrained BERT model a sentence and extract the embeddings for every word from the attention patterns the input evokes in the model. So, if we feed BERT the following two sentences

  I took my money to the bank. I took my guitar to the river bank.

the word *bank* will receive two different embedding vectors (768-dimensional, for BERT). The encoder layers redo their computation of key-query attention values, deploying the pretrained weight matrices for queries, keys, and values and generating contextual embeddings for the words in the input. This contrasts with Word2Vec, where we build a lexicon of words with generic vectors, packing (hopefully) all different contexts. Word2Vec only generates one vector for *bank*. In the next chapter, we will take a closer look at that.

9.4.2   *Fine-tuning BERT*

Once pretrained and similar to Word2Vec, a BERT embedding can be *fine-tuned* by connecting it to a classification problem, a so-called *downstream task* (figure 9.19). The loss on the classification predictions is fed back end to end into the pretrained BERT model. Fine-tuning BERT is no more complex than switching on a subset of the layers of a pretrained BERT model for fine-tuning (making them trainable, just as we did for Word2Vec). Importing a BERT model and adding a softmax layer plus labeled data is all we need to fine-tune the model.

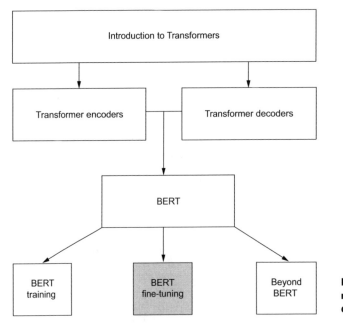

Figure 9.19   Pretrained BERT models can be fine-tuned with downstream tasks.

For instance, we can fine-tune a pretrained BERT model for sentiment analysis, leading to changes in the vector space spanned by BERT that reflect word similarities relevant for, for example, polarity classification. In the next chapter, we will see how to fine-tune BERT for such a task.

BERT-style language models have produced very competitive results across all NLP tasks (Devlin et al. 2018). As mentioned, BERT is an autoencoding model. It corrupts (masks) its input data during training and tries to find an optimal encoding to reconstruct the corrupted (masked) input data. Autoregressive models pair such an encoder with an explicit decoder, allowing for text generation. The GPT-3 model by OpenAI (Brown et al. 2020) has an additional decoder and a whopping 175 billion parameters. It can generate new texts word by word with its decoder, which is very hard to discern from human-produced text, causing quite a stir (and a lot of concern) in the scientific world (see, for example, McGuffie and Newhouse 2020).

9.4.3   *Beyond BERT*

One recognized shortcoming of BERT is its implementation of masking (figure 9.20). During pretraining, where BERT is trained to predict the words under masks and predict sentence pairs, the masks make perfect sense. But fine-tuning is a different story. The [MASK] tag is irrelevant for the data used for fine-tuning BERT, but it is still inserted during BERT's preprocessing stage. Furthermore, if multiple tokens are masked in the pretraining stage of BERT, the interactions between those tokens (and their possible contributions to each other) are lost: BERT makes an *independence* assumption and reconstructs every mask in isolation from neighboring masks. Unlike

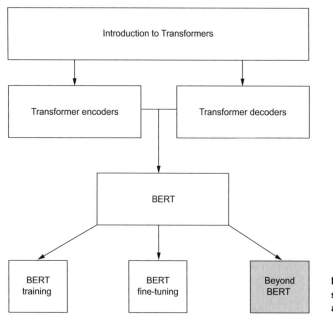

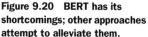

Figure 9.20   BERT has its shortcomings; other approaches attempt to alleviate them.

autoregressive language models, where probabilities of word sequences are based on products of all probabilities for words in the context, BERT addresses every masked word in turn, and its unmasking of one mask will not influence the unmasking of another masked word.

So, for example, if BERT receives the following sequence

```
[MASK] [MASK] and a Happy New Year
```

it will maximize the following sum of probabilities, since for the two masks, `Merry` and `Christmas` are the prediction targets:

```
log(P(Merry|and a happy New year))+log(P(Christmas|and a happy New Year))
```

but none of the probabilities is conditioned on the other, although they clearly are related.

For these reasons, an alternative Transformer-based encoder for creating word embeddings saw the light in 2019: XLNet (Yang et al. 2019). XLNet takes a different approach and optimizes the following in our example:

```
log(P(Merry|and a happy New year))+log(P(Christmas|Merry, and a happy New Year))
```

How does it do that? It deploys *permutation language modeling*: words are predicted for different *factorizations* (permutations). Let's re-address our example

> *The nurse performed an echoscopy*

This sequence has 5! = 120 different permutations. XLNet uses a subset of these permutations (and addresses a subset of the positions in these permutations based on a cutoff estimated hyperparameter). XLNet is autoregressive like Transformers: it does not peek into the future, and every word w at position i is predicted based only on words preceding i. But this is implemented differently: XLNet is autoregressive over the permutations it generates. It uses a permutation language model. Let's look at the following permutation of our example:

> *nurse, The, an, echoscopy, performed*

We can represent this permutation with numbers indicating the original word positions:

> *[2,1,4,3,5]*

Being autoregressive over a permutation means we can only look to the left (the past) when predicting a token in the context of a permutation; this leaves open the possibility that words from the right of a current token will emerge in the left (permuted) context.

To predict word 2, there is no left context, so XLNet needs to optimize as follows:

```
P(nurse|_)
```

For the next token, word 1, there is a left context: word 2. So, we have

```
P(The|nurse)
```

For the next token, word 4 (*echoscopy*), the available context is words 1 and 2. XLNet encodes this context with a mask applied to the permutation at hand.

For word 2 (*nurse*), the mask is

```
[0,0,0,0,0]
```

meaning none of the words in the permutations serves as a context for predicting *nurse*.

For word 1 (*The*), we have

```
[0,1,0,0,0]
```

meaning the original token at position 2 (*nurse*) serves as context for predicting *The*.

For word 4 (*an*), we have as context (1,2), which is *The nurse*, leading to the mask

```
[1,1,0,0,0]
```

and so on. These masks are applied one by one in the model. Notice how the original permutation can be fully reconstructed from these masks. Since XLNet is autoregressive and always *left-looking*, we can directly read the precedence relations between the words in the permuted sequence from the binary masks:

- Word 1 has mask [0,1,0,0,0], implying {2} < 1.
- Word 2 has mask [0,0,0,0,0], implying {}<2: nothing precedes 2. Therefore, 2 must start the permutation sequence.
- Word 3 has mask [1,1,0,1,0], implying {1,2,4} < 3. We can conclude 2,1,4,3 or 2,4,1,3 at this point.
- Word 4 has mask [1,1,0,0,0,0], implying {1,2} < 4. We know that {2}<1, so we can decide for 2,1,4,3.
- Word 5 has mask [1,1,1,1,0], implying 5 closes off the permutation sequence. We have reconstructed 2,1,4,3,5.

With these ingredients, the story is not complete yet. XLNet has no real sense of word order at this point, and it cannot learn that in

```
P(The|nurse)
```

The is in the first word position and *nurse* in the second. We would like XLNet to condition this probability as follows:

```
P(The|pos=1, nurse~2~)
```

In BERT, we solved this by adding positional information vectors to the embeddings. In this case, doing so would lead to an anomaly like

```
P(The|The+pv~1~, nurse+pv~2~)
```

where pv_i is the positional vector for position *i*. This makes the prediction task trivial. XLNet puts forward a dual self-attention mechanism to solve this conundrum;

basically, it carefully separates the token information from the positional information to omit this situation and inserts an extra 1 for every token in their permutation mask to be able to inspect itself. We will not go any deeper into this; you're invited to look at Yang et al. (2019) for further details.

Performance-wise: what has this given us? XLNet appears to outperform BERT by sizable margins throughout (refer to Yang et al. [2019] for experimental results).

To recap, XLNet does away with explicit masking, which creates a disadvantage for BERT during fine-tuning. It uses a smart trick: a form of permutation language modeling. XLNet also overcomes the independence assumption BERT makes for multiple masks in one sentence. It turns out XLNet performs better than BERT across a wide range of applications. This comes—as always—at a price: permutations are costly to compute and process, and XLNet consequently makes a number of simplifying assumptions for practical reasons.

It is time we turn to practical implementations. In the next chapter, we will implement the necessary methods for working with BERT on actual problems.

Summary

- Transformers are complex encoder-decoder networks based on self-attention.
- BERT is a Transformer encoder.
- BERT derives attention-weighted word embeddings using masked language modeling—a complex attention mechanism—and positional encoding.
- BERT differs from Word2Vec by creating dynamic embeddings that discriminate between different contexts and is similar in its downstream fine-tuning facilities.
- XLNet differs from BERT by omitting the masking of words using a permutation language model, and it may be a better option in some circumstances while being more costly from a computational point of view.

Applications of Transformers: Hands-on with BERT

This chapter addresses the practicalities of working with the BERT Transformer in your implementations. We will not implement BERT ourselves—that would be a daunting job and unnecessary since BERT has been implemented efficiently in various frameworks, including Keras. But we will get close to the inner workings of BERT code. We saw in chapter 9 that BERT has been reported to improve NLP applications significantly. While we do not carry out an extensive comparison in this chapter, you are encouraged to revisit the applications in the previous chapters and swap, for instance, Word2Vec embeddings with BERT embeddings. With the material in chapters 9 and 10, you should be able to do so.

10.1   *Introduction: Working with BERT in practice*

The financial costs of pretraining BERT and related models like XLNet from scratch on large amounts of data can be prohibitive (figure 10.1). The original BERT paper (Devlin et al. 2018; see chapter 9) mentions that

> *[The] training of BERT – Large was performed on 16 Cloud TPUs (64 TPU chips total) [with several pretraining phases]. Each pretraining [phase] took 4 days to complete.*

If the authors used Google Cloud TPUs, which are GPUs optimized for TensorFlow computations (TensorFlow is Google's native deep learning formalism), at the current TPU price per hour of $4.50 to $8.00, this would amount to a total pretraining price of $6,912 to $12,288 (16 TPUs × 96 hours × $4.50—$8.00 per hour).

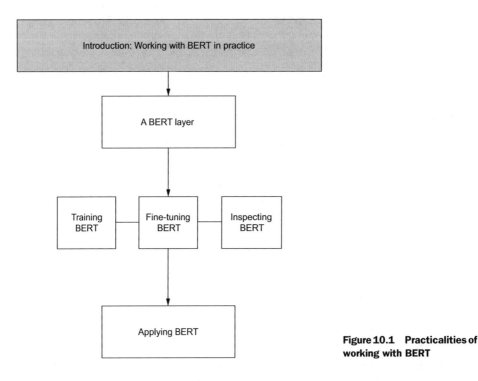

Figure 10.1   Practicalities of working with BERT

For XLNet, with its more complex permutation language modeling approach, non-official estimates amount to a steep pretraining cost of $61,440 (Bradbury 2019). Likewise, the cost of training a Transformer for the GPT-3 language model, which was trained on 1 billion words, has been estimated at a whopping $4.6 million (Li 2020), and such models are only available through commercial licenses.

Luckily, smaller pretrained BERT or XLNet models are becoming increasingly available for free, and they may serve as stepping stones for fine-tuning. For example, see https://huggingface.co/transformers/pretrained_models.html for an overview of many Transformer models for a variety of languages.

In practice, you can download a pretrained BERT or XLNet model, incorporate it into your network, and fine-tune it with much more manageable, smaller datasets. In this chapter, we see how that works. We begin by incorporating existing BERT models into our models. For this to work, we need a dedicated BERT layer: a landing hub for BERT models.

10.2 A BERT layer

In deep learning networks, BERT layers (figure 10.2), like any other embedding layers, are usually positioned right on top of an input layer, as figure 10.3 shows. They serve a purpose similar to any other embedding layer: they encode words in the input layer to embedding vectors. To be able to work with BERT, we need two things:

- A pretrained BERT model
- A facility for importing such a model and exposing it to the rest of our code

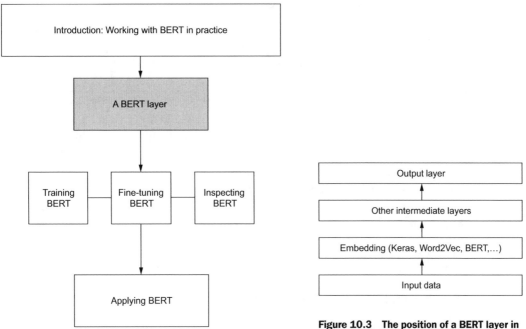

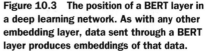

Figure 10.3 The position of a BERT layer in a deep learning network. As with any other embedding layer, data sent through a BERT layer produces embeddings of that data.

Figure 10.2 Creating a BERT layer in which we can load BERT models

Google has made available to a general audience a very valuable platform for obtaining pretrained BERT models: TensorFlow Hub (www.tensorflow.org/hub). This is a platform for downloading not only BERT models and the like but also functional parts of preconstructed deep learning networks, which, in Google's idiom, are subgraphs of TensorFlow graphs. Recall that TensorFlow is Google's native deep learning formalism.

> **NOTE** Starting with Keras version 2.3 (2019), Keras stopped supporting Theano as a backend and now uses TensorFlow exclusively. It is advisable to use the TensorFlow-embedded version of Keras. The BERT libraries we use in this chapter depend on TensorFlow 2.0 and above. You can read more in Aj_MLstater (2020) and Rosebrock (2019).

This means we can download both models and other useful code from TensorFlow Hub. At https://tfhub.dev/google/collections/bert/1, you will find a large list of all kinds of BERT models. One set of models is based on the official implementation of Devlin et al. (2018); although this implementation has been superseded by others, we will use one of its models.

Let's first define a special-purpose layer to which to attach downloaded models. Recall from chapter 5 that we can define our own layers in Keras as classes. Such class definitions need only three obligatory methods: `init()`, `build()` and `call()`.

Scenario: Working with BERT

You would like to use existing BERT models in your applications. How should you attach such models to your code? You decide to implement a dedicated Keras layer for harboring BERT models.

Listing 10.1 shows how to implement such a Keras BERT layer. Calling this layer entails downloading a BERT model and optimizing it for fine-tuning if desired. The fine-tuning consists of specifying the number of BERT attention layers to be fine-tuned. This is a crucial parameter that determines both the time complexity of the operation and the quality of the final model: fine-tuning more layers generally leads to higher quality, but it comes with a time trade-off.

> **NOTE** The layer used in this example is currently found in many implementations, including those at https://freecontent.manning.com/getting-started-with-baselines and https://gist.github.com/jacobzweig/31aa9b2abed395195 d50bf8ad98a3eb9. Its origins are unclear.

Listing 10.1   A dedicated Keras layer for BERT models

```
class BertLayer(tf.keras.layers.Layer):

    def __init__(
        self,
        n_fine_tune_layers=12,
```

The first obligatory method to implement when defining a Python class: initializing the class object

Set the number of layers that need to be fine-tuned if we choose to fine-tune an imported BERT model.

The path to a downloadable (or locally installed) BERT model. This particular URL leads to an uncased (lowercase) ready-made BERT model with 12 hidden layers and a standard output dimension of 768 (see chapter 9).

```
        bert_path=
        ➥"https://tfhub.dev/google/bert_uncased_L-12_H-768_A-12/1",      ◁
        **kwargs
    ):
```

Set the output size (again, standard 768 for BERT).

```
        self.n_fine_tune_layers = n_fine_tune_layers
        self.trainable = True                          ◁
        self.output_size = 768
        self.bert_path = bert_path
```

Switch the trainable flag to True so the standard setting will be to fine-tune the imported BERT model.

```
        super(BertLayer, self).__init__(**kwargs)
```

The trainable variables refer to layers in the BERT model we're using. Since BERT models are complex and have many layers, we can opt to limit training (fine-tuning) to a subset of these layers. The BERT model has been loaded into self.bert; it has a folder structure in which paths not containing the string "/cls/" lead to trainable layers (for idiosyncratic reasons).

```
    def build(self, input_shape):         ◁
        self.bert = hub.Module(
            self.bert_path,
            trainable=self.trainable,
            name=f"{self.name}_module"
        )
        trainable_vars = self.bert.variables
        trainable_vars =
        ➥[var for var in trainable_vars if not "/cls/" in var.name]
        trainable_vars = trainable_vars[-self.n_fine_tune_layers :]    ◁
```

The build method does administrative work on the weights of the layer. This method will be called automatically by call() on its first invocation.

Create the subset of layers to be fine-tuned.

```
        for var in trainable_vars:        ◁
            self._trainable_weights.append(var)
```

Append the trainable layer variables to the (initially empty) list of trainable weights.

Store the non-trainable variables (the remaining variables).

```
        for var in self.bert.variables:
            if var not in self._trainable_weights:
                self._non_trainable_weights.append(var)

        super(BertLayer, self).build(input_shape)
```

The call method defines what happens if we call the layer: that is, apply it as a function to input data.

```
    def call(self, inputs):                                    ◁
        inputs = [K.cast(x, dtype="int32") for x in inputs]
```

Base the input data to 32-bit integers to avoid unexpected numerical values.

```
        input_ids, input_mask, segment_ids = inputs      ◁
```

Decompose the inputs into token IDs, an input mask (defining which tokens the model should attend to), and a list of segment IDs. See listing 10.7 for details.

Store these ingredients as key/value pairs in a dictionary.

```
        bert_inputs = dict(
            input_ids=input_ids, input_mask=input_mask,
            ➥segment_ids=segment_ids
        )
        result = self.bert(inputs=bert_inputs, signature="tokens",
        ➥as_dict=True)[                   ◁
            "sequence_output"
        ]
        return result
```

Define the result as the application of a self.bert function (referring back to the TensorFlow Hub model) to the input.

An obligatory function that computes the shapes of input and output

```
    def compute_output_shape(self, input_shape):          ◁
        return (input_shape[0], self.output_size)
```

As mentioned, the trade-off we make between trainable and non-trainable variables allows us to directly balance time complexity and quality. Fine-tuning fewer attention layers leads to producing lower-quality embeddings but also guarantees a shorter training time. It's up to the developer to balance this trade-off. Before we dive into fine-tuning an existing BERT model, let's take a quick look at the alternative: building your own BERT model and training it on your data from the start.

10.3 *Training BERT on your data*

If you have enough resources available (data, GPU quota, and patience), it is possible to bootstrap a BERT model from your data (figure 10.4).

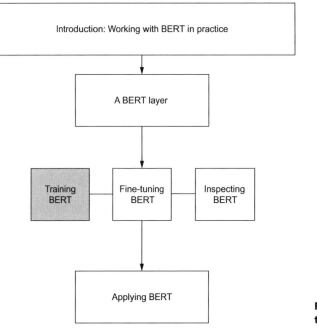

Figure 10.4   The process of training BERT on your data

Scenario: Training BERT on your data
You choose to build a BERT model entirely from scratch. Maybe you want full control over the data you base your BERT model on. This is possible—at the cost of lots of GPU cycles if your dataset is large.

Currently, many Python frameworks based on Keras allow us to work smoothly with BERT, such as `fast-bert` (https://pypi.org/project/fast-bert) and `keras-bert` (https://pypi.org/project/keras-bert). For other options, https://pypi.org/search/?q=bert. `keras-bert` offers simple methods for directly creating a proprietary BERT model, and we use it in our examples in this chapter. Needless to say, training BERT starts with prepping our data in the right format. Recall from chapter 9 that data comes in the form of paired sentences, because BERT is also trained on the next-sentence-prediction task.

Let's assume we process a set of documents beforehand into a newline-separated list of sentences, like this fragment of Edgar Allen Poe's *The Cask of Amontillado*:

> *He had a weak point — this Fortunato — although in other regards he was a man to be respected and even feared. He prided himself on his connoisseurship in wine. Few Italians have the true virtuoso spirit. For the most part their enthusiasm is adopted to suit the time and opportunity—to practise imposture upon the British and Austrian millionaires.*

Using a simple sentence splitter will get you to this point. Optionally, you can split not just on closing punctuation like periods but also on commas, dashes, and so on; doing so would create additional (pseudo-)sentences like

> *He had a weak point this Fortunato although in other regards he was a man to be respected and even feared*

and would lead to more sentence pairs.

The following function turns such a list into the paired data we need for training a BERT model.

Listing 10.2 Processing input data for BERT

```
def readSentencePairs(fn):
    with open(fn) as f:
        lines = f.readlines()

    pairs=zip(lines, lines[1:])
    paired_sentences=[[a.rstrip().split(),b.rstrip().split()]
       for (a,b) in pairs]

    tokenD = get_base_dict()

    for pairs in paired_sentences:
        for token in pairs[0] + pairs[1]:
            if token not in tokenD:
                tokenD[token] = len(tokenD)
    tokenL = list(tokenD.keys())
    return (paired_sentences,tokenD,tokenL)
```

Invoke the function with a filename.

All lines in the files are read into one list.

From this list, pairs are created with the Python built-in zip().

All sentence pairs in this list are split into words, and newlines are removed.

keras_bert has a base dictionary containing a few special symbols like UNK, CLS, and SEP. This dictionary will be expanded with the words in our data.

Gather all tokens in the dictionary into a list.

For every pair of sentences, any words in the sentences that are not already in the dictionary are added with a new index number.

Return the paired sentences, token dictionary, and token list.

For our example, this produces a nested list of paired sentences split into words:

```
[
  [['he','had','a', 'weak', 'point','-','this', 'Fortunato',...],
```

```
[['He','prided', 'himself', 'on', 'his', 'connoisseurship', 'in', 'wine']
 ...,
]
```

Next, leaning on the precooked methods in keras_bert, we can build and train a BERT model quite swiftly (see https://pypi.org/project/keras-bert). We start by defining a generator function that produces an iterable object with pointers to the next data points. So, instead of generating all the BERT data in one go (which can be prohibitive for large datasets), this generator creates an object for working in an effective and memory-friendly way through large amounts of data.

Listing 10.3   Generating batch data for BERT

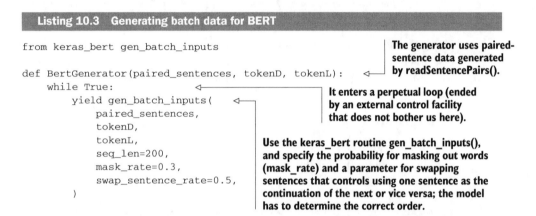

```
from keras_bert gen_batch_inputs

def BertGenerator(paired_sentences, tokenD, tokenL):
    while True:
        yield gen_batch_inputs(
            paired_sentences,
            tokenD,
            tokenL,
            seq_len=200,
            mask_rate=0.3,
            swap_sentence_rate=0.5,
        )
```

The generator uses paired-sentence data generated by readSentencePairs().

It enters a perpetual loop (ended by an external control facility that does not bother us here).

Use the keras_bert routine gen_batch_inputs(), and specify the probability for masking out words (mask_rate) and a parameter for swapping sentences that controls using one sentence as the continuation of the next or vice versa; the model has to determine the correct order.

Here is how this generator will be used.

Listing 10.4   Training a proprietary BERT model on data

```
from tensorflow import keras
from keras_bert import get_model, compile_model

def buildBertModel(paired_sentences,tokenD,tokenL, model_path):
    model = get_model(
        token_num=len(tokenD),
        head_num=5,
        transformer_num=12,
        embed_dim=256,
        feed_forward_dim=100,
        seq_len=200,
        pos_num=200,
        dropout_rate=0.05
    )
    compile_model(model)

    model.fit_generator(
        generator=BertGenerator(paired_sentences,tokenD,tokenL),
        steps_per_epoch=100,
        epochs=10
    )
```

The model-building function takes the paired sentence data and a model path as input parameters.

The keras_bert method get_model instantiates a model structure with values for the number of attention heads per layer, the number of transformer layers, the embedding size, the size of the feedforward layers, the length of the token sequences, the corresponding number of positions (for positional encoding), and a dropout rate.

The model is fitted on the data produced by the generator for the number of epochs specified and for a specified number of steps within every epoch.

Save the model after training.

```
        model.save(model_path)
```
> **This is how everything comes together.**
```
sentences="./my-sentences.txt"
(paired_sentences,tokenD,tokenL)=readSentencePairs(sentences)
model_path="./bert.model"
buildBertModel(paired_sentences,tokenD,tokenL,model_path)
```

Under the hood, `keras_bert` inserts the `CLS` and `SEP` delimiters in the paired-sentence data and tokenizes the words in the inputs into subwords using the `Word-Piece` algorithm (see chapter 9).

Let's use a manual approach to clarify what's happening. We first define a simple class called `InputExample`.

Listing 10.5   `InputExample` class

```
class InputExample(object):
    def __init__(self, text, label=None):
        self.text = text
        self.label = label
```

NOTE   This code is based on and extends a few existing repositories: https:// towardsdatascience.com/bert-in-keras-with-tensorflow-hub-76bcbc9417b,   https:// github.com/strongio/keras-bert/blob/master/keras-bert.py,   https://www.kaggle .com/igetii/bert-keras,   and   https://github.com/huggingface/transformers/ pull/2891/files.

Instances of the class are just containers holding labeled text items. We need them to store our labeled BERT sentences.

Next, we need a tokenizer to tokenize our input text. We will use another handy BERT Python library: `bert-for-tf2` (BERT for TensorFlow version 2 and above). We install this library under Python3 as follows:

```
sudo pip3 install bert-for-tf2
```

After this, it can be loaded with

```
import bert
```

The following listing shows how to obtain a tokenizer from TensorFlow Hub.

Listing 10.6   Obtaining a tokenizer from TensorFlow Hub

```
import tensorflow_hub as hub
import tensorflow as tf
from bert import bert_tokenization

def create_tokenizer_from_hub_module(bert_hub_path):
  with tf.Graph().as_default():
    bert_module = hub.Module(bert_hub_path)
    tokenization_info = bert_module(signature="tokenization_info",
    ⮡as_dict=True)
```
> **We are operating on a TensorFlow graph (https://www.tensorflow.org/ api_docs/python/tf/Graph).**

> **The path to our BERT model on TensorFlow Hub**

```
with tf.compat.v1.Session() as sess:
    vocab_file, do_lower_case = sess.run([tokenization_info["vocab_file"],
                                tokenization_info["do_lower_case"]])
return bert_tokenization.FullTokenizer(
    vocab_file=vocab_file, do_lower_case=do_lower_case)
```

We obtain vocabulary and case information from the BERT model. The case information expresses whether the model uses lowercase to represent words.

Create a fresh tokenizer that stores the vocabulary and case information.

We invoke the tokenizer like this:

```
bert_path="https://tfhub.dev/google/bert_uncased_L-12_H-768_A-12/1"
tokenizer = create_tokenizer_from_hub_module(bert_path)
```

For a specified BERT model from TensorFlow Hub, this returns a tokenizer that contains a token dictionary mapping words to integers. Given this tokenizer, for a given `InputExample` instance, we can now generate the feature representation a BERT model wants: a tokenized text, an input mask that selects the tokens the model should pay attention to, and a set of labels.

NOTE   Remember that we will teach the labeling and, on the fly, fine-tune the BERT model, just as we did with Word2Vec in chapter 3.

Listing 10.7   From `InputExample` to features

Begin populating the tokens array. It starts with the pseudo-token [CLS], indicating the start of a sequence, and it ends with [SEP], which is why we reserve two extra positions and check that we do not exceeding max_seq_length-2. The segment_ids array is just a list of zeroes proportional to the length of the token array. Its first and last positions implicitly (and redundantly) encode the start and end positions of the current text.

Invoke the method with a TensorFlow Hub tokenizer, an instance of InputExample, and the maximum sequence length we allow, set to a standard value of 256.

Tokenize the input text with the tokenizer, obtaining a list of tokens.

```
def convert_single_example(tokenizer, example, max_seq_length=256):
    tokens_a = tokenizer.tokenize(example.text)
    if len(tokens_a) > max_seq_length - 2:
        tokens_a = tokens_a[0 : (max_seq_length - 2)]
    tokens = []
    segment_ids = []
    tokens.append("[CLS]")
    segment_ids.append(0)
    for token in tokens_a:
        tokens.append(token)
        segment_ids.append(0)
    tokens.append("[SEP]")
    segment_ids.append(0)

    input_ids = tokenizer.convert_tokens_to_ids(tokens)

    input_mask = [1] * len(input_ids)

    while len(input_ids) < max_seq_length:
```

Specify an input mask—a list of ones that correspond to our tokens—before padding the input text with zeroes. Only nonzero tokens are attended to by BERT.

Convert tokens into token IDs with the tokenizer.

Pad all arrays with zeroes.

```
        input_ids.append(0)
        input_mask.append(0)
        segment_ids.append(0)

    return input_ids, input_mask, segment_ids, example.label
```

Return the token array, input mask, segment array, and label of the input example.

We do this for a bulk of examples as shown next.

Listing 10.8   Converting examples into features

```
def convert_examples_to_features(tokenizer, examples, max_seq_length=256):
    input_ids, input_masks, segment_ids, labels = [], [], [], []
    for example in examples:
        input_id, input_mask, segment_id, label = convert_single_example(
        ➥tokenizer, example, max_seq_length)
        input_ids.append(input_id)
        input_masks.append(input_mask)
        segment_ids.append(segment_id)
        labels.append(label)
    return (
        np.array(input_ids),
        np.array(input_masks),
        np.array(segment_ids),
        np.array(labels).reshape(-1, 1)
    )
```

Convert a single example.

Add to the collective array.

Return the results.

The diagram in figure 10.5 describes the process.

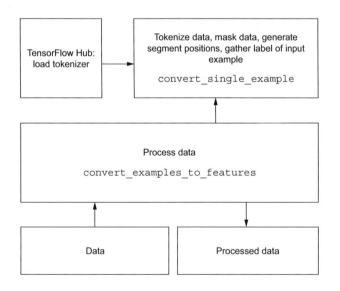

Figure 10.5   Processing data for BERT. Data is tokenized and masked, and segment positions are generated.

Now, suppose we have labeled data stored in CSV format:

```
text,label
I hate pizza, negative
I like icecream, positive
```

Such pairs of texts and labels, once extracted from the CSV data, can be converted into `InputExamples`.

Listing 10.9 From pairs of texts and labels to `InputExamples`

```
def convert_text_to_examples(texts, labels):
    InputExamples = []
    for text, label in zip(texts, labels):
      InputExamples.append(
        InputExample(text=text, label=label)
      )
    return InputExamples
```

Let's process this CSV data using the previously defined conversion methods and our tokenizer. We will generate a number of arrays holding the conversion results.

Listing 10.10 Processing CSV data

```
import pandas as pd
from sklearn.preprocessing import LabelEncoder

def loadData(trainCSV, testCSV, valCSV, tokenizer):      ◁─┐
    max_seq_length=256

    train = pd.read_csv(trainCSV)      ◁─┐
    test = pd.read_csv(testCSV)
    val = pd.read_csv(valCSV)

    label_encoder = LabelEncoder().fit(pd.concat([train['label'],
    ➥val['label']]))                                            ◁─

    y_train = label_encoder.fit_transform(pd.concat([train['label'],
    ➥val['label']]))
    y_test = label_encoder.fit_transform(pd.concat([test['label'],
    ➥val['label']]))
    y_val = label_encoder.fit_transform(pd.concat([train['label'],
    ➥val['label']]))

    train_examples = convert_text_to_examples(train['text'], y_train)
    test_examples = convert_text_to_examples(test['text'], y_test)
    val_examples = convert_text_to_examples(val['text'], y_val)

    (train_input_ids, train_input_masks, train_segment_ids, train_labels) =
    ➥convert_examples_to_features(tokenizer, train_examples,
    ➥max_seq_length=max_seq_length)                              ◁─
    (test_input_ids, test_input_masks, test_segment_ids, test_labels) =
    ➥convert_examples_to_features(tokenizer, test_examples,
    ➥max_seq_length=max_seq_length)
    (val_input_ids, val_input_masks, val_segment_ids, val_labels) =
    ➥convert_examples_to_features(tokenizer, val_examples,
    ➥max_seq_length=max_seq_length)
```

Invoke the method with CSV filenames for training, testing, and validation data and a tokenizer.

Use pandas to read the CSV text into dictionary structures. Our CSV data has just two fields: text and label.

Use the sklearn LabelEncoder (see previous chapters) to convert the labels into numerical values.

Convert the texts in our training, test, and validation data into InputExamples.

Convert the various InputExamples into array tuples (features).

```
           return [(train_input_ids,train_input_masks,train_segment_ids,
               ➥train_labels),
Return  ⌐       (test_input_ids,test_input_masks,test_segment_ids, test_labels),
the results. └─▷  (val_input_ids,val_input_masks,val_segment_ids, val_labels)]
```

Figure 10.6 illustrates this flow.

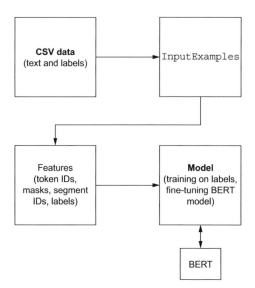

Figure 10.6 Processing CSV data for fine-tuning BERT. CSV data is processed (tokenized, segmented), and masks are generated.

Now we are ready to feed our data to a BERT model that will be fine-tuned while learning an additional labeling task.

10.4 Fine-tuning BERT

Scenario: Fine-tuning BERT with your own data
You downloaded a pretrained BERT model, and you want to fine-tune it with your own data, labeled for a certain labeling task.

As we did in chapter 3 for Word2Vec, we will now fine-tune a BERT model (figure 10.7) by picking up a pretrained model and using a labeled dataset, to which we apply the various conversion routines discussed in the previous section. We add the BERT model as a layer to our overall model that learns the labeling task. The following listing shows a method to create that model. It uses the `BertLayer` we defined earlier, in which we can specify the model we wish to download from TensorFlow Hub and fine-tune.

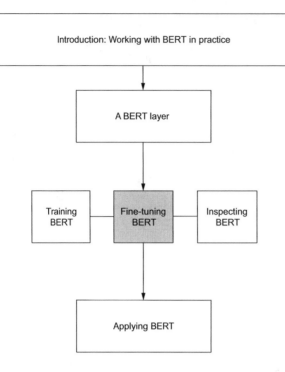

Figure 10.7   Fine-tuning a BERT model: tying it to a downstream (extra learning) task. Learning this task will force BERT to optimize its word embeddings accordingly.

Listing 10.11   Building the BERT model

We feed three types of inputs to the BERT model: the token identifiers (in_id) corresponding to our tokenized input texts, the input mask (forcing the model to pay attention to non-padded token positions only), and the segment identifiers. For each of these, a separate InputLayer is defined.

```
import tensorflow.keras.backend as K
import tensorflow as tf

def buildBertModel():
    max_seq_length=256
    in_id = tf.keras.layers.Input(shape=(max_seq_length,),
    ➥name="input_ids")
    in_mask = tf.keras.layers.Input(shape=(max_seq_length,),
    ➥name="input_masks")
    in_segment = tf.keras.layers.Input(shape=(max_seq_length,),
    ➥name="segment_ids")

    bert_inputs = [in_id, in_mask, in_segment]

    bert_output = BertLayer(n_fine_tune_layers=10)(bert_inputs) 3((CO9-3))

    drop = keras.layers.Dropout(0.3)(bert_output)
    dense = keras.layers.Dense(200, activation='relu')(bert_output)
```

Gather the three inputs in one list.

Define the output of the BERT model as the application of the BERT layer to these inputs. Notice how we override the standard number of fine-tunable layers (12) with 10.

Define custom network layers consisting of two dropout layers and two dense layers. This part is fully open to experimentation, and optimal choices depend on the labeling task at hand.

```
drop = keras.layers.Dropout(0.3)(dense)
dense = keras.layers.Dense(100, activation='relu')(dense)
pred = keras.layers.Dense(1, activation='sigmoid')(dense)

session = K.get_session()                          ◁─┐  While not required, it is a good
init = tf.compat.v1.global_variables_initializer()    │  idea to initialize all variables in a
session.run(init)                                     │  TensorFlow computation like this.

model = tf.keras.models.Model(inputs=bert_inputs, outputs=pred)   ◁─┐
model.compile(loss="binary_crossentropy", optimizer="adam",          │
➥metrics=["accuracy"])                                Define and compile
model.summary()                                        the final model.
return model
```

With this method in place, we can begin training the model and fine-tuning the BERT model stored in the BERT layer on the fly.

Listing 10.12 Fine-tuning the BERT model

```
def finetuneBertModel(trainT, valT):
    model=buildBertModel()
    (train_input_ids, train_input_masks, train_segment_ids,
    ➥train_labels)=trainT
    (val_input_ids,val_input_masks,val_segment_ids,val_labels)=valT

    model.fit(
        [train_input_ids, train_input_masks, train_segment_ids],
        train_labels,
        epochs=10,
        batch_size=64
    )
```

We will not use any validation data at this point, but it can be used in `model.fit` by inserting

```
validation_data=(
        [val_input_ids, val_input_masks, val_segment_ids],
        val_labels,
        )
```

The next listing ties everything together.

Listing 10.13 Overall procedure for fine-tuning BERT

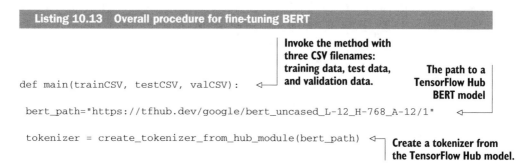

```
                                            Invoke the method with
                                            three CSV filenames:
                                            training data, test data,    The path to a
                                            and validation data.       TensorFlow Hub
def main(trainCSV, testCSV, valCSV):   ◁─┘                              BERT model

  bert_path="https://tfhub.dev/google/bert_uncased_L-12_H-768_A-12/1"   ◁─

  tokenizer = create_tokenizer_from_hub_module(bert_path)   ◁─┐  Create a tokenizer from
                                                               the TensorFlow Hub model.
```

```
[trainData,testData,validationData]=loadData(trainCSV, testCSV, valCSV,
    ⮑tokenizer)
finetuneBertModel(trainData)
```

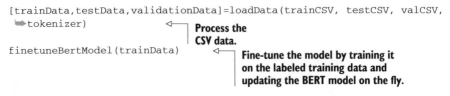

Process the CSV data.

Fine-tune the model by training it on the labeled training data and updating the BERT model on the fly.

Once this has run, you can save your model and use it for prediction purposes.

Exercise

Experiment with these methods, and fine-tune a BERT model using labeled data. A suggestion is to deploy the IMDB sentiment data (see https://keras.io/api/data-sets/imdb), but any labeled data will do.

10.5   *Inspecting BERT*

In this section, we inspect BERT models for the contextual, semantic word distances they infer (figure 10.8). Does BERT generate different vectors for homonyms (words with the same spelling but different meanings)? If so, it lives up to its promise of contextual word embeddings. Unlike Word2Vec, which combines all different meanings of one word into one vector, BERT was designed to generate a different vector for a homonym given its specific context in a sentence. Let's find out if it does.

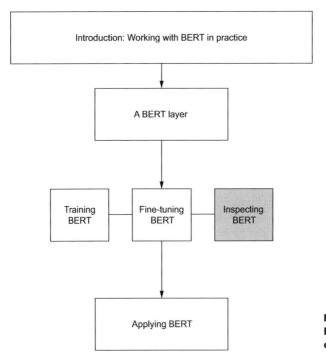

Figure 10.8   Inspecting BERT models for inferred contextual distances

10.5.1 *Homonyms in BERT*

Homonyms are words that are spelled the same but have different meanings. Perhaps the most well-known homonym is *bank*:

- *bank₁*—A financial institution
- *bank₂*—The slope beside a body of water, such as a river or a lake

How does BERT deal with homonyms? We know that BERT assigns contextual vectors to words in a dynamic fashion, without a fixed lexicon derived from data. So, unlike Word2Vec, BERT should assign different embedding vectors to the two instantiations of *bank* depending on their context. Let's verify this empirically.

> **Scenario: Inspecting BERT for homonyms**
> You would like to see for yourself how BERT handles homonyms by examining their embeddings produced by a BERT model.

The idea is as follows. Following McCormick (2019) and his code, we hand BERT a sentence in which we infuse homonyms for the word *bank* with different local contexts. Subsequently, we extract the BERT word embeddings for each word, select the ones for the different homonyms, and inspect their vector similarity. We hypothesize that words with different meanings will have measurably different vectors. We will measure vector similarity through a distance metric.

Listing 10.14 implements a callable function that applies the BERT model to input and returns its output, which consists of embedding vectors. To be precise, for a set of tokenized input texts, this function will return an input mask and segment information: a three-dimensional array of predictions. We'll refer to that array as P. Then, most importantly,

- P[0] refers to the input texts.
- P[0][i] refers to the *i*th text.
- P[0][i][j] refers to the vector representation (embedding vector) of the *j*th word of the *i*th text.

Listing 10.14   Creating a BERT function

```
import tensorflow.keras.backend as K

def createBertFunction():
  max_seq_length=256
  in_id = tf.keras.layers.Input(shape=(max_seq_length,),
  ⮑name="input_ids")
  in_mask = tf.keras.layers.Input(shape=(max_seq_length,),
  ⮑name="input_masks")
  in_segment = tf.keras.layers.Input(shape=(max_seq_length,),
  ⮑name="segment_ids")

  bert_input = [in_id, in_mask, in_segment]
```

As before (listing 10.11), we define three Input layers holding the input data for the BERT model.

The BERT model input consists of a list with these three inputs.

Apply the BERT layer to the input. The BERT layer will have the reference
to the TensorFlow Hub BERT model hardcoded, but you may want to
supply it as an initialization parameter for reasons of elegance.

Create a function
that maps input to
output through the
low-level backend
interface to Keras.

```
bert_output = BertLayer(n_fine_tune_layers=10)(bert_input)

func = K.function([bert_input], [bert_output])

session = K.get_session()
init = tf.compat.v1.global_variables_initializer()
session.run(init)

return func
```

Optionally, instantiate
TensorFlow variables
(listing 10.11).

The function is returned
and can now be called.

Our data is stored in CSV format like this:

```
text,label
"I took my money to the bank and put it on my bank account after which I
➥laid down on the river bank",0
```

This data is converted to BERT feature format (and subsequently is analyzed) as
shown next.

Listing 10.15 Reading from BERT

A few necessary imports: a cosine distance for vector
similarity and a TextBlob for part-of-speech tagging

Invoke the method with
a tokenizer, our BERT
function, and an input
CSV file with labeled text
(the labels are ignored
in this experiment).

```
from scipy.spatial.distance import cosine
from textblob import TextBlob

def readOutBertModel(tokenizer, functionBert, textCSV):

    examples=convert_text_to_examples(textCSV)
    features=convert_examples_to_features(tokenizer,examples)

    pred=functionBert(features)

    tags=TextBlob(examples[0].text).tags

    vectors=[]
    text=""
    for i in range(nb_words):
        if tags[i][1] in ['NNP','NN','NNS']:
            vectors.append(pred[0][0][i])
            text+=words[i]+" "

    # Words: money bank bank account river bank

    same_bank  = 1 - cosine(vectors[1], vectors[2])
    other_bank = 1 - cosine(vectors[1], vectors[5])
```

Input text is converted
to features, as before
(listing 10.10).

Apply the BERT function to
the converted input data.

For the first example (our data
contains just one example),
words are part-of-speech tagged.

We are only interested in the nouns,
and our zero-based vectors array
contains vectors for money, bank, bank,
account, river, and bank (in that order).

Compare vector 1 (referring to the second word, "bank")
with the third word ("bank"). These occurrences of
"bank" should have similar meanings (financial).

Compare vector 1 (financial bank) with vector
5, the sixth word, "bank" (river bank). These
words should have different meanings.

```
print('Vector similarity for  *similar*  meanings:
➡%.2f' % same_bank)
print('Vector similarity for *different* meanings:  %.2f' % other_bank)

return (vectors, text)
```

Return the extracted vectors (word embeddings) and the corresponding words.

Print out the results.

The vector similarity between the first two similar meanings of *bank* (financial) appears to be .62. The vector similarity between the two different meanings of *bank* (comparing the first *bank* with the last *bank*) is a meager .43, which shows that different homonym meanings are reflected in the BERT word embeddings. We can plot these results with T-SNE.

Listing 10.16 Plotting BERT vectors with T-SNE

```
from sklearn.manifold import TSNE
import matplotlib.pyplot as plt

def plotTSNE(bert_vectors, text):
    tsne = TSNE(n_components=2, init='pca')
    output = tsne.fit_transform(bert_vectors)

    x_vals = []
    y_vals = []
    for xy in output:
        x_vals.append(xy[0])
        y_vals.append(xy[1])

    plt.figure(figsize=(5, 5))

    words=text.split(" ")
    for i in range(len(x_vals)):
        plt.scatter(x_vals[i],y_vals[i])
        plt.annotate(words[i],
                     xy=(x_vals[i], y_vals[i]),
                     xytext=(5, 2),
                     textcoords='offset points',
                     ha='right',
                     va='bottom')
    plt.savefig('bert.png')
```

Import T-SNE from sklearn along with the necessary Matplotlib routines for plotting.

Run T-SNE on the vectors, creating a 2D version with principal component analysis (PCA).

Create a 2D array from the T-SNE output.

Invoke the method with the vectors and text (words) created by readOutBertModel() (listing 10.15).

Set up a 5 × 5 figure grid.

Create a scatter plot from the T-SNE values and the words linked to the vectors.

Save the picture as a PNG image.

This produces the picture in figure 10.9 (the x- and y-axes encode the values produced by T-SNE for the input data when it compresses the high-dimensional input vectors to 2-D).

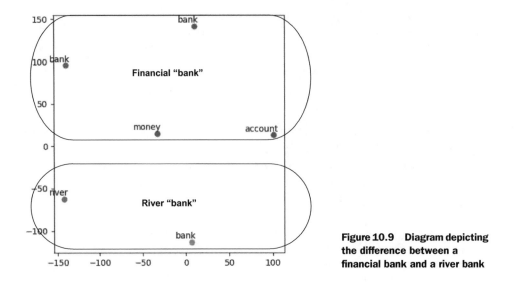

Figure 10.9   Diagram depicting the difference between a financial bank and a river bank

The lower *bank* is the river bank, and the two other *bank*s are the financial banks. They appear far apart in this 2D representation.

Finally, we combine all this in the following code.

Listing 10.17   Tying it together

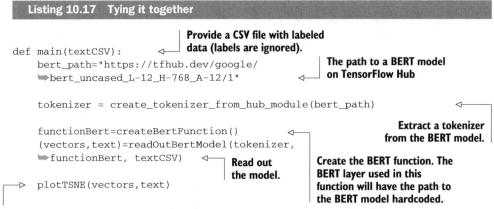

```
def main(textCSV):
    bert_path="https://tfhub.dev/google/
    ➥bert_uncased_L-12_H-768_A-12/1"

    tokenizer = create_tokenizer_from_hub_module(bert_path)

    functionBert=createBertFunction()
    (vectors,text)=readOutBertModel(tokenizer,
    ➥functionBert, textCSV)

    plotTSNE(vectors,text)
```

Provide a CSV file with labeled data (labels are ignored).

The path to a BERT model on TensorFlow Hub

Extract a tokenizer from the BERT model.

Read out the model.

Create the BERT function. The BERT layer used in this function will have the path to the BERT model hardcoded.

Create the plot.

10.6   *Applying BERT*

Based on what has been presented in this chapter, you can now start experimenting with BERT (figure 10.10). You can load an existing, pretrained model and fine-tune it on your supplementary labeled data, or train your own BERT model from scratch. You saw in the previous section how to obtain contextual vectors per word. This allows you to combine vectors for separate words into composite vectors for paragraphs or longer documents. The previous chapters described techniques that are agnostic with respect to the data representations you want to use. For instance, you can replace a Word2Vec

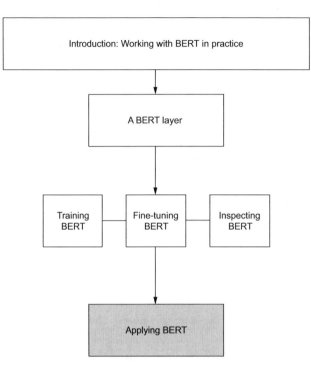

Figure 10.10   **Applying BERT
after pretraining and/or fine-tuning**

embedding with a BERT embedding and check whether the results improve (they should!).

> **Exercise**
> Go back to the many applications in this book, and swap a BERT model for the embeddings used. Compare the results by keeping the overall model organization stable and working on the same data.

One caveat: In recent research, it has become apparent that large, off-the-shelf word embedding models like Word2Vec and BERT display bias due to a skewed selection of textual sources underlying the models. For one thing, it has been demonstrated that these models exhibit strong gender biases, associating, for instance, male pronouns more strongly than female pronouns with high salaries and scientific professions (see Bolukbasi et al. [2016] for Word2Vec and Bhardwaj et al. [2020] for BERT). This may have societal effects since word embedding models are part of many search engines (including Google and search engines for recruitment). Several tests have been developed for measuring and even counteracting such bias, including the Word-Embedding Association Test (WEAT; Kurita et al. 2019) and the Relational Inner Product Association (RIPA; Ethayarajh et al. 2019). Incidentally, the RIPA paper authors have found that WEAT overestimates bias. Findings like these underline the importance of carefully handling large, hard-to-inspect, off-the-shelf language models. As an AI engineer, you have a responsibility here that reaches beyond mere technical skills.

Summary

- Existing BERT models can be imported into your Keras network.
- You can train BERT on your own (raw text) data.
- Fine-tuning BERT models on additional labeled data (downstream tasks) may be beneficial.
- As with any data-driven model, BERT is susceptible to bias and may produce undesirable associations between words, reflecting cultural and societal biases that have crept into the raw data underlying a BERT model. It is important to be aware of this as an NLP engineer.

bibliography

Aj_MLstater. 2020. "Why does Keras need TensorFlow as backend?" Stack Exchange. https://datascience.stackexchange.com/questions/65736/why-does-keras-need-tensorflow-as-backend.

Ba, Jimmy Lei, Jamie Ryan Kiros, and Geoffrey E. Hinton. 2016. "Layer Normalization." https://arxiv.org/abs/1607.06450.

Bhardwaj, R., N. Majumder, and S. Poria. 2020. "Investigating Gender Bias in BERT." arXiv preprint arXiv:2009.05021.

Bolukbasi, Tolga, Kai-Wei Chang, James Y Zou, Venkatesh Saligrama, and Adam T. Kalai. 2016. "Man Is to Computer Programmer as Woman Is to Homemaker? Debiasing Word Embeddings." In *Advances in Neural Information Processing Systems*, 4349–4357. MIT Press.

Bottou, Léon. 1998. "Online Algorithms and Stochastic Approximations." In *Online Learning and Neural Networks*, edited by D. Saad, 9–42. Cambridge University Press.

Bradbury, James. 2019. Tweet, June 25. https://twitter.com/jekbradbury/status/1143397614093651969?s=20.

Brown, Tom B., Benjamin Mann, Nick Ryder, Melanie Subbiah, Jared Kaplan, Prafulla Dhariwal, Arvind Neelakantan et al. 2020. "Language Models Are Few-Shot Learners." https://arxiv.org/abs/2005.14165.

Chen, Hung-Yu, Adrian W. Gilmore, Steven M. Nelson, and Kathleen B. McDermott. 2017. "Are There Multiple Kinds of Episodic Memory? An fMRI Investigation Comparing Autobiographical and Recognition Memory Tasks." *Journal of Neuroscience* 37 (10): 2764–2775.

Chollet, François. 2017. *Deep Learning with Python*. Manning Publications.

Clark, Kevin , Urvashi Khandelwal, Omer Levy, and Christopher D. Manning. 2018. "What Does BERT Look At? An Analysis of BERT's Attention." https://arxiv.org/abs/1906.04341.

Daelemans, Walter, and Antal van den Bosch. 2005. *Memory-Based Learning*. Cambridge University Press.

Daelemans, Walter, Antal van den Bosch, and Jakub Zavrel. 1999. "Forgetting Exceptions is Harmful in Language Learning." *Machine Learning* 34 (1): 11–41.

Devlin, Jacob, Ming-Wei Chang, Kenton Lee, and Kristina Toutanova. 2018. "BERT: Pre-training of Deep Bidirectional Transformers for Language Understanding." https://arxiv.org/pdf/1810.04805.pdf.

Ethayarajh, K., D. Duvenaud, and G. Hirst. 2019. "Understanding Undesirable Word Embedding Associations." arXiv preprint arXiv:1908.06361.

Harris, Zellig. 1959. "Linguistic Transformation for Information Retrieval." In *Proceedings of the International Conference on Scientific Information, 1958*, vol. 2, 937–950. National Academy of Sciences.

Ivakhnenko, A.G. 1971. "Polynomial Theory of Complex Systems." *IEEE Transactions on Systems, Man and Cybernetics* SMC-1 (4): 364–378.

Ivakhnenko, A.G., and V.G. Lapa. 1965. *Cybernetic Predicting Devices*. CCM Information Corporation.

Karpathy, Andrej. 2015. "The Unreasonable Effectiveness of Recurrent Neural Networks." http://karpathy.github.io/2015/05/21/rnn-effectiveness/.

Kumar, Ankit , Ozan Irsoy, Peter Ondruska, Mohit Iyyer, James Bradbury, Ishaan Gulrajani, Victor Zhong, Romain Paulus, and Richard Socher. 2016. "Ask Me Anything: Dynamic Memory Networks for Natural Language Processing." In *Proceedings of The 33rd International Conference on Machine Learning, PMLR 48*, 1378–1387. MLR Press.

Kurita, K., N. Vyas, A. Pareek, A.W. Black, and Y. Tsvetkov. 2019. "Measuring Bias in Contextualized Word Representations." arXiv preprint arXiv:1906.07337.

Le, Q. and T. Mikolov. 2014. "Distributed Representations of Sentences and Documents." In *Proceedings International Conference on Machine Learning (ICML)*, 1188–1196. Association for Computing Machinery.

Lee, Honglak. 2010. "Unsupervised Feature Learning Via Sparse Hierarchical Representations." PhD dissertation. Stanford University, Computer Science Department.

Li, Chuan. 2020. "OpenAI's GPT-3 Language Model: A Technical Overview." Lambda. https://lambdalabs.com/blog/demystifying-gpt-3.

Luong, Minh-Thang, Hieu Pham, and Christopher D. Manning. 2015. "Effective Approaches to Attention-based Neural Machine Translation." https://arxiv.org/pdf/1508.04025.

McCormick, Chris. 2019. "BERT Word Embeddings Tutorial." https://mccormickml.com/2019/05/14/BERT-word-embeddings-tutorial/#34-confirming-contextually-dependent-vectors.

McGuffie, Kris and Alex Newhouse. (2020). The Radicalization Risks of GPT-3 and Advanced Neural Language Models. https://arxiv.org/abs/2009.06807.

Mikolov, T., I. Sutskever, K. Chen, G.S. Corrado, and J. Dean. 2013. "Distributed Representations of Words and Phrases and Their Compositionality." In *Advances in Neural Information Processing Systems*, 3111—3119. Curran Associates.

Mikolov, Tomas. 2013. "Distributed Representations of Words and Phrases and Their Compositionality." *Advances in Neural Information Processing Systems*. arXiv:1310.4546.

Pang, Bo, and Lillian Lee. 2004. "Movie Review Data." https://www.aclweb.org/anthology/P04-1035. Accompanying paper: "A Sentimental Education: Sentiment Analysis Using Subjectivity Summarization Based on Minimum Cuts." In *Proceedings of the 42nd Annual Meeting of the Association for Computational Linguistics (ACL-04)*, 271–278. ACL. https://www.aclweb .org/anthology/P04-1035.

Peters, L. 2018. "Deep Contextualized Word Representations." In *Proceedings of the 2018 Conference of the North American Chapter of the Association for Computational Linguistics: Human Language Technologies, Volume 1 (Long Papers)*, 2227–2237). Association for Computational Linguistics.

Posner, Michael I., Mary K. Rothbart, and Pascale Voelker. "Developing Brain Networks of Attention." *Curr Opin Pediatr* 28 (6): 720–724.

Ratnaparkhi, Adwait, Jeff Reynar, and Salim Roukos. 1994. "A Maximum Entropy Model for Prepositional Phrase Attachment." In *Proceedings of Human Language Technology, Workshop held at Plainsboro, New Jersey, March 8-11, 1994.* Association for Computational Linguistics.

Remy, Philippe. 2016. "Stateful LSTM in Keras." http://philipperemy.github.io/keras-stateful-lstm.

Rosebrock, Adrian. 2019. "Keras vs. tf.keras: What's the difference in TensorFlow 2.0?" PyImage-Search. https://pyimagesearch.com/2019/10/21/keras-vs-tf-keras-whats-the-difference-in-tensorflow-2-0.

Schmidhuber, J. 1992. "Learning Complex, Extended Sequences Using the Principle of History Compression." *Neural Computation* 4 (2): 234–242.

Schuster, Mike, and Kaisuke Nakajima. 2012. "Japanese and Korean Voice Search." International Conference on Acoustics, Speech, & Signal Processing.

Squire, L.R. 1986. "Mechanisms of Memory." *Science* 232 (4758): 1612–1619.

Stamatatos, Efstathios. 2009. "A Survey of Modern Authorship Attribution Methods." *Journal of the American Society for Information Science and Technology* 60 (3): 538–556.

Sukhbaatar, A., A. Szlam, J. Weston, and R. Fergus. 2015. "End-to-End Memory Networks." In *Proceedings NIPS 2015*, 2440–2448. MIT Press.

Taylor, W.L. 1953. "Cloze Procedure: A New Tool for Measuring Readability." *Journalism Quarterly* 30 (4): 415–433.

Tulving, Endel. 1989. "Memory. Performance, Knowledge, and Experience." *European Journal of Cognitive Psychology* 1 (1), 3–26.

van der Maaten, L.J.P., and G.E. Hinton. 2008. "Visualizing Data Using t-SNE." *Journal of Machine Learning Research* 9: 2579–2605.

Vaswani, Ashish, Noam Shazeer, Niki Parmar, Jakob Uszkoreit, Llion Jones, Aidan N. Gomez, Lukasz Kaiser, and Illia Polosukhin. 2017. "Attention Is All You Need." In *Proceedings NIPS 2017*, 6000–6010. Curran Associates.

Vossel, Simone, Joy J. Geng, and Gereon R. Fink. 2014. "Dorsal and Ventral Attention Systems: Distinct Neural Circuits but Collaborative Roles." *The Neuroscientist* 20 (2): 150—159.

Weston, Jason, Antoine Bordes, Sumit Chopra, Alexander M. Rush, Bart van Merriënboer, Armand Joulin, and Tomas Mikolov. 2015. *Towards AI Complete Question Answering: A Set of Prerequisite Toy Tasks.* https://arXiv:1502.05698.

Weston, James, Antoine Bordes, Sumit Chopra, Alexander M. Rush, Bart van Merriënboer, Zavrel, Jakub, Walter Daelemans, Jorn Veenstra T. and Mark Ellison. 1997. "Resolving PP Attachment Ambiguities with Memory-Based Learning." In *Proceedings CoNLL (ACL), 1997*, 136–144. Association for Computational Linguistics.

Xu, Kelvin, Jimmy Ba, Ryan Kiros, Kyunghyun Cho, Aaron Courville, Ruslan Salakhutdinov, Richard Zemel, and Yoshua Bengio. 2015. "Show, Attend and Tell: Neural Image Caption Generation with Visual Attention." https://arxiv.org/abs/1502.03044.

Yang, Zhilin, Zihang Dai, Yiming Yang, Jaime Carbonell, Ruslan Salakhutdinov, and Quoc V. Le. 2019. "XLNet: Generalized Autoregressive Pretraining for Language Understanding." In *Proceedings NIPS 2019*, 5754–5764. Curran Associates.

Zavrel, Jakub, Walter Daelemans, and Jorn Veenstra. 1997. "Resolving PP Attachment Ambiguities with Memory-Based Learning." In *CoNLL97: Computational Natural Language Learning.*

index

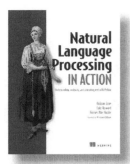

Natural Language Processing in Action
by Hobson Lane, Cole Howard, Hannes Hapke
Foreword by Dr. Arwen Griffioen

ISBN 9781617294631
544 pages, $49.99
March 2019

Deep Learning with Python, Second Edition
by François Chollet

ISBN 9781617296864
504 pages, $59.99
October 2021

Inside Deep Learning
by Edward Raff
Foreword by Kirk Borne

ISBN 9781617298639
600 pages, $59.99
April 2022

Getting Started with
Natural Language Processing
by Ekaterina Kochmar

ISBN 9781617296765
456 pages, $49.99
September 2022

For ordering information, go to www.manning.com

A new online reading experience

liveBook, our online reading platform, adds a new dimension to your Manning books, with features that make reading, learning, and sharing easier than ever. A liveBook version of your book is included FREE with every Manning book.

This next generation book platform is more than an online reader. It's packed with unique features to upgrade and enhance your learning experience.

- Add your own notes and bookmarks
- One-click code copy
- Learn from other readers in the discussion forum
- Audio recordings and interactive exercises
- Read all your purchased Manning content in any browser, anytime, anywhere

As an added bonus, you can search every Manning book and video in liveBook—even ones you don't yet own. Open any liveBook, and you'll be able to browse the content and read anything you like.*

Find out more at www.manning.com/livebook-program.

*Open reading is limited to 10 minutes per book daily